Date Due

EDUCATIONAL FOUNDATIONS OF
✠ THE JESUITS IN ✠
SIXTEENTH-CENTURY NEW SPAIN

Educational Foundations of ✛ the Jesuits in ✛ Sixteenth-Century New Spain

✛

By Jerome V. Jacobsen, S.J.

University of California Press · Berkeley · 1938

UNIVERSITY OF CALIFORNIA PRESS
BERKELEY, CALIFORNIA

CAMBRIDGE UNIVERSITY PRESS
LONDON, ENGLAND

PRINTED IN THE UNITED STATES OF AMERICA
BY SAMUEL T. FARQUHAR, UNIVERSITY PRINTER

THE PUBLICATION OF THIS VOLUME
WAS MADE POSSIBLE BY
THE GENEROSITY OF AN ALUMNUS OF
THE UNIVERSITY OF CALIFORNIA

CONTENTS

ILLUSTRATIONS

EDITOR'S PREFACE

THIS VOLUME *is the first of a series, already well under way, devoted to the activities of the Jesuits in Spanish North America between 1572, when they first arrived in Mexico City, and 1767, when they were expelled from all Spanish dominions. The work of the Jesuits in New Spain has long been an almost forgotten chapter in the history of the Western Hemisphere. Learned volumes were written on the subject by the early sons of Loyola themselves, but since their day it has received little attention either by scholars or by writers for the general public. The oblivion into which these pioneers of New Spain have fallen is quite in contrast with the lively interest shown in the Jesuits of New France, to whom Parkman devoted one of his brilliant volumes; whose* RELATIONS *were published by Thwaites in seventy-one monumental tomes; and whose work is the theme of many recent scholars and popular writers. This contrast is all the more notable since the labors of the Spanish Jesuits in North America were vastly more extensive than those of their contemporaries in New France.*

A few years ago a revival of interest in the history of the Jesuits in Western North America was begun at the University of California as one of the themes of a seminar in Spanish-American history. Numerous Jesuits and other advanced students have been attracted to the subject, and their researches are now bearing fruit.

An extensive collection of old and modern printed works has been assembled in the Bancroft Library. From European and Western Hemisphere archives a large mass of facsimiles and transcripts of unpublished manuscript materials has been acquired and is constantly being enlarged. These resources form a rich mine of unexploited data for writing the history of the truly remarkable contribution of the Jesuits to the cultural history of Western North America.

Dr. Jacobsen's volume on the EDUCATIONAL FOUNDATIONS OF THE JESUITS IN SIXTEENTH-CENTURY NEW SPAIN *stands logically at the beginning of the series, since it tells of the coming of the Black Robes to Mexico, and the founding of the central establishments from which the work of the order spread. It is an illuminating chapter in the history of education in America. Later volumes of the series will deal with the labors of the Jesuit missionaries on the frontiers of Western North America. Since it emanated from the same seminar, the volume by Dr. William Eugene Shiels, S.J., on* GONZALO DE TAPIA, *founder of the West Coast missions, would logically stand next in the series, although published elsewhere. Other volumes completed or in preparation will tell the story of the Jesuit missions on both slopes of the great Sierra Madre in Sinaloa, Durango, Chihuahua, Sonora, Pimería Alta, and Lower California. Documentary volumes as well as monographs are in preparation.*

HERBERT EUGENE BOLTON

AUTHOR'S PREFACE

"**F**OR MORE THAN *one hundred years nearly all the foremost men throughout Christendom, both among the laity and clergy, had received the Jesuit training, and in most cases retained for life an attachment to their old masters.*" This is the tribute to the Society of Jesus of one of England's foremost nineteenth-century writers on education, R. H. Quick. The manifold achievements of the Society in Europe have been recorded by numerous writers. Its labors in the missions of New Spain also have been described in some part; little attention, however, has been given to its educational efforts in the Western Hemisphere. One searches in vain for any extensive account of the great system of education which the Jesuits constructed and maintained in the American colonies. Yet within two hundred years after their first arrival and permanent establishment in Mexico City in 1572, they had created a network of free colleges and seminaries which became nurseries of European culture in North America.

It is the purpose of the present book to reveal the foundation of the Jesuit system of education in New Spain and to describe its growth up to the opening of the seventeenth century. Obviously, such a study necessitates a consideration of the educational efforts of those who preceded the Jesuits in the New World—the Franciscans, the Dominicans, and the Augustinians. Nor can the contributions of the followers of Loyola be understood or appreciated apart from some knowledge of his life, and of the Jesuit character developed through the system of spiritual and intellectual training *which was gradually evolved and carefully organized; for the character of the Jesuit educator was a most important factor in the building of the system of colonial colleges. Such, then, is the aim and scope of the study which follows and which, it is believed, will constitute a new chapter in the history of education.* J. V. J.

The Background

Chapter I

JESUIT INSTITUTIONS AND CONSTITUTIONS

EARLY IN THE SIXTEENTH CENTURY the Catholic Church had fallen upon troublous times. She was intent upon checking the paganizing elements of humanism and upon correcting abuses in the papal court when there loomed before her the great division in the Christian ranks known as the Protestant Revolt. Religious reforms had to be inaugurated. Political crises arose. With these affairs and with an educational program for clergy and laity, the Church was very much occupied. Then at an inopportune moment for her a vast new world had been opened up by Spain for colonization. The colonizing movement undertaken by their Most Catholic Majesties inevitably involved the Church in a new task. The prospect of an empire of souls awaiting the gospel tidings was inspiring, but it seemed she was in no position to widen the sphere of her activity, lest by scattering her energies she might everywhere become haphazard. However, with the opening of the new fields there came to her hands new instruments of cultivation, for, besides others, the Society of Jesus was being trained to carry ultimately a share of the burden of instruction and religious care in the Americas.

By 1572 a small group of the already far-flung cohorts of the Jesuits had arrived in Mexico. It is not our purpose to trace the history of their missionary and exploring activities, but of their educational developments and establishments in New Spain. They came as men fitted and inspired for any and every religious task. Very soon they were found at all occupations just as their brethren were in Europe, India, Japan, China, and South America.[1*] This ubiquity presupposed adaptability to race, language, climate, and position, to cultured and unlettered, to pagan and Christian. What was accomplished by the foremost members of the order in the missions of America has been told by sundry writers; the labors of those who remained in the obscurity and drudgery of the classroom have been left unsung. Still, all the Jesuits, in cities or on the frontier, had a single purpose and a common adaptability. Whence? The secret of their fitness lies in the Jesuit system of training. Because this has not been changed in essentials since the beginning of its practice, it will be useful to view the whole process in its setting, briefly, with an eye to the cardinal points. For this system of training is what the Jesuits brought to America, even as it was this system which inevitably had caused their coming to America. After we have seen the general rules pertinent and essential to the formation of the Jesuit character, and acting as the animating force of the whole Company, we may particularize concerning the day-by-day development of a Jesuit.

A year before the discovery of America the birth of Ignatius, an event seemingly of no more than ordinary significance, happened in the castle of Loyola which still stands in the town of Apeitia in the land of the Basques.[2] As a boy he served in the court of Ferdinand and Isabella, where he grew up listening to firsthand stories of the Moorish battles and of the novel lands across the sea. His cherished ambition

* Superior figures refer to notes on pp. 250–284.

to be off to the wars was realized early, and a right good soldier he proved to be.[3] The turning point of his career was owing to a minor battle between French and Basques at the town of Pamplona, just below the Pyrenees. Stranded there with a small detachment, he chose not to surrender, and he stood battling on the ramparts until a cannon ball shattered one of his legs. To while away convalescence he called for novels, which formed little part of the Loyola library. In place of these somebody gave him a "Life of Christ" and biographies of the saints. Ideas different from those of military glory came to Ignatius. Questions which were to influence the stream of history kept bobbing up: "What will it profit me to gain the whole world and lose my soul?" "Is there not something higher for me? Cannot I do something as the saints did for God and for my neighbor?"

THE SPIRITUAL EXERCISES

Thinking thus, he soon betook himself to prayer in a cave now famous as the Grotto of Manresa. The spirit of the Society of Jesus was born there during the many days of his meditations. This spirit is incorporated in what he wrote as the little book of the *Spiritual Exercises.*[4] The Exercises, or meditations, are the answers to his questions. They are of cardinal importance in the training of every Jesuit. Ever since the first retreat made by Ignatius, the Jesuits have followed him and his development according to the Spiritual Exercises. At some time each year every member must set aside all other occupations and meditate for eight days in silence upon the truths presented in this book. This essential act is termed making a retreat. Twice during his life as a

Jesuit, namely, at the beginning and about fifteen years later at the end of his training, every member makes such a retreat for thirty days. The retreat, to Ignatius, was a way to self-conquest; in other words, it was a means of establishing in his mind his relation to his Creator and to all things created, and the relative import of time and eternity. It is likewise an instrument for all Jesuits for a renewal of their spiritual life and ideals, and a check against the dangers of laxity. Consideration of the great truths fashioned out of Ignatius, the soldier, a man confirmed in purpose to devote his entire energy to the warfare for souls. He would be a soldier in the cause of a King not of this world.

The book is now four hundred years in the using by all classes of persons. For four hundred years it has exerted a tremendous influence upon the practice of Christian ideals, by reason of its content and the approbations of pope after pope.[5] It was a big factor of the Catholic Reformation. By nature it is not merely a guide for the exercises of the retreat itself; it is the manual of Jesuit doctrine, and it is, moreover, suitable to all persons, a complete and practical art of training for a lifetime of interior progress.[6] It was eternal principles derived from its use that carried Kino and Salvatierra into the far places and guided their every action. As a result of absorbing its truths, Jesuits were willing to preach as Bourdaloue did to kings, or as Jogues did to savages. Of temporal failures it made spiritual success for the Jesuits. It is the clue to their quiet acceptance of the Suppression; it is the moving force behind all their educational work; it is the ballast of the ship of the Society sailing unsmooth seas.

A study of the Exercises which effected the transformation of Ignatius would do much to elucidate what was meant by the sixteenth- and seventeenth-century thinkers when they spoke of supernatural ideals and what the teachers of those times endeavored to inculcate both in Europe and in America. Present writers are inclined to classify education which sets forth these ideals as "otherworldly"; and so it was. Religion and education went hand in hand in the earlier centuries, and the dominance of the former as a motive for education was a matter-of-course disposition of mind among all educators.[7] During the age of religious revolutions and revivals, educators strove to ingrain certain principles which would insure correct moral and ethical conduct on the part of their students. Teachers were responsible for the spiritual as well as for the intellectual growth of their hearers. Religion was to be taught and practiced. The basis for the authority of the teacher to demand from his students obedience to this code and procedure was ultimately the highly vivid actuality of the spiritual world and of spiritual forces. To the people of those generations in Europe of whatever Christian denomination, Heaven, Hell, and Eternity were states about which everybody was intimately concerned. Thoughts of a reward of eternal happiness were strong motives for doing good; fears of an eternal punishment were a deterrent from doing evil and a source of penitence. The Devil prowled with his minions as a real menace, a wolf in sheep's clothing, a serpent, a roaring lion. Prayer, penance, watching were necessary for overcoming his suggestions.[8] Strong faith in the doctrines of Christ and in the mercy of God was the keynote of every undertaking and of all activity in education before deism intruded its tenets of an aloof God, or rationalism of a God after man's own reason, or materialism its denial of any God.

Small wonder is it, then, that with discoveries of new lands, seas, and peoples, and with an intellectual and spiritual renaissance going on, the little book written by Ignatius became a sensational textbook, based as it was in the main upon cold reasoning while at the same time it was inclusive of all the traditional realities of the spiritual world familiar to the people. Here was a new ideal: to strive to be a good Christian by obedience to the laws not so much through fear of punishment or hope of reward, but simply for the glory of God. Nor was there question of coercing people, religious or lay, so to strive. Neither was it dictatorial. It was invitational; that is, a person was invited to share in the hardships attendant upon the spiritual warfare that involved perfection. Again, it was essentially an individual appeal to those who wished to signalize themselves in virtue's ways, an extension of Christian asceticism, in its broader sense of the teachings of Christ, to all peoples. But, if followed, it meant perfection in whatever state or profession a man found himself. The terse contents of the book, however, may prove an enigma to one who selects it for casual reading. Only when the points for consideration are amplified and illustrated by a competent director, and only when the system is followed as prescribed by the author, does the whole reveal itself as a masterful treatise on spiritual psychology.

Ignatius penned the text laboriously during the process of his spiritual development and handed it down to his

Company as a dynamic legacy. The meditations have been the dynamos for the power of the Jesuits of all times, and the ultimate secret of their success.[9] They presented Christ as an ideal for the lives of the members and demanded of them a striving for perfection. To the flesh, or to natural inclinations, the Exercises offer an audacious program of self-abnegation. And, although on its personal side the program was invitational, the philosophy of Christian charity embodied in the treatise of Ignatius and his zeal for the extension of Christianity to all parts of the earth were bound to bring the Jesuits ultimately to the New World.

Having made resolutions which flowed logically from his intimate realization of great Christian truths and having schooled himself in his principles, Ignatius was in a position to train others. He was aware of the vastness of the labor to which he had set himself. It would comprehend all classes and nations.[10] His first efforts at preaching got him haled before the Spanish Inquisition. He was shortly released. He concluded that if he wished to have any telling influence upon the savants, he must prosecute a fitting course of studies and become a priest. At the age of thirty-three, therefore, he was humble enough to sit in the classroom with little boys learning Latin rudiments. It required eleven years for him to complete his courses at the Universities of Alcalá, Salamanca, and Paris, during which period he won over to his mode of thinking nine university graduates. Several years after their organization, in 1537, they knelt before the pope and received an approval[11] of their principles and learning. The spirit[12] of the Society of Jesus was then safely housed in a body.

THE CONSTITUTIONS

The founder thought there would be no need of a code of laws with a group of men trained according to the *Spiritual Exercises,* but the example of governments of all sorts indicated the necessity of a written code. By 1541 Ignatius had completed a first draft of his regulations called by him *Constitutions.* In the succeeding nine years rules were added or modified as practice dictated. It was not until the year of his death (1556) that the final draft appeared. The Constitutions were the second instrument of cardinal importance in the training of a Jesuit; for they guided him in whatsoever occupation he found himself.[13] The fourth section of the Constitutions, dealing with the educational plan, was slowly evolved into the famous *Ratio Studiorum* during the forty years following the death of Ignatius. This *Ratio* became the third cardinal instrument for the training of a Jesuit. It is absolutely necessary to consider the Spiritual Exercises, the Constitutions, and the Ratio as instruments working simultaneously toward the formation of the Jesuit character. They are inseparable. They made of the individual Jesuit at once a religious, a schoolmaster, and a missionary.

The original Constitutions have never been changed. As time went on, however, new regulations and ordinations, either of the general congregations or of the generals of the Company, came into being, with the result that there grew up an official body of documents known as the *Institute of the Society of Jesus.* This includes everything of which we have been speaking, and the volumes are best described by an outline of their contents. The Institute is divided into the following ten sections:[14]

(1) Pontifical documents approving the Company and establishing it in its ecclesiastical relations
(2) The *Constitutions* written by Ignatius
(3) Decrees of the General Congregations of the order
(4) General and particular rules
(5) Methods of holding congregations
(6) Ordinations of the generals of the Company
(7) Various instructions for superiors
(8) Counsels for superiors
(9) The book of the *Spiritual Exercises*
(10) The *Ratio Studiorum*

Thus with the spread of the Society the original plans of Ignatius evolved. There will be need in the present work to make allusion to details of government and to institutions. We may reasonably anticipate difficulties by devoting some space to the government of the Society according to the Institute. European and American Jesuits enjoyed quite the same government. It was practically the same for the sixteenth as it was for the later centuries; consequently the second part of this book will not only afford many examples of the government in operation, but it will be also an unfolding of the Institute in the early history of the Province of New Spain. The life of a Jesuit according to the Constitutions will be discussed in the succeeding chapter. The tenth section of the Institute, the *Ratio Studiorum*, has recently been translated[15] and has been appraised by every writer who has interested himself in the history of education. The other parts will be elaborated so far as they become pertinent to educational development in New Spain.

Among those competent by reason of their close association with the founder to know his mind, there was the unanimous conviction that Ignatius had conceived a speculatively perfect instrument of government.[16] After years of practical experiment and modification in nonsubstantial matters had rounded out the scheme, the Jesuit government bore superficial likenesses to every known form of rule. Some thought it monarchical, others thought it absolutistic, others thought it democratic.[17] Pages could be filled with the various criticisms, good and bad, of this government. We cannot linger with these, but must turn to particulars concerning the governing personnel.

THE GENERAL

"As in all well-ordered commonwealths," it seemed necessary that one person have universal charge of the Company.[18] This one was designated the general. He was to be most carefully chosen for his outstanding virtue, judgment, prudence, and courage. He was elected for life by a general congregation of representatives from the various provinces, and he could be deposed by the same. A vicar-general, previously appointed by him with the approbation of the provincials, was to take over the control in the event of the serious sickness or the incapacitating old age of the general. Both of these must be from among the professed fathers. Although the general's authority over the members was universal and his power the fullest, it was never arbitrary and undefined, because he, like any subject, had to obey the Constitutions. Above all, he was bound by the law of charity. His was the power to admit the gift of houses, colleges, and goods. He admitted new members or delegated someone to do so, and papers of dismissal had to be signed by him. He might on consultation erect new provinces. He appointed rectors and provincials on receiving written advices, but did not regularly appoint his own admonitor nor the assistants. He could send a member to work in any part of the world, but he could command nothing in violation of the Constitutions, much less of the laws of the Church or of God. He must be accessible to each member of the Society directly or by letter, and with him rested an ultimate appeal. The mere academic statement of these powers does not touch the salient feature of the general's supreme authority, which was that it must be used according to the great principles and spirit spoken of in the treatment of the Spiritual Exercises. For the general was no high king or military chieftain, but rather a vicar of Christ for his subjects.

THE OTHER SUPERIORS

The members of the Society were grouped geographically into provinces or territorial units. Designated groups of provinces were termed assistancies, of which there were four in 1558. A professed father from each assistancy, as for instance from the Spanish or Italian, was chosen by the general congregation to reside at the Jesuit headquarters as a member of the general's *curia*.[19] He was known as an assistant. The assistants were to be counselors of the general in matters of graver import. They were to meet at least every three months to consider if the general was too lax or too severe in his administration, and each was to be an intermediary between his group of provinces and the general.

With the early spread of the Company it was necessary to appoint heads of the different provinces (1546), who were known as provincials. These were to exercise immediate jurisdiction over their respective groups of subjects; to compare the ecclesiastical hierarchy, they were to the general as bishops were to the pope. They were appointed from the ranks of the professed fathers of a particular province by the general for a term of three years. Information regarding the qualities of members for this office was submitted according to the Constitutions to the general prior to his choice. Once chosen, the provincial disposed of the individuals under his authority to the houses in his territory and to the missions attached to his province. Although he had ample administrative faculties under the Constitutions, the provincial was limited in certain respects. He could not accept any foundation, nor build, nor disburse a large sum, without the permission of the general. He was to make a visitation of each house within his jurisdiction once in a year and have during the visitation a conference with every member. With the advance of the mission frontier, provincial visitations became impossible in so vast a province as New Spain. Each subject was at liberty to expose any grievance and to offer suggestions. An annual complete inventory of the province was to be prepared by the provincial and his secretary, or *socius,* and a report sent to the Roman headquarters. This was called the *carta anua.*

The rector of a house or college was another superior appointed by the general. The choice might be made from among the nonprofessed, except in the case of a rector of a professed house or of a college wherein the younger Jesuits were taught their philosophy and theology.[20] The rectors were subject immediately to the provincial, and it was their chief duty to enforce observance of the Constitutions regarding the government of their respective houses or colleges. The rector was to exercise paternal care over his community, and he assigned positions within his house. He had four consultors with whom he was to confer about administrative matters. His term of office was three years, although like the provincial he was removable. Superiors of groups of missions, as, for example, those of the northern frontier of New Spain, were appointed by the general.

All the superiors and consultors were required to write letters. The regulations concerning letter writing have occasioned vast amounts of documentary sources for historians. The provincial had to write once a month to the general; the consultors of the province twice a year; the secretary of the provincial once a year; the rectors twice a month to the provincial and four times a year to the general; the deans of the colleges twice a year to the provincial, once a year to the general; the consultors of every house, twice a year to the provincial, once to the general; the superiors of missions wrote each two months to the provincial, each three months to the general. There were several minor offices which required their incumbents to write. Although in the later centuries all letters were composed according to formulae, in the sixteenth century the superiors wrote more at length to inform the general of their particular worries, plans, and progress. One readily sees how the archives of the Jesuits became abundantly stocked.

Besides the ordinary superiors there were the extraordinary—the visitors. The visitor was sent to the province by the general at any time he considered an inspection necessary, or when the province requested one. The *visitador* had any authority or jurisdiction over the members of the province visited which the general saw fit to delegate. His duties as outlined were to urge the members to unity and charity, to apostolic labors, and to observance of the Constitutions. He was to smooth difficulties; he was to confer with each subject, and finally was to submit an accurate report to the general concerning the condition of the province.

The superintendence of the household affairs and of the buildings was always the care of a local official known as the minister. The father so designated took the place of the rector upon the illness or absence of the latter. Each house and each province gradually developed a set of local customs concerning apparel, diet, and other details; the minister was to see to their observance. Likewise, he was to watch over the health of his community. His office required him to keep a diary of daily happenings of importance in the house or college, and many such diaries have become important manuscripts for historians.

THE LEGISLATIVE BODY

Such in substance was and has been the administrative scheme of the Society. The power to legislate, however, belonged not to the general but to the General Congregation.[21] Its origin is not obscure. According to the papal bull of establishment (1540), a congregation of all the fathers was to be called for deciding serious problems. Within ten years such a procedure proved impossible, because the number of members had increased and the fathers were at work in distant places. To settle the constitutional point of a meeting of all of the fathers, Pope Julius III interpreted the mind of the former pope to mean that the major portion of the membership should assemble.[22] To assemble even this majority was impracticable long before 1593; consequently the pope left the question to the decision of the congregation of Jesuits then convened to interpret the Constitutions as it saw fit.[23]

The General Congregation represented juridically the Society of Jesus and was the sole legislative body. It elected the new general on the death of the old; it was to be summoned by the general for business of great concern; it had the power to depose a general. What was its personnel? Representing each of their respective provinces by election were two professed fathers; the provincials were present, as were the assistants; the general or the vicar-general presided. Others though not professed might be present, but they did not vote after the deliberations. If it were a congregation called for the election of a general, any of the professed in or out of the congregation was eligible for the office. All political maneuvering directed to the voting for a general or to the voting upon laws was proscribed under penalty. Laws once passed by the General Congregation affected all members of the Society.

Another congregation, which met usually every three years with the general, was an instrument of contact between head and members. In advance of this convention at headquarters, in each province forty fathers, including the provincial and rectors, convened in a provincial congregation and elected one from their midst to represent the province in the triennial, or procurators', congregation. Through the one chosen, petitions and complaints from the province in administrative and other affairs went to headquarters and answers were returned. Any member of the provinces was free to use this personal avenue of approach to the father general by writing a statement of his cause.

Thus in as brief a compass as possible the instruments used in the Jesuit system, that is, the Spiritual Exercises and the governing Constitutions, are surveyed. In order to complete the survey the Ratio remains to be examined. Again it must be emphasized that these three instruments, even though the last named was not fully developed at the time of the arrival of the Jesuits in New Spain, operated at one and the same time in the formation of the Jesuit character and underlay all Jesuit activities. They are the fundamental answer to the question why the Jesuits came to America, and it is hoped that the following chapter will explain the state of preparedness of the Jesuit for his intellectual endeavors on American soil. Since the training which every member had to undergo was an element of his success, the preceding institutional approach was deemed basic for an outline of the method of fashioning the Jesuit character.

Chapter II

JESUITS IN TRAINING

ALTHOUGH ENTRANCE OF THE JESUITS into the field of education might have been forecast as an inevitable consequence of the principles contained in their Institute, the Company up to the year 1540 had no intention of building colleges.[1] The fathers drifted, little by little, toward their educational destination. Their earliest instructions, emphasizing religion and morality, were carried on in peripatetic fashion. Yet of course these "masters of arts graduated in the University of Paris ... teaching boys and unlettered people those things which are essential to the formation of the Christian man ..."[2] so as to merit the approval of Pope Paul III, had early to face the problem of training newcomers in their own organization. After halls of studies for young Jesuits were opened, the next step was to permit extern students to enter the classrooms with them. The final evolution revealed colleges for externs and colleges for Jesuits.

A "problem child" was occasion for much thought over educational beginnings. About the time of the papal approval of the Company, a Castilian youngster forced his way into the Jesuit house and adopted the learned masters of arts. Pedro Ribadeneira is well known to all Jesuits and is humorously referred to as the patron of those novices who sometimes enliven a novitiate with a prank at the expense of their more sober fellows.[3] This *españolito* had been brought to Rome in 1539 as page to the great Cardinal

Alexander Farnese. A diversity of opinion between the playful Pedro and the court major-domo, who happened to be intolerant of pranks, widened to vast proportions. As a result, one night Ignatius Loyola was called to the door, where he found the boy, bag and baggage. Pedro had heard of the Jesuits and had determined to join them. The grave benignity of the first Jesuit won his heart; he refused to do otherwise than to stay; he became the first illustration of the paternal forbearance which has won many a boyish heart. Ignatius saw the good qualities of the manly little lad and even indicated the great works he would perform in the Society. With a smile, the most serious companions bore the practical jokes of this lively spirit.

Pedro had to be trained, however, for he was only fourteen; and the necessity of training this and other youthful entrants drove the fathers into planning the education of young Jesuits. All the members at the time were priests and scholars, yet here was a problem: what to do with young members who would be admitted to the Company. It had papal permission to increase to the number of sixty. By 1541 a short draft of the Constitution was ready, and in them Pedro and other young companions were implicated. A set of rules marked out the educational procedure they were to observe while studying at the universities to which they were sent. There was discussion of establishing Jesuit colleges for the training of subjects in a manner distinctive of the order.⁴ This discussion, with the repeated appeals which came to the Jesuits to open schools, ended in their getting into the classrooms (1543) and in their opening colleges (1545). The spread of colleges and the rapid growth of membership,[5] developments which belong to the European history of the Company and to the history of education, demanded organization and a teaching code.

It is important to note that the early popularity of the Company as a teaching body did not depend upon the Ratio Studiorum. In its final form this did not appear until 1599. Numerous plans (*rationes*) were used during the intervening years to guide the Jesuit teacher of extern students, but a uniform plan was in vogue for the training of Jesuit teachers.[6] We shall see presently what the latter was, after a few words about the evolution of the former, because both were transplanted to America and both affected the collegiate foundations of the Jesuits in the New World. It is remarkable that the experiment stations for polishing the famous plan of studies of the Jesuits which came to be fundamental to the educational revival in Europe were certain classrooms in America.[7]

The writings about the pedagogics of the Jesuits have been copious. How did they become "the most efficient corporation of schoolmasters then at work"?[8] We repeat the answer, it was their spirit engendered by training.[9] It is said at times that the Company borrowed,[10] to put it politely, the ideas of the Ratio from the great German educator, Johann Sturm, or again from the Spaniard, Juan Luis Vives. Sturm himself, whose course of studies was externally different[11] from that of the Jesuits, made no direct accusation to this effect, although he did say, "So little different is this from our system and rules that it would seem they had borrowed from us."[12] This was written in 1565, years after the Jesuit beginnings of education. There is no one who can say just how much the Company gleaned from the other great teachers of Europe. What Sturm and Vives did not have, and therefore what the Jesuits originated and perfected, was the whole system of training and motivation. Undoubtedly they assimilated any good pedagogical rules of the time, but who can say these were not the common heritage of European education?[13]

Vives, too, manifests a difference of ideals from those of the Jesuits, even though superficially there are many points in common between his system and that of the Society.[14] Manifestly the universities exercised a great influence upon the system of Jesuit pedagogy, since all the first generation of Jesuits was graduated from them, particularly from the University of Paris, and many of the succeeding members, who were superiors and deans at the time of the drafting of the Ratio, had received their intellectual training at Rome, Alcalá, Salamanca, and Paris.[15] The mistake lies in supposing that ordinary affairs underwent a complete transformation in the year 1517 with the inauguration of the Protestant Revolt.[16] It seems more likely that the educational policies of the Brethren of the Common Life, and many of their pedagogical principles, were utilized by Vives, Sturm, and the Jesuits.[17] Vives certainly was familiar with the methods of the Brethren by reason of living near one of their great schools. Sturm actually spent three of his formative years (1521–1524) in their college at Liége, and the Jesuits took over that college in 1580.[18]

In view of the translations of the Ratio and of the many and varied criticisms it has received, there is no need here of considering it as it was applied in the instruction of the youth of Europe. It is pertinent, however, to explain the Ratio as an instrument for the training of the Jesuit—an instrumental attribute which places it beyond Sturm and Vives in scope. It was a guide in the Jesuit's intellectual expansion, but at the same time it aided in disciplining his spirit and so in impressing upon him a missionary-schoolmaster character.

In the abundant short biographies of the Jesuit fathers and in the provincial menologies we find descriptions of the spiritual and intellectual qualities for which each is noted. Invariably the virtues most extolled were obedience, humility, charity, self-sacrifice, and mortification. The narrators may appear to harp with unnecessary frequency upon the edifying qualities of the deceased priest or brother, but the point of the matter was to encourage younger members by giving every example of the effects of a difficult training courageously undergone and thus to keep before them the ideal *esprit de corps* of the Company. There was no successful character building, in the mind of Ignatius and the early superiors, unless a deep foundation had been laid in virtues such as ordinarily escape the eye but become manifest in action and crises. Once he was grounded in the fundamentals and particularly in obedience, no task would appear to the member to be impossible of accomplishment. But sturdy virtue for schoolmasters, missionaries, and priests could result only from patient attention to a highly detailed course of training, and hence the first fifteen years of the life of a Jesuit have always been the burnishing time for his character. The system of intellectual and spiritual training set up by Ignatius gradually crystallized into an art of warfare against natural inclinations, with no conspicuous or fundamental difference appearing in its application from generation to generation throughout these four centuries. Still, various fundamentals of the routine of Jesuit training must be considered here, even though it has been treated at length by others from diverse standpoints.[19]

In the early days of the Society an applicant for admission came to Ignatius or to a provincial appointed by him, who accepted or rejected the man after weighing his qualifications. Soon the increasing number of applications and certain regulations of the Council of Trent gave rise to a policy of procedure for receiving men into the order. Thereafter, when anyone applied for admission he was sent to confer with several fathers who returned separate verdicts regarding his acceptability. Each examiner asked prescribed questions and formed an opinion from several considerations, namely, the suitability of the candidate for the life and work of a Jesuit, his gifts of nature in respect of health, intellect, and good judgment, his external appearance and personality, and his antecedents. A deficiency in any of the points eliminated the candidate.[20] If he had been in any manner cajoled or coerced into applying, he could not validly become a member of the Society; and the examiner was bound very solemnly to investigate these possibilities. Afterwards he submitted a written report to the provincial, including his opinion that the candidate should or should not be admitted.

THE TWO YEARS OF PROBATION

Arriving at the place of his noviceship, the candidate spent a number of days apart from the already enrolled novices, during which time he was informed of all the rules and regulations. These preliminary days were called the first probation. At their completion the candidate received a cassock, became a novice, and entered his second probation,— unless he had decided to withdraw, as he had been free to do at any time and as he would be free to do until the taking of his religious vows. The length of this second period or novitiate is now two years, but in the sixteenth century it was not so definite, being shorter or longer according to individual circumstances. The place of the probation was not always a house set apart as it is now; the novice underwent his probation in some Jesuit abode,[21] or, as at least a few did, even with missionary fathers in the wilds of Florida[22] or Brazil.[23] Once a novice, however, he was dependent upon the Society for the necessaries of life and was relieved of financial worry.

Rather in anticipation of the account of the Jesuit novitiate at Tepotzotlán in New Spain, mention must be made here of items in the novices' program of life which may appear insignificant unless the general purport of this character study is kept in view. Although novices rarely attained historical importance in the annals of Jesuit accomplishment, the significance to them and to the Society of their daily occupations should not be obscured.

A day in the house of probation demanded constant obedience to bells, orders, and regulations.[24] The novice rose at a set hour of four, five, or six o'clock, according to local custom. He meditated on some spiritual truth for an hour, then heard Mass and breakfasted. He was then assigned to manual tasks about the house or garden, and since in Europe such occupation was normally that of servants it was indeed humbling to many a youthful Jesuit hitherto accustomed to receive service. Prescribed for the later hours of the morning were study, class, reading of spiritual books or biographies of the saints, and self-examination regarding progress. At lunch and at dinner he heard reading in the refectory as was the custom in all communities, except when there was a sermon instead of reading. Occasionally the rector granted permission for all to talk while at table. During the day the novice's tasks were performed in silence, but after the principal meals he was allowed to speak in the vernacular with his fellows. If it was necessary during the day's silence to say anything, Latin was the vehicle. In the afternoon, exercises similar to those of the morning engaged the novice, and others were added. Sermons were written and delivered before the others for criticism. The catechism was explained to children, to the poor, and to prisoners in jails. Daily instructions were given by the master of novices on individual rules of the Institute. Conferences were held with the master, who alone could guide the novice and correct his mistakes. In the evening, half an hour was spent in Latin conversation, after which prayer and penance concluded the novice's day.

Such, then, was the daily order for the novices, with the exception of Sundays and the greater feasts of the Church, on which occasions there were several hours of recreation.

Besides this routine there were probations within the probation. The first of these was the thirty days' retreat made at the beginning of the novitiate. At another time the novice was put to work in the kitchen or refectory for a month or so. Sometimes novices were sent to help in a hospital where spiritual development was to be rounded out through performance of distasteful services. At times, too, a pair of novices were sent forth on a begging tour after the apostolic fashion, depending upon the charity of strangers for their sustenance.

In view of the strictness and duration of the religious probation, people neither chosen for nor inclined toward such a life were and are apt to pity the young Jesuit's lot. Commiseration may well be spared, for happiness was ever the mark of him who has foregone such things as men ordinarily hold dear. The bells and orders were not difficult to obey when they meant the summons of God. Correction and reprimand were accepted cheerfully from superiors who stood in the place of God, and the superior was always paternally watchful to lay a restraining hand on the probationer who inclined toward the excesses of youthful enthusiasm in piety or study. There was happiness in brotherhood with men of like ideals, and from his earliest days there grew in the Jesuit a deep love for the Society and a charity which influenced profoundly his attitude toward other members of "the same Society." The training and its derivatives in this latter respect might well be likened to those of a West Point or an Annapolis, but only as to externals, since the goal of the Jesuit was a maximum of spiritual motivation and a minimum of service through fear of demerit.

If, however, one failed to absorb the spirit of the Company of Jesus he could not long survive in its ranks. But if the novice proved during his probation that he had assimilated this spirit and could act according to the Institute, he was permitted to pronounce his vows of poverty, chastity, and obedience, and thus to bind himself perpetually to the Society. After this pronouncement he passed on to his studies and was termed a scholastic until his ordination to the priesthood.

THE JUNIORATE

The second stage in the development of the Jesuit character had in view the beginnings of his intellectual training according to the Ratio Studiorum. The young Jesuit studied the ancient classics during a period which is now of two years. In the time of Ignatius and for some years following, many of the scholastics attended some neighboring college, but when the Jesuit colleges began to flourish, the religious took their courses in them under Jesuit instructors. The students were called juniors and the period the juniorate. Later on, separate quarters and buildings were assigned them together with a dean, and the dwelling became known as the juniorate.

The order of the day in the juniorate as distinct from the novitiate changed to one almost entirely of lecture and study.[25] The essential spiritual concerns of meditation, Mass, and self-examination continued, but many of the exercises of prayer of the novitiate were omitted. Instead, study with a proper intention became a means both of praising God and of perpetuating the training process begun in the novitiate. The hours of the day, except the one or two devoted

to healthful recreation, were spent in mastering the classics
with the objective of one day teaching them in the colleges.
In the time allotted it was not difficult for juniors to read
Cicero, Livy, Tacitus, Vergil, Juvenal, and others in Latin,
and Xenophon, Homer, Sophocles, and the philosophers in
the Greek. Hebrew was also in the curriculum. The junior
likewise had to study the prose and poetic masterpieces of
the country in which he resided. Even though he had had
such courses before his entrance into the Society, the junior
frequently had to repeat them during his years of humanities and rhetoric as part of his teacher training. Supervised
classes were conducted regularly by the junior before his
companions, who acted as critics of the method and arrangement followed. The traditional pedagogical principles of the Jesuits were transmitted from generation to
generation, with emphasis laid upon exposition, drill, repetition, and composition in the classical Greek and Latin and
in the vernacular. Sermons and orations in Latin were of
frequent occurrence, and classes were conducted in the re-
fined tongue of Cicero. Such procedure was necessary to the
scholastic's future study and work; and when it was completed the junior passed on to a college of the Society for
philosophical studies.

THE THREE YEARS OF PHILOSOPHY

There were definite objectives for the intensive courses in
scholastic philosophy prescribed by the Jesuit plan of studies.
The three-year curriculum in the philosophate, as both the
period of study and the place of study were termed, called
for lectures in logic, epistemology, ontology, psychology,

ethics, cosmology, theodicy, natural science, and mathematics. These constituted an essential intellectual background for the study of theology.[26] They were a rationalizing check on the previous study of the humanities; they gave reasons for man's creation and existence, they gave form to the scholastic's thought, balance to his opinions, and stabilization to his purpose in life. The hard, unbreakable chain of Aristotle's logic gave mental sureness to his ways. Philosophy, moreover, was studied for itself and was a prime academic field in those times; it was at once speculative and realistic to a generation of schoolmen which had uncomplicated leisure and a desire to argue and to refute.[27] In practical aspect, philosophy was necessary as an aid to faith and a weapon against heresy.

Philosophy classes were conducted in Latin. There was a daily quiz, a repetition quiz on Saturdays, an examination for each philosopher before a board of four at the end of the third year.[28] Most distinctive was the disputation, for which, at least twice a week, a full hour was set apart.[29] The procedure was this: One of the scholastics was assigned some theses which he must prepare to explain and defend; two others were appointed to gather objections against one of the theses; on the day appointed, after all had assembled in the hall of disputations, the defender and objectors took places on the platform much after the fashion of a college debating circle. The defender expounded his proposition, gave a bibliography including authorities who held with him and against him, presented a survey of ancient and modern views, and finally worded his proof in strict syllogistic form. The batteries of the objectors were then opened for a quarter of an hour before the discussion went to the floor. This intellectual joust in Latin, at times wearisome, was conducted at other times in so heated a manner that an outsider might readily suppose the good people, professors included, were on the verge of a major schism. These jousts, or *actas,* while admirably suited to sharpen the mind to a keen point for perception of truth, falsity, and distinctions, had a reflex in external attitudes and go a long way toward explaining the combative and controversial spirit of some religious.

What limited scientific courses were taken during these years were conducted in Latin. A survey course in the undeveloped sciences of physics, chemistry, geology, and biology was probably less important than the two in mathematics.[30] As a student in philosophy, the scholastic picked a hobby for specialization, which might be linguistic, classical, scientific, or technically philosophical. The method of carrying on this special work is interesting in this, that the philosopher usually gathered together several kindred spirits into what was known as an academy, which met regularly during some recreation period to discuss its project. The extracurricular group was expected to give at some time in the year a public exhibition of its findings or progress, as, for instance, a lecture in science or an interpretation of a French or Spanish drama.

THE REGENCY OF THE SCHOLASTIC

With some seven years of training behind him, the Jesuit student emerged qualified for teaching the younger boys in one of the Jesuit colleges. He did not choose his position;

he was sent and appointed to his class. Teaching was an experiment for himself and for the order. It was a test of his training, and he might be kept at it variously from one to five years, depending sometimes on the need of teachers, sometimes on the age of the individual, sometimes on the necessity of experience. His community life and spiritual practices were unchanged; his duties and the many regulations of the teachers made life more complex. The teacher was given several weeks' summer vacation with the community at some villa, where the religious life persisted but studies were omitted. After the vacation there were summer school and private study. The villa season, with summer study, was the regular custom for the scholastic each year of his philosophy, teaching, and theology periods.

THE YEARS OF THEOLOGY

Theological studies based on Thomas Aquinas occupied the Jesuit for the four years following his teaching and were the direct preparation for his priestly life.[31] For some less gifted in philosophical or theological attainments, the courses were less intensive or the period might be shortened to three years. Ordination to the priesthood, the goal of religious ambition, generally took place at the end of the third year: it was as a priest that the Jesuit concluded his four years of study. The lectures covered apologetics, dogmatic and moral theology, scripture, canon law, and ecclesiastical history. As in the days of philosophy, there were quiz periods, disputations, and yearly examinations; a final comprehensive examination demanded a knowledge of all the matter worked at in both philosophy and theology.

THE FINAL PROBATION—TERTIANSHIP

It would appear that the eleven years of study exclusive of the regency might be sufficient training, but there was another year called the tertianship, or third probation, which usually followed theology.[32] It was a year devoted to final spiritual formation and was probationary in view of the similarity it had to the novitiate. The tertian father studied the Institute in his seclusion, made the thirty days' retreat, wrote sermons and meditations for the retreats which he intended giving to others, catechized children, helped in parish work on occasions, and administered the sacraments in hospitals. Meantime, at home, he performed manual work about the building or in the kitchen for an hour or two a day. After this final test of his humility and obedience the father entered upon the active work of his life.

THE GRADES

The idea of probations and training suggests the likelihood of reward or distinction. Were Jesuits given a classified status at the end of their training in accordance with the degree of their spiritual and intellectual attainment? They were, but, so far as the external world was able to detect, there was no difference between one Jesuit and another because of this rating. Nor would the peculiar distinction conferred upon the father who had manifested the greatest progress in the course of his training be considered by lay folk precisely as a reward. The distinction lay in several extra vows which some fathers were permitted to make.[33] Usually, within the year following the conclusion of the

last probation, every father repeated his three vows publicly
and finally, after having renounced in legal form all prop-
erties and possessions. The procedure according to the custom since the first days of the Society was to have the father
kneel in the sanctuary of the church immediately behind
the celebrant of the Mass. At the solemn moment of the
Communion he read aloud his three vows, written in his
own hand, and then placed the paper in the hand of the
celebrant, the father rector customarily, who accepted them
in the name of the general.

Those fathers, however, who had been deemed highly
eminent in virtue, who had excelled in learning, who had
good health and judgment, and who had reached the age
of thirty-three years, were notified that they were to take
vows termed solemn, and thus to become professed fathers.
The vows included, besides the usual three of the religious
life, a fourth one, which was to go whithersoever the pope
might wish to send the father. Added to this vow were several simple vows that bound the professed, among other
things, never to give way to ambition for any dignity or
prelacy in or out of the Society, and never to relax the requirements of the vow of poverty—if anything, to make
them more strict. The professed father, therefore, has ever
been the particular protector of the institutions of the Jesuits.
The extra vows were not taken in public. When conditions
permitted the ideal to be followed, the professed resided in
what was known as the professed house, which will be described later, but in the want of such an abode he lived
more frequently in one of the colleges. He was eligible for
the offices of provincial and general; he sat in the provincial

councils and was eligible for election as representative of his province in the triennial congregation at Rome or at the time of the election of a new general.

The other fathers, who for lack of health or preëminence in theological or philosophical learning did not take the fourth vow, became spiritual coadjutors. At times the profession has been given to these when the necessities of administration or hitherto undiscovered talent, judgment, or virtue indicated such a procedure. The general alone admitted fathers to their respective grades. The distinction between members of the order has rather lapsed in practice, since both professed fathers and spiritual coadjutors have invariably followed the same domestic life and have worked together in similar public occupations; thus, although certain offices are reserved for his grade, the professed has sometimes found himself teaching in a college wherein a nonprofessed is dean or rector.

There was from the beginning another grade in the Society, that of the temporal coadjutor. The lay brothers belonged to this. They were not to become priests; but they were none the less Jesuits, by reason of their having taken the three vows and obeying the same Constitutions. They did not follow the scholastic courses of study. They devoted themselves to the manual and secretarial work of the houses, churches, and colleges, and occasionally one was found teaching boys in the lower classes. The Society was ever quick to appreciate the efficiency and self-sacrifice of these capable members, and the Church has canonized more than one of them.

In a summary of these two chapters it is well to empha-

size again that the institutional standpoint, with the resultant survey of the evolution of the Jesuit character, was not
chosen to distress readers familiar with Jesuit life; the intention, rather, was to afford a comprehensive view of the
operations of the Jesuits prior to their arrival in North
America. The logical procedure now would be to give a
description of a typical Jesuit as Macaulay and others have
done. But there is no typical Jesuit character; there never
was a lone mold waiting for every young man who entered the Society. This fact is manifest in the remarkable
diversity of interests, tastes, occupations, and achievements
which history has attributed to individual members. There
was a typical method of training which was and is Ignatian;
nevertheless, in the Company, there was allowed the widest
latitude for individual broadening and assertiveness within
the Constitutions. The superiors, from the master of novices
on through the rectors and provincials to the generals, have
not been of a mind to distort the characters of men in their
care but rather to develop to a useful point the natural gifts
of the individual while they inculcated the supernatural outlook. There was never the idea among them of destroying
first the subject's individuality, then of fashioning what
would prove to be a new and superficial character. In fair-
ness it must be said that sometimes the training was not
successful, so that sometimes men left the order or were
expelled. At times it was only partially successful, so that
members continued in the ranks only to become "family
concerns."

The complete organization of the Society with its particular *esprit de corps,* supernatural motivation, and individual

loyalty, together with the very simplicity of its objective, has given rise to misconceptions about Jesuit motives which carry on like the sturdy myths of Spanish gold. The particular armor of the Jesuit has been simplicity of purpose, of soul, and of manner of life; but to many this very simplicity has been perplexing. The pages to follow, it is hoped, will reveal a typical method of Jesuit procedure and development. Since it would be necessary, in the Jesuit way, to see at least vaguely the possibilities in the field which lay ahead in America, a glance at conditions there should prove useful.

Chapter III

THE BEGINNINGS OF EDUCATION
IN NEW SPAIN

THERE HAD BEEN VARIOUS FORMS of education in vogue in what is now Mexico long before the arrival of the Jesuits. It might prove enlightening indeed to search among the ancient ruins abounding in the lower portion of North America, and to scan the old picture writings, for indications of the existence of public schools in the ages of the Mayas, Toltecs, and Aztecs. It seems that at times efforts were made toward the education of youth among the early peoples of lower North America who for centuries had been holding the land against the coming of the Europeans.

The Mayas are reported to have had centers of learning where boys were taught, along with the arts of warfare, the history of their nation, astronomy, and music.[1] There must have been some teaching method in use for the tradition of their lore and handicrafts. We are told there was in one place a seminary whose faculty consisted of seventy masters supported by the treasury, but we must be wary of the terminology used by writers of the conquest times. The exact history of the Mayas, if that is what is carved on their stelae and monuments, remains a perennial puzzle awaiting a Rosetta stone. The peoples of Yucatan, even though they may have bequeathed some culture to the other tribes, do not come into the scope of this book. The Toltecs, too, persist in being enigmatical; to some they are purveyors of the ancient civilization of the Mayas, to others they are a mythical tribe. Traces of their barbarian culture had vanished before the coming of the whites. The Aztecs are better known, chiefly by reason of the great Spanish power which overtook them in the days of their cultural decadence. As recipients of the foreign impact their history and customs came under closer scrutiny, and their institutions were glorified by men accustomed to the less polished savagery of the Caribbean islands.

The tribes in and about Mexico had no alphabet and were illiterate except for the few who could convey an idea by picture writing.[2] They seem to have had some teachers who aided in the transmission of knowledge of tribal affairs to the younger generation. The teachers forced the chosen boys to memorize the oral traditions, and they arranged pageants commemorative of the past. Singularly enough, the Christian priests used two methods of instruction which, whether invented or adopted, appealed immediately to the native intelligence. One was to illustrate pictorially the Catholic doctrine,[3] and the other was to explain ideas by pantomime plays. We may suppose, therefore, that these methods had been familiar to the natives. Schools of a sort existed, but they brought nothing to sixteenth-century intellectual life in the Spanish colony, and they were not schools in any modern sense of the word.[4] Nor was there any general public education, although there were forms of training for specific duties in pre-Cortesian times. Select groups of girls were sheltered in a building adjacent to the temple. These devoted themselves to the work of keeping the temple clean and of serving the local religious chief in his household affairs, receiving in return some religious

instruction. Their after-careers as concubines of the Mocte-
zuma or as wives of favorite soldiers indicate ulterior objectives for the girls' schools.[5] Two prevalent types of schools
for young men have been called colleges. In one, chosen
sons of the chiefs learned to chant the historical episodes
of the nation's past and the ritual of religious ceremonies.
The other gathering of youths was a quasi-military school
wherein an almost inhuman discipline prevailed.[6] Thus all
the existing education was limited to small groups and
was far removed from learning in arts or letters. The sha-
man elders and military chiefs developed privately what
oratory and astronomy the natives are reputed to have had.
How the vast masses of people employed their leisure for
learning is open to conjecture. The similarity of procedure
in education adopted by the Nahuan leaders and the Franciscan friars is striking, for both brought groups of natives
together into halls of instruction which stood hard by the
religious edifices. The significance lies in this, that to men
from Christian Europe and to men in pagan America religion and culture appeared closely associated.[7]

These few echoes of a cultural past, the picture writings,
the pageants, and the groups of youngsters near a temple,
were all that remained to the Aztecs when education in
a modern signification took up its abode in Mexico. The
Christian education was strange to the land, and the land
made resistance; the essential circumstances of popular
education were against the Europeans; all had to be built.
Fortunately a number of real builders arrived, ready to lay
the foundations of an educational system. The Franciscans,
Dominicans, Mercedarians, and Augustinians set hand to

the labor of organization of instruction while far-reaching plans were being pushed forward with earnest impatience by such leaders as Bishop Zumárraga, Bishop Quiroga of Michoacán, and Viceroy Mendoza.

Rudimentary and primary education followed the steps of the conquest. We are aware that the Franciscans who were told by Columbus to construct a stone monastery at Nueva Isabella attached a little school to their completed building in 1502. At the same time a similar school for the instruction of Indian boys in reading, writing, and singing was in progress beside the convent of La Vega. One of these was the first grade school in the New World.[8] Convents were founded later in Cuba beginning with 1505, San Juan (1511), and Darién (1512), but the founders confined themselves principally to missionary work. We are more concerned with the base for an educational spread, which was established in New Spain.

The first educator to command attention is Pedro de Gante.[9] This nobleman who had turned friar, besides tempering the later phase of the Central American conquest and influencing greatly the civil and ecclesiastical policy during the formative years of New Spain, threw the weight of his astounding educational personality into what loomed as the hopeless task of cultivating aboriginal minds. He is the focal point for all primary educational progress in the area of Mexico City between the years 1523 and 1572. His real name was Peter Van den Moere, which he Latinized into Petrus de Mura; but having been born in a suburb of Ghent, Flanders, he became best known as Pedro de Gante. The year of his birth was 1479. Somehow he has been referred to erroneously as a brother, a half-brother, and even as a natural son of Emperor Charles V, who was born in 1500.[10] Gante studied at Louvain and was engaged before entering the Franciscan convent in legal cases for the crown.[11] After spending some years as a lay brother in a Belgian house, together with Fray Juan de Tecto, the guardian of the convent, and Fray Juan de Aora, he moved to Spain in July, 1522, where he tarried until May of the following year. The three arrived in the New World August 13, 1523, which indicates that at the age of forty-four Gante began almost a half-century of labor in New Spain.

He and his two companions remained in Mexico City for a short while, considering the various angles of their work. They found themselves as poor as the Indians of the city and as ignorant of the Aztec idiom as the Aztecs were of theirs. The Spaniards, busy about the conquests and rebuilding, were of no help to them.[12] Furthermore, the altars of the natives were not yet cold; the military organization of the conquered people, so closely linked with religion, was shattered, but steeped as they were in the inhuman sacrificial worship of centuries, the people could not be expected suddenly to adopt a new theology. Above all, the distressing time of conquest and plague seemed no likely time to begin education. Consequently, the three hied themselves to the abode of the friendly chief at Tezcoco, where, heeding the warnings against appearing in public, they learned the language and customs of the land.

In 1524 the famous "twelve apostles" of the Franciscans arrived. Gante moved from place to place a tireless teacher and builder. The results of his efforts viewed in their en-

tirety give us a panorama of progress which affords cause
for wonderment. He labored day and night instructing natives in reading, writing, singing.[13] He taught the sons of the
chief men how to compose and deliver sermons. The boys
taught others. He had classes which totaled five hundred
natives in and about Mexico City. He made the city appear
like another Rome, for he had constructed more than a
hundred churches and chapels by the year 1529. Springing
up with these were the school buildings housing numbers
of children.[14] In the patios between church and school instructions in religion were in progress at all hours of the
day. It must have been a strange sight to the eyes of the
conquistadors, this scene of quiet learning on the part of
natives whose war cries of the earlier battles could still be
remembered; remarkable likewise was the picture of the
older Indians squatting in the patios in the morning before
trudging to their labor, and the picture of the sons of a
proud race being instructed in the manner of delivering a
Sunday sermon. But what appeals to the educator is the
establishment which grew under the careful administration
of Pedro de Gante and the other Franciscans into the College of San Francisco.

This college, which was erected behind the conventual
church called San José de Belén, was in the heart of Mexico
City. It took care of a thousand children in its early days,
and later included Latin and drawing in its curriculum. As
Icazbalceta informs us:

Not satisfied with working for the children, Pedro de Gante gathered together the adults, for whom he established a school of trades
and fine arts. He provided the churches with religious paintings,

statuary, embroidered vestments, crosses. . . . He was also able to supply workmen. . . . In his school he had painters, sculptors, carvers, stonecutters, carpenters, embroiderers, tailors, shoemakers, and other tradesmen of whom he was not only the supervisor but the teacher. The Herculean labors of this lay brother arouse in us the profoundest admiration. Without resources other than his indomitable energy which was born of a flaming charity, he built and for many years maintained a magnificent church, a hospital, and a huge establishment which was at the same time a school of primary education, a college for higher education, a home for religious training, a trades school, and an academy of fine arts: in a word, a center of civilization.[15]

From this Franciscan center radiated in all directions the light of spiritual and intellectual progress.

Patience is a fundamental virtue for those who intend to stay in a classroom for any great length of time. The estimable Brother Pedro made Mexico his classroom for nearly fifty years. It required patience to master the Mexican dialects. The restlessness of untamed children to many of whom he had to be father, mother, and teacher, meant trying days. Nevertheless, so diligently content was he with his lot that several times he refused to accept clerical orders and ecclesiastical dignities, even the archiepiscopal, in order to remain laboring at his real vocation. His influence was so great that Archbishop Montúfar is quoted as having said, "It is not I who am archbishop of Mexico, but Pedro de Gante, lay brother of the Order of St. Francis."[16] If a patron saint of hardworking American schoolmasters is ever sought, Gante, founder of the first primary school system in the New World, would prove a suitable choice.

The other friars were probably not far behind Gante as skilled instructors. Fray Jacobo de Tastera, for instance, with his invention of visual aids, paintings and picture writings, and others with translations of the catechism into the native tongues, captured the attention of the pupils even as Gante did.[17] Religion appears to have been the main content of the courses, but incidentally the children were acquiring new customs and manners, and reading and writing, and they were learning to grasp concepts that were poles apart from the natural morality, the tribal religion, and the urges of their environment. An atmosphere of study was created. The religious training awakening many minds to the interests of civilized life made primary and secondary education an inevitable consequence. In short, the work of the friars was really the beginning of the transmission of European culture.[18]

Besides being an educator, Brother Pedro de Gante has been called "a star of the first magnitude in the ecclesiastical and civil history of New Spain."[19] His influence on two generations of natives who hastened to him with their concerns was of far-reaching importance. His life epitomizes the ideal which Church and Crown had for apostles; it is a summary of the task of elevation and civilization of the natives which the Church was undertaking. Mexicans today honor his memory. He is a competitor for the honors of "apostle of the Indies" which have been bestowed upon Bartolomé de Las Casas with far less reason in achievement. Gante must be forgiven for shattering idols when we consider the ideals he fostered. The idols upon which he waged war had for him the hideous implication of human sacrifices, of the lifeblood of infants shed at times by parents, of mutilation of high-born victims, of death on the altars for strong men

and for the flower of Mexican maidenhood. Gante died in
1572 and the span of his life serves as a connecting link between the pagan past and the arrival of the Jesuits.

Many worked with Gante at the foundations of Christian culture. If life among the Mexicans was arduous and
hazardous for the sturdy friars, what must it have been for
the first nuns who came? The Tertiary Sisters were actually
in the capital in 1525 teaching the native girls, and the Poor
Clares were brought from Spain by the wife of Cortés.[20]
They were engaged in primary instruction in religion and
in sewing and domestic arts, and proved worthy pioneers
in the field of child psychology and social endeavor in
America. In 1530 the Empress sent a group of six ladies
from Spain to train native girls. In 1534 Zumárraga introduced six nuns. The great bishop saw the need of schooling
for girls, and with the help of the Franciscans opened classes
for them in Huejotzingo, Otumba, Tlascala, Cholula, Tepe-
aculco, and Coyoacán.[21] A college for *mestizas* named Nuestra Señora de la Caridad is mentioned in the cedulas from
the year 1530. These are typical examples of the attempt of
churchmen to elevate women and to free her kind from the
evils of the chattel state.

In the early days there was a street called San Juan which
led past the central monastery of San Francisco. Across this
road, opposite the monastery, was a market place, where
children gathered with their parents. There the friars were
wont to instruct the children in religion, and soon discovered that many of them were sick. The guardian petitioned
the *cabildo,* or city council, for the grant of a site whereon
an infirmary, or clinic, might be built. The *cabildo* donated

the land in legal form,[22] and the building was constructed with living rooms on the main floor for the little boarders and for the sick. The institution thus begun in 1529 was called San Juan de Letrán. Now, one of the evil effects of the conquering soldiery upon the land was the birth of mestizo infants who were in a way of becoming children of misfortune.[23] When at length ordinances commanding mothers to bring such children to stated places for ascertaining parentage, failed to remedy the evil, the wide doors and kindly hands at San Juan welcomed the orphans.

In time the shelter became a primary school for both boys and girls of the mixed caste. In 1545 it came under the king's patronage. Aided by donations from the king, it grew until 1547, when Viceroy Mendoza confiscated the building for the purpose of establishing the College of San Juan de Letrán for more advanced students, promising the friars a new building in return. The promise was unfulfilled, but the college for mestizos prospered. Several additional endowments came from the king (1548, 1552, 1557), and it had attained to the character of a normal school by 1557.[24] Three theologians were in charge, who filled annually in turn the offices of rector, master of schools, and Latin teacher. The less apt pupils were set to learning trades for three years, while each year six of the more promising were permitted to study letters for an additional seven years. These latter are they who became teachers and prominent civic leaders and aroused the envy of Creole and Spaniard.[25] There were two hundred boys being educated in San Juan de Letrán in 1553, of ages varying between nine and fourteen. In the same year Gregorio Pesquero, supervisor of the school, journeyed to Rome to ask Ignatius Loyola for Jesuit teachers for his college.[26] The Jesuits did not accept the offer. A decline set in when Gante, who was responsible in great part for the kingly interest and favors from the royal treasury, passed away. Plagues interfered with the work, and the mestizo population declined with the correction of the original evil to which the school owed its origin. By 1579 San Juan had only seventy students. Archbishop Moya y Contreras, according to the wishes of Philip II, asked the Jesuits to take it over in 1580. Again the Jesuits declined the offer, because of a lack of men and because there were girls being trained in one section of the institution and hospital inmates in another section.[27] But San Juan de Letrán lingered on, in a checkered career, until its doors were closed in the middle of the nineteenth century.

San Juan de Letrán College for mestizos could scarcely be categorized as a secondary school from its curriculum, if we neglect the Latin being taught in its upper division. Its seven-year course is difficult to classify. Nor could Gante's College of San Francisco be termed a secondary school according to modern standards, since in its final form it had technical courses and instruction in a remarkable number of pursuits from reading to theology and sermon writing; yet both institutions were excellent feeders for high school and even for preliminary college work. After a few years they had created a demand for higher learning, and hence it was that a standard college came into being. We judge the need of further studies from a petition which went to Charles V in 1533 from Bishop Sebastián Ramírez de Fuenleal, president of the famed second *audiencia*.[28] His letter

contained a plea for a specified amount of goods and money
to support a house and a group of students, and appears to
have been written on behalf of the Franciscans of Mexico
City. Grants were made and a site was selected at Tlatelolco
in the northern environs of the city near the lake. The germ
of the idea lay in the fact that the Franciscans had received
great aid in the planting of the faith from those to whom
they had taught the Latin language.[29] When it was concluded that the boys and the people were capable of the
same knowledge and the same virtues as the Spaniards,[30]
the great-minded friars urged the establishment of the college for culture's sake.

El Colegio de Santa Cruz de Tlatelolco opened solemnly
on January 6, 1536. Sixty students were in attendance, and
from that day the numbers constantly increased. The clien-
tele was native, the better students being selected from the
neighboring schools in Mexico and the villages. The building must have been hastily constructed, for within a few
years it began to totter a bit. At news of this, the very busy
emperor manifested his interest to the degree of telling
Viceroy Mendoza to see that the edifice was permanently
constructed. Otherwise, what with alms, a gift from Bishop
Zumárraga of some rentals, and another of some haciendas
from Mendoza, the college progressed rapidly for the first
five years.[31]

The faculty of this first American college deserves mention. It was organized from members of the near-by Franciscan convent and was composed of such learned men as
Fray Arnaldo de Basacio, probably the first teacher of Latin
in New Spain, Fray García de Cisneros, pioneer and first

provincial of the Franciscans in Mexico, Fray Andrés de Olmos, the missionary of holy renown who knew many languages, Fray Juan de Gaona and Fray Juan Focher, both distinguished graduates of the University of Paris, and Fray Bernardino de Sahagún, the distinguished writer and Father of the Indians. It was a very notable faculty; if we remember the year, the conditions, and the native students, it was a remarkable faculty. The lecturers offered courses in reading, writing, Latin, rhetoric, philosophy, music, Mexican medicine, and printing, the last named probably connected somehow with the newly introduced printing press. Many of the graduates later came to occupy chairs in the college and to administer its affairs. They became instructors of the young religious in native languages, and even of the sons of the conquerors. Thus there arose the astounding paradox of natives teaching Europeans and Creoles and spreading European culture. According to Sahagún, this progress continued for twenty years before a decline set in, partly because of a change of faculty and partly because a lay Spaniard became major-domo. The friars resumed charge and Sahagún, who had a great share in the foundation, also had part in the reform of the ordinances.[32]

Meanwhile one of the students, the cacique Carlos de Tezcoco, unfortunately went home and developed a system of beliefs of his own. This episode brought to a head the dispute about the advisability of higher instruction for natives. In spite of its good work the college was receiving the attention of conscientious objectors. It was argued that since the young men were not going to be priests there was no need of teaching them. Besides, they would be in danger

of heresy in reading the Scriptures, and there was sufficient
work for the friars without trying to teach all those courses.
One particular objector was the counselor of the viceroy,
Gerónimo López, whose animosity to the program reveals
itself in a letter[33] to the emperor and has the gratifying effect of a flood of light on what was being done in education. He affirms in effect that the friars, not content with
teaching the natives how to play musical instruments and
with giving them primary education, must needs train
them to read, write, and speak like Cicero, and to write
heroic verses in Latin; moreover, they put in their hands
the Scriptures and sciences which are likely to bring about
their eternal damnation.

Additional objections came from the Dominican provincial, Fray Diego de la Cruz, and his subject Fray Domingo
de Betanzos.[34] From their standpoint nothing was to be
hoped for from natives. Light-minded, they had no standing in the community; newly converted, they knew not the
import of the sacraments. They should be excluded from
higher education and never be ordained to the priesthood.
As Betanzos was an advisor of Bishop Zumárraga, his opinion had considerable weight. The bishop had previously
transferred some house rentals from the college to the Dominican convent for hospital purposes. Consequently, the
College of Santa Cruz was left dependent on the Franciscans for its support.[35] Sahagún wrote a loyal defense for it
in his later years when he said, "More than forty years has
this college persevered and the collegians have been delin-
quent in nothing either against God or Church, or king or
state."[36] The college passed through the vicissitudes which

seem to be a heritage of all colleges in Mexico, and ultimately, after several expirations and resuscitations, gave up
the ghost in 1811.

The logical consequence of the construction of the educational edifice, namely, the foundations of primary education
in the above-mentioned institutions and in almost all the
convent schools in the cities of New Spain, and the superstructure of secondary education and college beginnings,
was that there should be a demand for a university. It was
curious that all had been built for the benefit of natives and
mestizos. The Spaniards and Creoles, growing in numbers
toward the middle of the century, demanded attention.
What had been done for them? About 1536 a university
graduate, Gonzalo Vasques de Valverde, was appointed by
the king to act as a private teacher of grammar to the Spaniards.[37] There were other teachers later. Besides this private
tutoring, some instruction was given to the Spaniards at
Franciscan convents, but we may presume that this was for
future priests and brothers. The Augustinians also had a
house of studies for similar purposes at Tiripitío, in reality
the first seminary officially designated. The presence of tu-
tored students and of clerical students indicates that some
Spaniards and Creoles were ready for university work. Only
the rich could go to Spain for studies, and hence petitions
went to the king from the various interested persons, stating
the financial difficulties, the needs, the necessity of training
men for the priesthood, for jurisprudence, for medicine, for
civic life, and in the arts. The letters requested the foundation of a university. The king heard and responded.

The dispute for the distinction of priority of foundation

in the New World lay for years between Lima University and the Old University of Mexico, but really the first university in the Americas, as Dr. Priestley points out, was begun years before at Santo Domingo.[38] There in 1538 the Dominicans had had their College of Santo Domingo raised to the rank of a University. The first of a long list of laws[39] regarding universities in the New World, dated September 21, 1551, "creates, founds and constitutes in the City of Lima and in the City of Mexico, universities and liberal arts." In Mexico the solemn opening of the University took place on January 21, 1553. The story of its long life of 312 years with its development along the traditional lines of a continental *universitas,* of its achievements within hallowed halls, of fiestas, processions, and occasional brawls, and especially of its influence in the Mexican national, cultural, and political advance, has already been well told.[40] It will be referred to again in these pages.

Thus in brief survey a narration of the coming of a "more abundant life" has been given, together with a view of the educational structure in New Spain prior to the arrival of the Jesuits. In later pages, schools and colleges outside the capital in cities and on the rancherias will be touched upon. With the early labors of Gante in primary and secondary schooling for natives at the College of San Francisco there had been begun and developed a regular system of free public and private intellectual training for natives, which included the facilities of the College of Santa Cruz. Care of the mestizos was in the hands of the Franciscans at the College of San Juan de Letrán. University work was in progress. It is noteworthy that this foundation of culture had been laid in the heart of the new land within a few decades of its barbarous days. Mexico City was to remain the center for the transmission of a civilization which Europe had been nurturing for centuries, or even a center for the development of a new American culture. Still, while interest in learning was not much diminished by 1572, the founders of former times were passing on, and, with a new horizon of Mexican affairs widening in the northern frontier, were scattering. There was need of more workers both in the missions and in the schools. The Jesuits in Spain were now prepared to take up the burden of education in the New World.

Why was it that the Jesuits, famed for their colleges in Europe and represented in the missions of every continent but North America, did not enter the Mexican sphere of their future triumphs until 1572? Certainly the reason was not fear of the dangers of the way, even though whithersoever they turned a hazardous life or a sudden death seemed to lurk. The precariousness of their existence was a fact not only in African and Indian missions which named their first Jesuit martyrs before 1561,[41] and on the high seas where sixty-eight members were slain by pirates, but also in Catholic France and Ireland and in England.[42] In the eyes of the early members martyrdom, rather than being a bar to a projected course, was an expected and for many a Black Robe a desired goal. The desire of the martyr's crown was so strong with some Jesuits that the general, Father Borgia, cautioned them to "conserve their lives for the service of our Lord."[43] The wish of death cannot be said to have imparted to the fathers a morbid outlook on life; on the contrary, they moved about the pagan strongholds buoyantly and found therein a rather cheerful existence. Yet it illustrates the point that places more dangerous than Mexico City were sought, and that the pull of the missions was stronger than the pull of classrooms in North America.

Lack of numbers was only a partial obstacle to the appearance of the Jesuits on Mexican shores as educators. Jesuit colleges had sprung into being with marvelous rapidity during the generalates of Ignatius and Laínez (1556–1665), and each clamored for more man power. By the time Francis Borgia, the former Duke of Gandía, became general in 1565, there were 18 provinces, 130 establishments, and 3500 members.[44] But petitions were being received from prince and prelate for an assignment of the Jesuits for pastoral works, for the conduct of seminaries, for lecturing in colleges. With these many new points of contact the increase of membership is not surprising, and yet there were not enough Jesuits to satisfy the requests from Europe and Asia. All this while, letters urging an establishment in New Spain were reaching the three generals and the king.

Certain oppositions were not of sufficiently great importance to prevent the Company's advance to New Spain. Charles V and Philip II had maintained stringent ordinances against works of evangelization in the colonies by other than the ancient orders of religious.[45] It might be inferred that the Jesuits, like other innovators of the times, were still under the cloud of suspicion which hung over the early life of Ignatius. It might be presumed that the Jesuits had multiplied points of antagonism in the body cleric, since their diversified efforts in social works, catechetical and pastoral duties, philosophical writings, and general educational movements, each seemed to stamp them as competitors in a previously occupied domain. Competitors have a habit of arousing jealousy; therefore, it is assumed, religious and secular clergy must have opposed their advance in Europe and in America and must have influenced the state authorities to discourage the spread of Jesuit activities. Charles V and Philip II are supposed to have disliked the Jesuits until a blood relative of the reigning family bearing the powerful name of Borgia became general and by his political influence won for the order the right of way to the New World. Even though these assumptions may have had some slight foundations, they did not give rise to noteworthy hindrances to Jesuit movements.[46]

An underlying reason for the late appearance of Jesuits, over and above the presence in New Spain of religious of other orders who were carrying on splendidly, was the general plan for future operations of the Society. This program on the side of the Church authorities at Rome was concerned with the union of all missionary endeavor under what was to become in the next century the Congregatio de Propaganda Fide, and it was involved on the side of Philip II with the *Patronato*. Long before his election to the headship of the Society, Borgia had considered the inadvisability of dispatching individuals or isolated groups to faraway lands.[47] It grew increasingly apparent that while single missions might result in numerous baptisms, the new native Christians, unless properly ministered unto, would be lost leaven in the vast masses of pagans. The widening frontiers would have to be apportioned for evangelization

and instruction; there would have to be centers of missionary action as bases for thrusts into the new lands. The entire
plan signified the necessity of a directing force at Rome and
the protection of the rulers. There might conceivably be
difficulties with the plan if Philip II sought to dominate
missionary activities as he was seeking to dominate the
papacy.[48]

Loyola left the matter of sending Jesuits to New Spain
in the hands of the Spanish provincials.[49] Laínez could not
send any organized group. Borgia, however, had the numbers but was awaiting the maturity of his missionary plans.
With an eye to permanent establishment of missionary centers, he bided his time and considered the requests from
New Spain and Florida.[50]

The Jesuit Foundations

Chapter IV

THE COMING OF THE JESUITS

URING THE TIMES of the Spanish conquests of the
sixteenth century the name Florida was applied
generally to the whole southeastern section of North
America north of the Gulf of Mexico. It was always considered a beautiful country, but was made even more allur-
ing by the descriptions of its fountains, streams, pearls, gold,
and cities, painted in glowing colors, which appealed immediately to imaginations keenly aroused to receive such
tidings and which carried the conquerors on to a solution
of the northern mysteries.[1] Very soon beauties of land and
stream vanished in bewildering tangles of underbrush and
impenetrable swamps. Where each of the explorers or settlers trustingly hoped to find the rewards of health and
wealth, he found thorns of sorrow or death. Similarly,
Catholic missionaries[2] stalked out into the wildernesses in
their desire for the spiritual conquest of souls, only to be
thwarted by an obstinate generation of natives who returned them nothing but graves for their cherished hopes.[3]
In this land and among these peoples the Jesuits, in the
course of their initial sally into the North American missionary fields, likewise felt the sting of defeat and the joys
of death for the Faith.

At the request of the *adelantado,* Pedro Menéndez de
Avilés, two fathers of the Company of Jesus, Pedro Martínez
and Juan Rogel, with a lay brother, Villarreal, made their
appearance in 1566 on the Florida shores.[4] They had been

sent to reconnoiter. Martínez was killed by the natives even
as he entered the land. However, the report went back to
headquarters at Rome that with Havana as a base of activity
the outlook for missionary success on the mainland seemed
bright. Thereupon the islands and Florida were designated
as the territory of a vice-province of the Society, subordinate
to the Province of Peru.

In 1568 Father Juan Segura arrived as first vice-provincial
with five companions, two priests and three brothers. An
establishment was made in an old house in Havana. From
this abode the fathers went to the mainland in the following
year, and at San Agustín, Guale, Santa Elena, and Axacán
the customary missionary beginnings were made in the
catechizing of the natives. In Guale, along the coast at a
spot which is now St. Catherine's Island in eastern Georgia,
Brother Báez prepared a catechism and grammar in the
native language.[5] A little school was opened at the house
in Havana for a few natives. Two years later several new
members of the Company were admitted to the work, making, with the few who had lately entered the Society, sixteen Jesuits divided among the four missions.

Late in the springtime of 1571, Father Francis Borgia,
General of the Jesuits, received two important letters in
Rome.[6] One contained anything but good news. It was
signed at Havana by Father Antonio Sedeño, who had lately
put in there from Florida. It told the general the story of
the catastrophe that had befallen his subjects in the missions
of the mainland. Segura and seven other Jesuits had been
slain by the natives at Axacán, February 4 and 7, 1571. With
the vivid memories of such martyrdoms in the northern

missions still upon them, Sedeño and the brothers, Villarreal and Carrera, had sailed away from San Agustín in the company of Menéndez, and having arrived at Havana awaited new instructions at the mission base.[7] All told, six members remained of the sixteen that had come since 1566. The task of evangelizing Florida was temporarily at a halt. The letter went on to urge its permanent abandonment. "Since the natives are," as Sedeño informed the general, "fundamentally inconstant, cruel, and given over to their vices, there really is no hope of any permanent success among them. ... It would be better for the fathers to go to Sinaloa and New Mexico to preach the gospel; consequently your paternity ought to send a visitor to the four residences, namely San Carlos, San Agustín, Santa Elena, and Havana, who might inquire into their condition and see to their closing."[8] Defeat is recognizable in the letter, but not discouragement.

The other letter, dated May 4, was from King Philip II and asked for a contingent of Jesuits for New Spain.[9] For almost twenty years there had been requests for the new order from the viceroyalty of the West. One of the last of these to come to the notice of the Spanish authorities was the petition of the *cabildo,* or municipal council, in Mexico City, made just about the time of the disaster in the East and at a moment when the Jesuits would seem to have done entirely with the American project.

From what the *cabildo* says,[10] it was apparent that the uniform, pleasant climate of Mexico left the sons of the conquerors with little desire to exercise energy, and as a result of idleness they were inclined toward the easier ways of vice. There was not much left in the Valley of Mexico for those sturdy in the profession of arms; besides, those few who did follow it found many natives to carry on the arduous mechanics of camp life. Effeminacy seemed likely to ensue, and the soldiery might prove a menace to the young men about town. Furthermore, the sons of the merchants had little to occupy them. What time could be more propitious for exercising all the youths in letters? Quite true, they had the University of Mexico with learned doctors offering instructions; nevertheless, many of the young men attending the great institution were well on the way to breaking the hearts of their professors and to shattering their own nervous systems for lack of grounding in Latin and letters. Because of this deficiency both students and professors were at a disadvantage.[11]

Such was the purport of the letter to Philip II. To him it might have signified that education in Mexico was failing, or that the standards of Latinity were very high. It was clear, however, that since the professors lectured in Latin and since the texts were in that tongue there was a need of careful secondary training for the boys who matriculated in the University. This necessity caused him to turn his eyes toward Borgia for assistance; and thus, in the letter, he conveyed his wishes for Jesuit help and left the matter of appointments entirely in the general's hands.

Borgia, in spite of the first setback, had no intention of giving up any phase of his world-wide mission plan, let alone the one in the Americas.[12] This blood shed in Florida must surely produce fruit; hence, after some consideration of the letters, the idea of dropping the ill-starred venture and of proceeding to a new base in Mexico was adopted.

The incipient college at Havana would have to be closed as purposeless, because it was maintained solely as a starting point for missionaries going north. To speculate for a moment, we may say that if the eastern project had proved successful it might have altered the course of the history of our southland; as it was, its failure caused the fathers to move along with the ever-widening wave of the land conquest in the Southwest, where they played their part, sometimes following the soldiers, sometimes in advance of them, sometimes remaining far in the rear cementing with higher learning the foundations laid by their predecessors or preparing new missionaries for the outposts.

Borgia manifested his excellent will towards the overseas peoples by constituting New Spain a province and by appointing one of the most renowned scholars of Spain to lead the expedition as its provincial. This choice was tantamount to saying that Mexico was on a par with seats of the Jesuit foundations in Europe. The appointee to the provincialate was Doctor Padre Pedro Sánchez. He had been rector of the University of Alcalá before his entrance into the Society, and at the time of his appointment was lecturing in theology in the University of Alcalá, where he held the rectorship, and in the Colegio Mayor of San Ildefonso.[13]

So notable a selection is significant of the policy followed uniformly by the Jesuit superiors in choosing men for the missionary bands. Very frequently subjects of high intellectual attainments were moved from positions in which they enjoyed considerable esteem to places which in the eyes of Europe were quite obscure or, indeed, inferior. The policy has been criticized, but it brought results. It may

be that such learned divines were sent to distant places because the mandates of the kings demanded such a procedure;[14] it may be, too, that the virtuous were chosen because
they would be able better to resist the influences of the
pagan contacts; still, there remains an objective consideration, namely, that in the mind of the general and of the Society at large one soul was as good as another, and whether
it was a Castilian noble's or a dusky Aztec's made little
difference. Thus there was a certain democracy in the enthusiasm exhibited by missionaries for labors in far fields,
and a cosmopolitanism to their outlook.[15] Again, the wisdom
of centuries of human endeavor and Christianizing movements has taught churchmen how frequently great movements have humble origins. Who could predict what this
might lead to?

Anyhow, the scholarly Sánchez, imbued with these ideals,
now had to go about the provinces of Castile and Aragón
to gather up the nucleus of his province for the journey to
America. Although it was within the powers of the general
to send any member of the order to whatsoever spot he
wished,[16] a call for volunteers was issued. From those who
responded[17] Sánchez ultimately chose fifteen, and in thus
gathering more than the usual dozen, which was also the
number indicated by Philip,[18] he violated the pious prece-
dent—for such expeditions—of an "apostolic twelve." He
was given two other duties preliminary to founding a house
in Mexico. One was to act as visitor to the residences of the
former vice-province of Florida, and the other was to repair
to New Spain to arrange for the arrival of his cohort. He
himself did neither. He had a very good man for both du-

ties in the person of Father Sedeño, who was still on the scene in Cuba and was now subject to Sánchez' authority.[19] Leaving until a later time the closing of the houses on the east mainland, which resolved itself into simply declaring them to be what in reality they were—ruins,[20] Sedeño and a brother entrusted themselves to the boat for San Juan de Ulúa and to the waves,—and to whatever annoyance boat and waves could compound.[21]

When the pair arrived in Mexico City, Sedeño called upon the viceroy, Don Martín Enríquez, to inform him of the coming Jesuits. The viceroy, who was a friend of Borgia's and who had asked for the fathers at an earlier date,[22] expressed his happiness on hearing that the religious whose fame was so widespread in Europe would soon take up their abode in his territories. Then, since there was a vacancy in the archbishopric created by the death of Montúfar, Sedeño presented himself at the ecclesiastical court and also before the *inquisidor mayor,* receiving everywhere assurances of hospitality. This visit was late in July, 1572.

Even before Sedeño had reached Mexico, Sánchez and his band, divided between two ships, were a month on the way to Cuba. They had missed the fleet sailing from Seville in August of the preceding year[23] and had been forced to wait until June 13, 1572. The adventurous voyage toward the land of the setting sun, with all the anticipations and the novelty it offered, was a momentous episode in the life of each. Two months, however, is a long time on any boat, and these same Jesuit educators, it must be admitted, lacked certain qualities which went into the making of a robust seafaring character; they did not take to the rolling craft with the abandon of qualified navigators. Moreover, a disease of some sort joined up with the passengers. They were indeed glad of the respite granted them for a few days at Ocoa, ten leagues west of Santo Domingo.

They followed their religious order of the day so far as the sickness would allow. What might have been the subject of their conversations during the long days on the nar-

SITES OF THE JESUIT PROVINCE OF NEW SPAIN IN THE
SIXTEENTH CENTURY

row decks? Possibly it was of theology, of philosophy, of classroom affairs; or of the Council of Trent, whose reforms were now being felt. Then, too, John Knox had just carried all before him in Scotland; Mary Stuart was in the third of her twenty years of imprisonment; Calvin had died a few years before; Galileo was seven years old that year; Kepler was born in 1571; Titian was within about seven years of celebrating his hundredth birthday anniversary. The Morisco revolt in Granada had lately been squelched; Alva was in the Netherlands building up a reputation for cruelty, and William the Silent had now for two years been chartering the "Sea Beggars." The French pirates,[24] who were all around them, had slain forty Jesuits in 1570; the Turks were ravaging the eastern Mediterranean, and Lepanto was within some months of happening. The Jesuits did not, we are fairly certain, talk of the wars and strifes between the Christian princes, because these were prohibited topics for them.[25] Surely they knew of the mines of Zacatecas and of the push being made into Nueva Vizcaya, and in all likelihood of the Ibarras. Did they know of the Manila galleon which had come from the Philippines in the preceding year for the first official voyage? Or of what had happened to Drake and Hawkins a few years previously at the very port to which they were tending?

They might have talked of these events as the scenes and affairs of the Old World faded behind them and they came into the interests of the new hemisphere. They dropped anchor off San Juan de Ulúa on September 9 and went on to Vera Cruz, where they were given a heartening reception. It was the eighteenth before they set out for the highlands

and Puebla. The royal officials on their part did everything
to persuade the fathers to travel after the fashion of merchants, with a well-equipped and comfortable caravan; but
the fathers chartered a small pack train for their few books
and effects, and used coarse blankets for saddles. After a
journey of more than two hundred miles, finally the dusty
cavalcade of Black Robes rode[26] into Mexico City about nine
o'clock in the evening of September 28, 1572.[27] Three days
later, at Rome, Father Francis Borgia died. Three months
previously, in Mexico, Brother Pedro de Gante had been
called to his reward.

Sánchez, in order to avoid a repetition of the embarrassing
demonstrations he had received at Vera Cruz and Puebla,
and aware of the welcome which had been prepared for
his province by the viceroy and the inquisitor (Don Pedro
Moya y Contreras), delayed his entry until dusk had fallen.
Ably guided by Sedeño, they were soon at the doors of the
hospital founded by Cortés, where they were given lodging.
We wonder if Sedeño, when he was arranging for this, sus-
pected future contingencies.

Early morning found Sánchez, with the rector, Father
Diego López, on his way to visit Viceroy Enríquez. He discovered that his ruse of a delayed entrance the night before
had merely deferred the civic demonstration, for there was
a glad welcome by an immense concourse of people.[28] Then
there were speeches.[29] The viceroy voiced his greetings, his
anticipations of their forthcoming labors, and his gratitude
to God for moving the heart of the king to send the group
of fathers into the country. Sánchez replied in turn that
the Jesuits would try to live up to all his expectations, and

that they were ready to coöperate industriously with him in carrying out the wishes of the king as expressed in the cedula. This ordinance he then produced and presented to Enríquez:

Know ye, my Viceroy, Governor, and Captain General of New Spain, of the great devotion we have for the Company of Jesus; and because of the great esteem in which we hold the exemplary life and holy customs of these religious, we have determined to send some learned men of theirs to our Western Indies where we hope their doctrine and example will produce great fruit among our subjects and vassals, and that they will aid greatly in the instruction and conversion of the Indians. Wherefore we are presenting Dr. Pedro Sánchez and twelve other companions of his of the same Company who are going to place the first foundations of their order in these our kingdoms. Knowing then our resolve to aid them in every way, I command you that having at heart this work for the service of God and the glory of His Holy Catholic Faith, you do when these said religious arrive in that land receive them well and with affection, and that you do offer and give them all the favor and aid that may seem fitting for the founding of the said religion as a means of accomplishing the good for which we hope. And that they may know better what to do, advise them as one who understands the affairs in that country, assigning them sites and lands so that they may build a suitable house and church.[30]

We are struck not only by the general tone of this cedula, but in particular by the words "instruction and conversion"; they are the keynotes in a vast program of which the one in America was but a part. In its famous universities of Alcalá, Salamanca, Madrid, and in its colleges as well as in all forms of intellectual life, Spain had a tradition of culture. This must be perpetuated in the homeland, and (the more since the emperor—i.e., Charles V—had raised the American natives to the dignity of Spanish subjects) it follows that arts and letters must be extended, as they actually were being extended, to the Americans. Furthermore, the tradition of culture was so intimately related to religion as to be inseparable from it. It appears, outwardly at least, that the king, ruler of empires though he himself was, with multiplying concerns of government, realized his obligations in this respect toward all, even his least subjects.[31] The ruler's motives often were complex, but, above all, Philip II seems to have considered it his duty to put shoulder to the task of maintaining and spreading the Western civilization everywhere within his dominions, just as he felt it incumbent upon the Crown to bring about the conversion of the aborigines. It was for the Catholic cause that he came by the *Patronato Real*. It was such a conviction of and conscientiousness toward a duty that brought churchmen and statesmen of Spain to a harmonized effort to elevate entire races high above the moral and intellectual level to which by nature they seemed destined.[32] Missionaries, over and above attaining their immediate purpose of rescuing souls from paganism, acted as a wedge in the cultural advance; the educators would follow.

Now, while Church and State in Spain were inwardly persuaded of this duty, they could not avoid the realization that the natives had a corresponding right both to the privileges of Christians and to intellectual progress, or, to conversion and civilization, once it was proved that the natives were rational beings. The justification for bringing a new religion to uncivilized peoples has been questioned again in recent years; the right of infidel persons to any share in the Christian ceremonies and to membership in the Church, and so even their need of the same, is denied. The basis of the objection is probably this: natives should first be educated, then allowed a free choice of religion. The viewpoint is far from Catholic thought of any century and from Protestant thought of the sixteenth century, for then there was toleration only of the religion of the rulers of states, and nonconformity was tantamount to a political offense. The European attitude was applied to the natives in foreign lands. With respect to the invasion of human liberties, the Catholic Church had for centuries taught the right of all human beings to a knowledge of religon, and the duty of churchmen to spread that knowledge, and this by divine commission. It was considered wrong to deprive newly found peoples of their right to a knowledge of the Faith. This was a traditional aspect, and so the Catholic kings to all outward appearances considered it; likewise it was paternal, for ignorant subjects had to be told what was for their good, just as boys of today have to have things of the mind prescribed for them by parents and State. This concept of respective rights and duties was the basis for the spread of our Western civilization.

The Jesuits who were left standing before the viceroy were heirs to such weighty obligations in the New World, if we view things from the sixteenth-century position. They were in Mexico, trained men with a single purpose of aiding fellow men to salvation. While Spanish national educational objectives were general, the Jesuit aims were particular and personal. And the value of a soul to them as to other missionaries was inestimable.[33] Education was a great means to winning souls, and hence was a business, not a method of self-gratification; they were not thinking either of the hardships or of popular manifestations in their favor. Still, formalities had to be undergone, so the fathers began a round of visits to the notables of the city.

Among others the Augustinian provincial besought them to leave the hospital and accept his hospitality until they were properly housed; but, feeling that their presence would become a drain on his community's resources, they preferred not to do so. The people of the city were seeing to it that the hospital was supplied with food for them. Their presence proved somewhat of a boon to the hospital, because the baskets sent to it were so well filled with poultry, eggs, and preserves as to provide sufficient food for the entire establishment.[34] Another reason for remaining in the hospital soon evinced itself. One by one the Jesuits fell sick of the fever. Perhaps they were now feeling the full effects of the epidemic which had made the sea voyage so unpleasant. When Father Farfán of the Dominicans perceived how badly the Jesuits were affected, he gathered together the brains of the medical profession of the city and sent out word requesting prayers for the recovery of the newcomers. In spite of ministrations, prayers, and the efforts of the viceroy, the fever raged until it had taken the life of Father Francisco Bazán, who had endeared himself to all by his amiable kindness. Thus only a month after their arrival Mexico began to take toll of Jesuit lives.[35]

Hardly had the fever abated when the other Jesuits began to exercise their ministries while they were waiting for a site for a residence. There was in the capital a gruff old gentleman named Alonzo Villaseca,[36] one of the wealthiest Spaniards of the city and the same who six years previously had dispatched his brother to Spain to obtain the Jesuits for this field. He now appeared before Sánchez with an offer of some property and a house. The provincial was somewhat timorous about accepting, since he did not know how far an acceptance might infringe upon the jurisdictional rights of the other orders. He wanted no harsh feelings. On the other hand, a refusal might give offense to a man whose real heart was not revealed by his unprepossessing mannerisms. Moreover, the viceroy's plans had to be considered; inasmuch as the company was at his disposal he was obliged to provide for it.[37] In this dilemma Sánchez thanked Villaseca and informed him of the necessity of calling the fathers into consultation before acting. The consultors indicated that Enríquez had thus far made no move to place them; therefore, since a home hung in the balance, they had better go out quietly to take a glance at the proffered grounds. So that evening they went.

The site was about three short squares northeast of the present cathedral, just about the same distance as the hospital was to the south of the cathedral plaza. This left it *extra cannas*[38] as far as the other religious houses were concerned, yet sufficiently close to the center of the city's activities. When the fathers came upon the place it should have been painful to their eyes. No joy to the hearts of the European educators was this view of dilapidated burro sheds, huts of adobe with straw roofs, and odds and ends spread about in uninspiring disarray. Veritably it was a corral. Strange to relate, the fathers grouped together in the quiet of the Mexican twilight, seemed to peer through and beyond all that into the vistas of the future. They decided to accept the gift, and there was no dissimulation in their gratitude for it. They set themselves to work cleaning up the debris and making the quarters somewhat habitable. In the least unsuitable of the shacks they arranged their chapel for Masses in the morning.[39] The place whereon their first altar stood sustained later the main door to the Colegio Máximo. In such humble habitations the Company of Jesus found shelter for its Master and itself on its advent into New Spain.

The viceroy soon knew of the move. It was then that Sánchez was informed by him of his intention to give the province a site near the palace off the plaza. His declaration came too late; the Jesuits had grounded themselves in Mexico.

Chapter V

GROWTH IN MEXICO

NOW THAT THE JESUITS were settled on a plot of ground, we may observe how they went about their temporal concern of the moment, the building up of the material structure of their province. By the end of 1572 they were in their remodeled living quarters and had, besides this structure, a chapel. Their problem now was to erect a more commodious residence to care for the new subjects, a novitiate and house of studies for the student members, and colleges for extern students, as soon as they should have found themselves ready to take up their tasks in the classrooms.

Looking back, we may say that 1573 was a critical year. No end of problems confronted them and demanded solution before they could commence the educational enterprise; but principal among these was not the economic one, for ultimately they might reasonably rely upon the help of the king and his viceroy for the erection of a college building,—a justifiable presumption in the face of the many expressions of esteem and promises of assistance made by the rulers. The main idea now was to test the good will of the people whom they had come to help, and to establish the identity of their institute. Upon friendliness depended their whole moral and physical support, for they really were beggars. Consequently, even if they were not inspired by a zeal for the spiritual improvement of the natives and Spaniards in Mexico City, they would have to familiarize the townsmen with Jesuit methods and manner of life by going out among them in the capacity of missionaries.

The word *mission* ordinarily conveys to us an impression of the familiar church constructed for natives in a land beyond the jurisdiction of any bishop, an ecclesiastical outpost, as it were, differing from a parish of a diocese, and an economic unit capable of supporting itself and its spiritual head by means of its herds and gardens. By a missionary we usually mean a man in such a district as that described above, who has built up such an institution and who exercises his functions in it as minister of the gospel and the sacraments among the natives, independently of a local bishop. In this sense Mexico City of 1573 was not a mission nor might the Jesuits be termed missionaries, because they were within the well-defined limits of an archbishopric.

Still, in another sense they were missionaries, since by reason of their privileges as a religious order they were not subject to the disposition of the ordinary nor even to his jurisdiction, except so far as he could prevent their exercise of ministries in his diocese by refusing them diocesan faculties for administering the sacraments. Again, the Jesuits at this time had no parish which might have put them under episcopal control, for parishes are parts of a diocese and subject to their bishop.

Moreover, viewed as by the superiors who sent them, they were *missi,* or men sent for purposes of evangelization. Finally, with regard to the terminology, even within a bishopric, priests regular and secular who went from parish to parish giving a series of sermons in each for a week or two at a time were styled missionaries, and the series which they preached was called a mission. The status of the Jesuits as missionaries thus becomes clear. With the high approval of the archbishop they went about the city and its environs while they were putting up their dwellings; their voices were heard in the streets, in the plaza, in the hospital, and in their own chapel, at specified and unspecified times; their ministries were received with favor and the groundwork of good will was well laid.

Their contacts with the growing city and its inhabitants must have been interesting. It is not our good fortune to know the exact number of Spaniards, Creoles, Mexicans, and mestizos living in the capital of the Western World. A knowledge of the population statistics would be of great value in estimating exactly the number of children and young men who were being educated; to the Jesuits it was a fundamental consideration. If they opened a college, how many boys could they expect to attend it? How many instructible youths were there in Mexico and the other centers? What were the possibilities of candidates for the Society? Should their student body be drawn from the native or from the Spanish classes? To how many would a classical education appeal? All we can offer is a tentative survey with some awkward deductions.

A rough estimate based on various sources[1] leads us to the conclusion that there could not have been more than 150,000 people in Mexico City by 1570. Probably there were fewer.[2] If the Spaniards and Creoles were one-fifth of the population, which likewise is a top estimate, they were 30,000. On the basis of a family unit of six persons, the child population would have been 20,000; this divided equally between boys and girls gives us 10,000 boys under the matrimonial age, or at most 3000 of high-school age. If we go by the present military-service standards, the reckoning would be 10 per cent of the total population, or 15,000, which includes all men under twenty years and up to thirty, say a twelve-year span. This would give us 5000 eligibles of all classes for college work. From this, the conclusion would be that at the most there were 1000 Spanish and Creole youths who might be considered student possibilities. From these two computations it would be fair to place the number of instructible boys of high-school age somewhere between 1000 and 3000.[3] Some of these were at the University of Mexico, some were under private instruction, some at the conventual schools or in study for the priesthood, and some few in Europe. A number of boys were not being educated, and this number was increasing. The parents were the citizens of the capital, to whom the Jesuits would direct their instructions and sermons in the course of their missionary work about the city, and whom first of all they would have to inspire with educational ideals. They could be selective with the children of the natives, choosing the brightest from the various grade schools for future training.

Widespread is the despair of ethnologists who attempt to compute the numbers of natives in the districts beyond Mexico. The *visitador* Valderrama was receiving frowns from the king in 1564 because the royal coffers were not getting complete tax returns from the more than 440,000 Indians taxable in the viceroyalty,[4]—a fact which gives us some inkling of the numbers reduced by that time. Yet it must be recalled that Nueva España did not then include as taxable the natives in the vast uncolonized stretches of mountainous and desert regions to the north.[5] Indeed, not half of the present-day Mexican lands had been colonized, and accidentally the arrival of the Jesuits synchronized with the movement of Spaniards into the unbounded northern borderlands.

What hampered the growth of population in the capital besides the constant drift toward "otro México" and the southlands and the succession of settlements in the other cities of the new empire? It may have been in part the fear of floods, pestilences, and earthquakes which was engendered by certain European writers. Their fictions of the monstrosities one was likely to encounter in the Americas and of cataclysmic manifestations of physical law were written in vivid pages. Yet stories of temblors, tornadoes, wild animals, cold, heat, floods, and diseases were fearsome but not impeding obstacles to a steady stream of daring spirits from Spain, while they were part of the environment of the native sons. Mexico remained a wonderland even though it was establishing a tradition of suffering.

Plagues are ever most harrowing visitations, and all countries have felt their destructiveness. Sixteenth-century New Spain was no exception. The whites feared them, but the natives were they who felt them most. The pestilence prevalent in many cities of the viceroyalty in 1544 took a tremendous harvest of native lives.[6] With unabating fury it scourged the land during the following year until its ravages cost an estimated 800,000—10,000 of these in the Tepotzotlán subdivision of Mexico City.[7] Intermittently it returned to the whole land or struck in localities; in 1575 it became a general smallpox epidemic which cut down thousands.[8] Even though the numbers seem exaggerated, it is clear there were other depopulating forces at work besides the exploiting Spaniards.[9] Whether these were attributable to stagnant waters or insanitation or mosquitoes makes little difference to us now, but they undoubtedly were a source of fear and trembling to everybody who heard of them, and a devastating force as far as the native population was concerned. Echoes of such catastrophes, together with reports of earthquakes, volcanic eruptions, and floods should have convinced European peoples that the New World was an unlikely land in which to make out a temporal existence, but ideal for those who desired a speedy consummation of earthly cares.[10]

No such thoughts regarding their adopted country entered the minds of the Jesuits. The Mexico City which was a Venice in the time of the Moctezumas had much changed in appearance since the conquest.[11] The Lago de Texcoco, in which it had rested from the period when the old Aztecs built it there as an island of refuge, had failed the city as a watery bulwark in its moment of need against the Spaniards. The conquerors set about extending the limits of the city fast developing into the hub of an empire. Most of the canals were filled in; the lake front was pushed out in all directions. By the time the Jesuits arrived, Mexico was more than a mile from the lake.[12] Its streets even in preconquest times had never been devious like those of the European towns of that day, and so the conquerors continued many of the olden ways and laid out the other streets with similar regularity in squares.[13] Dwellings above two stories in height were rather infrequent, and hence the height of the city was rather even except where the towers of the churches jutted upwards. From the belfries rang out the summons to prayer, the joyous peals for fiestas, and the solemn tones for the *De profundis*.

In the heart of the urban life close by the spot where the old altar of sacrifice stood, a hideous emblem of paganism to the Spaniards, there was now a cathedral.[14] Before it was a plaza, the forerunner of many an American town square. It was flanked by the façades of official buildings, and notables and officials of all sorts had their residences in the immediate vicinity. Near the center of the town were many of the other Spanish households, with their servants and slaves.[15] In the outlying districts, which were at their extremities marshy, were three large areas occupied and tilled by the Indians under Indian governors. The Venetian streets, or canals, negotiable by small boats, ran through these areas and well into the center of the city. In times of a great flood similar to that of 1553, or 1629, all the streets were canals; but normally the streets were neither so dirty nor so muddy as their European counterparts.[16]

Rich with color was a day on the plaza where the mingled brilliant hues affected by Mexicans and Spaniards, in apparel and decoration, stood forth in the bright sunshine of the high altitude and caught the eye from great distances, even as they do at the present day in the western lands. About the great square the notables moved with the natives, and on Sundays and feast days shared democratically the same religious edifice. In the plaza the public crier read aloud the edicts in the presence of the viceroy, *oidores, visi-*

tadores, and notaries.[17] There the concourses gathered for religious processions, and there the bickerings with merchants took place over goods from Orient and Occident. There likewise, unless human nature of that day was vastly different from ours, Spanish gentlemen sunned themselves of a late afternoon and unavailingly ran the affairs of gov-

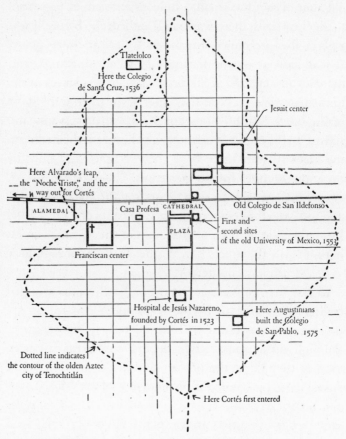

Tlatelolco

Here the Colegio
de Santa Cruz, 1536

Jesuit center

Here Alvarado's leap,
the "Noche Triste," and the
way out for Cortés

ALAMEDA

Casa Profesa   CATHEDRAL   Old Colegio de San Ildefonso

First and
second sites
of the old University of Mexico, 1553

PLAZA

Franciscan center

Hospital de Jesús Nazareno,
founded by Cortés in 1523

Here Augustinians
built the Colegio
de San Pablo, 1575

Dotted line indicates
the contour of the olden Aztec
city of Tenochtitlán

Here Cortés first entered

SIXTEENTH-CENTURY MEXICO CITY: EDUCATIONAL SITES

ernment to suit themselves, or awaited the coming and going of the mail.

In the plaza and cathedral the Jesuits preached. People of all classes were generally eager to hear simple sermons of the instructive and constructive type in which the Jesuits specialized. Occasional and grandiloquent discourses and panegyrics had their place in the ceremonies of some big religious or civic affair. In a later century, because these latter were the types of sermon transmitted to posterity rather than the everyday beneficial instruction, they brought down on church orations the opprobrious adjective Gongoristic. The sincere directness of the Jesuits' words increased the numbers of their auditors to concourse proportions which could scarcely be cared for either in the plaza or in their small chapel. Something would have to be done to accommodate the masses. Remarkable it is to note how a native Indian solved the problem by voluntarily undertaking the burden of rearing a more spacious church.

The Indian was a noble, Don Antonio Cortés, cacique and governor of the populous city of Tacuba, situated a league to the west of Mexico. When he visited Sánchez with his proposal, he left no doubt in the provincial's mind concerning his lofty motives of zeal for the religious progress and civic betterment of his race.[18] Sánchez, moved by his earnestness, accepted the offer. Whereupon three thousand natives went singingly to work for the next three months, preparing the foundations, hewing the timbers, and fashioning a temple of worship on the site occupied later by the Collegial Seminary of San Gregorio and still later by the beautiful Church of Our Lady of Loreto. This was a gift

of manual labor and a concerted effort in a common cause
which savors of medieval times. Even though the product
did not bespeak the magnificence of a Gothic cathedral, it
expressed the degree to which the natives had grasped the
Christian ideals. The dedication ceremonies in April, 1573,
brought together all the city notables, the secular clergy,
and the religious orders in a solemn procession that assumed
the appearance of a spontaneous public demonstration in
favor of the Company.[19] What touched the fathers most was
the good will surrounding the entire endeavor. The consola-
tion was theirs now of knowing by this concrete expression
of appreciation that they could hasten the work of erecting
their province.

Shortly after this notable demonstration of good will, the
Jesuit provincial became peculiarly involved in the foundation of an eminent college. It happened that Doctor Don
Francisco Rodríguez Santos, the treasurer of the Metropolitan Church of Mexico, was so taken with the life of the
members of the Society that he asked admission to its ranks.
Father Sánchez gently refused his request on two scores,
namely, that at the age of sixty he would be unable to sustain the novitiate training, and, secondly, he was doing
plenty for the good of the Church where he was. The reasons were sufficient, but the answer was disappointing to
Doctor Santos. Nevertheless, since Santos could not give
himself, he asked the provincial to accept his possessions for
the establishment of a Jesuit college. Again Sánchez refused, explaining that Villaseca had already promised them
funds, although the real reason was that Borgia had told
him not to build a college until the way had been carefully

paved.[20] This order meant particularly that the provincial must wait until such time as he had looked over the ground and was assured of the coöperation of the citizens, the lay and ecclesiastical officials, and the other religious of the city.

Seeing the chagrin of the generous Santos, the fertile mind of the Jesuit leader was ready with a consoling suggestion. Why not, he proposed, erect a college for deserving and well-born poor students? The idea appealed immediately to Doctor Santos, who soon dedicated the major portion of his wealth to the founding, upon his own property, of a college which was called Santa María de Todos Santos. Among the recorders of the opening of the college there is confusion about the precise date.[21] Some affirm it was August 15, 1573, while others say it was November 1 of the same year. What happened was this: Santos nominated fifteen likely students who were to benefit by the burses. He did so on August 15 and lodged them in his own house. They heard preliminary lectures at the university while their college building was under construction. The official opening of the college occurred on the second date; hence it derived its name from the two Church festival days.[22]

The guiding hand of Father Sánchez was in the work of drawing up its constitutions. These had the approval of the new archbishop, Moya de Contreras, and were modeled after the rules of the College of Santa Cruz de Valladolid, Spain, the alma mater of the founder. Santos granted four bursaries, or fellowships, to students of theology, four to those of canon law, two to those of philosophy; the specified students must have shown aptitude in their earlier studies, and they were to be chosen from among youths who for lack of funds might be forced to forgo promising careers.[23] The burses, then, were to be an aid to graduate studies. One of the theological beneficiaries had to be in priestly orders that he might officiate as chaplain of the college. Other gifts of Santos were the library and some ample funds from rentals from his estates. All in all, it was a generous foundation and a typical college beginning. A glance at the list of its illustrious alumni will reveal as many graduates in the legal profession and in civil offices as there were in the pulpits and episcopal chairs.[24]

Thus Santa María de Todos Santos embarked upon its task of aiding in the cultural advance of New Spain. As time went on it developed its very distinctive traditions and functions, its gala days, commencements, customs, college colors and dress, its school spirit and cherished memories. Many justifiable boasts were made by students and alumni who gloried in having worn the picturesque scarlet capes and who ever blessed the name of Santos. The college lived on to receive the title of a Major College by a kingly cedula[25] of April 1, 1700, a welcome concession for which Señor Don Juan Ygnacio Castoreña y Ursua is chiefly to be thanked. From then on it continued caring for distinguished students until its suppression in 1843,—a remarkable span of 270 years of useful existence.

When Father Sánchez refused to admit Dr. Santos to the Society because of age, he was acting with rare prudence, and his refusal eventuated in the college we have discussed. He had refused a man who was wealthy and influential. Yet when he did accept the first novice whom the province of New Spain received in America, he got a sexagenarian who was not learned as learning went, nor influential. He was the licentiate Don Bartolomé Saldaña, a humble priest, familiar by long service with the ways of the natives. He left his ministries in the little parish of Santa Catarina Mártir for the Jesuit novitiate, and, living with the Jesuit fathers, went through his period of trial. The province having begun to grow, we should cast a glance at the new candidates, since they were to be not only the future teachers but also the first to embark on the course of studies in the Jesuit normal schools of America.

A prebendary of the metropolitan church and secretary of the *cabildo,* Juan de Tobar, next applied.[26] Along with him came Don Alonzo Fernández, a native of Segura de la Sierra, a doctor of canon law. This latter, in spite of his sixty years and the cares of his office, went through the probation and lived an exemplary religious life for fourteen following years, expending his zeal at Puebla. Within a short while eight students entered the novitiate, and among them was the first of the native races, Antonio del Rincón, a descendant of the old kings of Tezcoco. A Creole applied, but Father Sánchez refused to admit him unless he should have previously obtained his father's permission to join the Company. He happened to be the only son of wealthy Rodrigo de Albórnoz, the *regidor* of the city. When Rodrigo found out his son's plight, he betook himself to the Jesuit church with the archbishop-elect of Mexico, who was to receive his official appointment in the same edifice. He created a sensation during the solemnity.[27] In the presence of all the notables and the fathers he announced his offering of his son to the Society; and the son embraced the Jesuit life.

With the coming of novices provision had to be made for their housing and instruction.[28] Father Pedro Díaz was appointed master of novices. The young men were housed in an adjacent buiding separate from the rest of the religious with whom they had been living. There they went through the days of their two-year novitiate and learned what would be expected of them as members of the order. They studied and recreated and performed the menial services about the house, and periodically they were sent to the hospitals to help the sick. They might be seen carrying water through the streets or working in the gardens. Both of these acts were means of acquiring humility, for they were normally the tasks of servants.

One of the institutions of the Jesuits designed for the recreation of both novices and scholastics was the villa. By way of a change from the routine of the classrooms, one day a week during the school year and two or three weeks at the end of the term were to be spent at the villa. Here no study was permitted; villa days were occupied in games or walks. The Jesuits of Mexico were not bereft of this happy institution which aided so much in establishing a community of ideals and in recuperating their physical strength. A gift had been made to them of a hacienda three leagues southwest of the city, by Lorenzo López, who intended it for a farm which might produce vegetables for the tables of the fathers.[29] Its fine location in the highlands, with a glorious panorama of the Valley of Mexico, made it an ideal site also for villa purposes. Sánchez called it Villa de Jesús del Monte after a similar place outside Alcalá where he had spent many happy days. Its value was 14,000 pesos, but owing to the efforts of the several lay brothers who cultivated the grounds it was worth much more to the province as a source of food and physical health.[30]

It can be readily understood how there was a growing educational problem, because these novices, once they had pronounced their vows, would have to be housed in a place where they might begin their real normal-school training according to the Institute of the Society. To be sure, there was no grave objection to the young Jesuits' taking the courses offered at the existing conventual schools or under the professors at the University of Mexico, for several were doing just that. The scholastics, or student theologians, who had come across the waters with Sánchez, were completing their studies of theology in the Dominican convent, and by the middle of 1573 three had been ordained priests. If more were to come, provision would have to be made for their training under Jesuit theologians and philosophers. So also, if the provincial was to follow the traditional custom of the Company and educate the junior subjects under Jesuit auspices, he would have to act within a year in the matter of a juniorate for classical studies.

Since there was to be solved the problem of educating the young Jesuits, which would necessitate a teaching staff and classes, naturally there came in for consideration and debate the question of educating externs. Should the Company open a school which would admit extern students to the very courses given for the young Jesuits, or should it organize separate classes for both simultaneously? Just ahead of the offer made by Santos, representatives of the *cabildo* had come to present to the Jesuits a site in the very center of the city, "whence," as the city council put it, "all its vast circumference might enjoy equally the rays of their piety and wisdom."[31] What he thought about the compliment is not recorded, but Sánchez refused the offer, because the hustle and bustle of civic centers did not seem conducive to study.[32] This refusal might easily give rise to an accusation against Sánchez of procrastination. The ground had been surveyed and had not been found wanting. Why was he waiting to open classes?

The reasons for the hesitancy were twofold. Borgia, as we have said, had told him to wait two years. One may object that Borgia was now dead. Nevertheless, the order had come from the office of the general whoever he might be, and had not been rescinded. In the second place, to obtain gifts from particular donors which at best were sporadic and would supply the needs of the Company only for the moment, was an altogether different thing from the acquisition of a foundation. Sánchez was waiting for such a permanent subsidy for the carrying out of a college program, on the basis of the European houses of the Jesuits, namely, a free college where no tuition need be asked and whereon there would be no staggering burden of debts within a few years; white elephants were feared even in that day. He was following the Jesuit rule of giving all service gratis. A scheme of this type made his men dependent for their living upon the income from the foundation. He took it for granted that there was as much altruism in America as in Europe and prayed for a generous donor. While these considerations were being weighed, Sánchez partly was forced, partly put himself, into the position of founding several institutions, which proved to be the nucleus for his principal college and for a seminary.

The developments during the first year were slow, at least to the participants. They seem rapid to us. The growths we have discussed for the Jesuits were reflexes of the times in New Spain. The City of Mexico was growing; its Spanish population was increasing and settlements out beyond were getting more and more numerous; the mining people were opening the earth to the north, and the infant empire was well out of its swaddling clothes. Along with the social and economic growths there were the intellectual. And the whole progress had gone on, as solid developments usually do, against difficulties of land and disease and hardship. Similarly the Jesuit Province of New Spain, which had rooted itself quietly in the capital, had grown in numbers and in the good graces of the people, and its members even at this time were in other cities laboring at their calling.

Chapter VI

THE SEMINARY OF SAN PEDRO
Y SAN PABLO

FATHER PEDRO SÁNCHEZ, who was a real builder and a remarkable superior, had, as we have said, put himself into the occasion of starting the educational labors of his province. His interest was in seminaries for students, that is, in what we might term boarding halls adjacent to the lecture halls of a college.[1] He hoped that some of the students living a regulated life might enter the priesthood. When we are informed that he had been for years associated with the instruction of men for the priestly life while he was lecturer in theology at Salamanca and rector at Alcalá, we are not surprised to find him continuously thinking along the lines of clerical progress in his new environment. The stimulus given by the legislation of the Council of Trent was vigorous and new in the matter of conduct of seminaries and it was to bring the *Tridentinos* later to New Spain. As an active participant of the Counter Reformation, he carried in his heart the ideals for clerics which the Council of Trent wished to establish. His foresight of the required elements for the continuance of the spread of Christian culture in New Spain was keen and purposeful. To him halls, colleges, seminaries, and grouped students appeared as essential physical equipment for the program.

His many sermons and addresses delivered in the churches of the city had a threefold purport. He emphasized the dignity of the calling to the priesthood and the ideal of virtue and learning required for it. The development of a worthy and more numerous clerical body must be based on firm educational foundations. And material assistance for his project of education was necessary. His words delivered with telling sincerity from the pulpit and in private conversations convinced many of the people that their rich land was capable of producing a virile and saintly generation of servants of the altar.[2] The authorities were spurred on to their duty of supporting the ecclesiastical growth. It was clear that the religious of the other orders had more than sufficient work in the city, that they were not teaching orders as were the Jesuits, that there was a constant demand for their services in other cities and Indian villages, and that, in view of the expensiveness of a European training, a native American clergy would have to be developed and perpetuated. Sánchez was laying the foundations of the great work of clergy training for Creoles—that is to say, American-born Spaniards—which his province accomplished in succeeding years.

The ground for all studies, sacred and professional, was Latin. Now, the Old University of Mexico had only one chair in Latin, and the study was for advanced students.[3] The civil authorities and the people interested decided to hasten plans for getting the Jesuits into the classrooms in order to amplify possibilities of preparation for higher learning. In Jesuit halls the boys would receive the benefit of skilled spiritual directors, and of a training such as the Company was undertaking in many parts of Europe. The particular concern of officials was expressed in organized appeals to the citizenry for means of supporting a college.

Hence by no coincidence did a particular group of the wealthier citizens meet together after one of the discourses of Sánchez. They were anxious to found a collegial seminary. Father Florencia, a great enthusiast over the deeds of these early Jesuits, who wrote in the late eighteenth century, rejoices in an old manuscript which explains the "origin of the College of the glorious and blessed Apostles and Princes of the Church, San Pedro y San Pablo, in the City of Mexico." Since it is illuminative of both the sincerity and the dignity and legality surrounding the event, as well as instructive of the manner in which men of the colonies went about starting a college in America at that early date,[5] I present the manuscript in translation:

In the year 1573, a little after their arrival and establishment in the City of Mexico, the fathers and brothers of the Company of Jesus, the illustrious and Very Reverend Dr. Pedro Sánchez, Provincial of the same Company, being moved by a zeal to serve the divine Majesty and to come to the help and succor of the youth of this worthy City of Mexico in their spiritual necessities, made overtures to some of the principal people of the city to the effect that in their midst he might found a college. The patrons of this foundation would be the persons who would contribute 100 pesos of gold as a permanent annual gift which would be a subsidy whereby the college could be modestly sustained; and each patron should present the same sum to the said college, so that being founded in this manner, the Provincial and the fathers with him at the time and the others of the future might be able to assist in its development by instruction in letters and virtue for the good of the public, while leaving to the care of those same patrons the rule and government of the college in temporal concerns.

In respect to these overtures many notable persons with similar zeal for the service of our Lord and Master, from whose hand they had received the temporal goods which they possessed, in order that their sons might be reared in seclusion in laudable and holy habits, offered to establish the said annuity. Upon which the Father Provincial obtained permission and license for the establishment from His Majesty and his very excellent Viceroy in New Spain who at the time was Sr. D. Martín Enríquez. He, agreeing to such a holy project and with special zeal for the service of our Lord, to say nothing of that of this City of Mexico, not only permitted it but graciously gave license for the college in the following tenor:

"D. Martín Enríquez, Viceroy, Governor, and Captain General of this New Spain and President of the Audiencia which herein resides: Forasmuch as Dr. Pedro Sánchez, Provincial of the Company of the name of Jesus, has furnished me with a statement to the effect that with the intention of serving our Lord and of doing good to this City, he has treated with some rich and fervent men about the establishment here of a college under the name of San Pedro y San Pablo, who at their expense were to endow it with a subsidy for the building and for the support of the collegians who are designated for it as well as others who come to it, and by which subsidy the college may be provided with fellowships by those who found it; and whereas he and they are to make the laws and constitutions to assure its good government, I, on my part, having considered that the work is very suitable and necessary, do hereby give the license and faculty to the said Provincial that he and the persons who seem good to him may carry on the said affair with the persons concerned and with any who wish of their own good will to found and endow the said college, and that they may make the regulations and constitutions which seem suitable to them for its good government, and that the nomination of the collegians whom they are to have perpetually in the college be made by those persons who found and endow it, in accordance with the constitutions which they may make for it and the order established, and I, as has been said, in the name of His Majesty, assure them that they will be safeguarded in the aforesaid and will allow neither hindrance nor obstacle; and for the effectual founding and endowing and making of the constitutions and rules, they may join with the said provincial without risk of penalty. Done in Mexico the twelfth day of the month of August, 1573. D. Martín Enríquez."— *Por mandado,* etc.

In virtue of this permission Sánchez gathered together his group of founders from among the principal citizens.

On September 6 they met as a committee to launch the project and to settle all terms. Having reread the license of the viceroy, they declared themselves the board of directors, or governing *cabildo,* and drew up formal statements of their financial allotments. Each founder bound himself to set aside from his lands or wealth a sum of 2400 pesos; from this principal there would be an annual income of 120 pesos; this constituted a bursary, or fellowship, and was divided so that 100 pesos went toward the support of the collegian who was nominated and 20 pesos went toward the building fund. Then each had formally to name the student for whom the burse was intended. Thus we have the names of the founders and of the first students of the college:

Gaspar de Valdes provided for his two sons, Gaspar and Balthasar
Dr. Pedro López for his son, Agustín de León
Francisco Pérez del Castillo for his son, Luís Pérez
Bartholmé Domínguez for his son, Alonzo
Alonzo Jiménez for his son of the same name
Don García de Albórnoz for Baltazar de Castro
Doña Catarina de Avendaño, a widow, and her brother Juan named her son, Juan de Ayanguren[6]

The founders were constituted a board of directors, or collegial cabildo, for the purpose of administering the temporalities, which were to be no concern of the Jesuits. There was no college building at the time; so the cabildo asked Sánchez to let the students use a house which had been recently erected as a boarding college. When he consented, the founders granted him an additional sum of 1000 pesos for the support of poor collegians for the next few years until a separate building could be put up for them. The Jesuits were to teach all and take complete charge of the spiritual direction of the students. Sánchez was the provisional rector. The fathers who followed him in the direction of this college were destined to have a long pull in a sea of troubles set in motion by the bilateral arrangements which had been so nicely consummated on this day of foundation, September 6, 1573. It became a tale of too many directors. In order to understand completely the relation of the Jesuits themselves to the institution, it will be pertinent to summarize the agreements made between the provincial and the cabildo, or chapter.

There was first of all a total principal of 19,200 pesos legally set aside which nobody could touch. The income of 800 pesos annually was for the board and lodging of the eight students; there was no question of tuition. Any student had to be over twelve years of age, and his training by the Jesuits was to be a preliminary to an ecclesiastical career, even though ultimately he might not follow it. There were twenty-four additional founders to be admitted, each with appointment privileges.[7] This would bring the total number of founders and students up to thirty. If each founder gave the rentals from the stipulated 2400 pesos, the total principal would be 72,000 pesos and the annual income 3000 pesos for board money and 600 pesos for the building and its upkeep. Needless to say, the upkeep would not include coal for heating in a city blessed with such a mild climate.

The Jesuit rector, while he was supreme over the details of discipline and education, had no vote in the cabildo proceedings. The founders and the Jesuits were jointly responsible for the formulation of the constitutions and rules. The cabildo was to elect a chairman or president, called a

rector, for the administration of the temporalities. This office should have entailed no other difficulty than that of in-
suring the collection of the annual income and the erection
of a separate building for the collegial body. The cabildo
would have to meet to consider new applicants for the rank
of founders.

In spite of the good will of the first founders, the agreement between the two heads of the collegial group, or
house, for that is what it was rather than a college in our
modern sense of the word, was bound to become complicated with the rise of new and unforeseen problems. The
college could thrive only amid the sweetest concord. This
harmony could be attained only by an absolute definition
of and strict adherence to the rights and duties of each factor
of the government, the Jesuit and the secular. It was important, too, to have a few well-disposed members in the secular
cabildo for the smooth functioning of the ideal plan. The
plan was faulty, however, in that it did not make provision
for the increase of founders, who soon began to sign the
legal documents and to appoint their boys. The machinery
of government of the temporal side was bound to grow
heavy and to grind. To anticipate the story, this is precisely
what happened; factions formed in the governing cabildo.
The Jesuits remained aloof from the financial disputes over
the burses, but were necessarily involved by reason of their
ownership of the property upon which the small boarding
house for the seminary students was being built.

To get back to the chronological account, then, it was not
until November 1, 1573, that the next step was taken. Each
of the founders of the Colegio de San Pedro y San Pablo

had provided a habit for his chosen student, who dutifully donned it on the appointed day. What the well-garbed young collegian of that day had to wear whenever he appeared in the streets, arouses our curiosity. The background of the ensemble was a woolen tunic, or cassock, of a dark red hue, whose sleeves were black serge. The cape also was of woolen cloth, and purple. Unfortunately there is no description of the color or shape of the distinctive college cap which had to be worn.⁸ Thus proudly robed, the young student accompanied by his sponsor and the others and their sponsors hied themselves to the house of the Jesuits.

In the presence of the fathers the newly appointed majordomo, Juan de Hermosa, conducted the ceremony of the presentation. Each founder formally presented his appointee; the provincial formally gave to the appointee his fellowship; and then there was a solemn Mass, at the conclusion of which Sánchez blessed the garments and then delivered a Latin address. He urged the wearers of the maroon habit to obedience and to the pursuit of letters and virtue, for the honor of their parents and for the good of their country. A little later the students were presented to the viceroy. In the course of the day they visited the college of Santa María de Todos Santos, which we have described in a preceding chapter, and there presented their felicitations. The collegians of that institution headed by Dr. Santos returned the visit, and this was the beginning of a great friendship and scholastic rivalry which grew up between the two institutions. The students ever felt themselves bound by a common obligation of gratitude to Pedro Sánchez, whom they revered as the father *fundador* of both.

Thus launched upon its career, the Colegio de San Pedro y San Pablo was little more than a nominal institution, a college in that it was a group of students bound to a common pursuit. It should not be confused with the Colegio Máximo de San Pedro y San Pablo founded—as we shall see—shortly afterwards as a Jesuit college entirely. This mistake has been made by those who composed the plaque which rests today on the wall of the old Colegio Máximo in Mexico City, and which reads "Here was founded by Father Pedro Sánchez the Colegio Máximo de San Pedro y San Pablo in 1573."[9] The foundations of the two colleges were distinct; the connecting link between them was the Jesuit teaching staff.

It was not until early January, 1574, that all the constitutions were approved in their informal draft, which with some alterations became formal only in 1581. Whereas until October 12, 1573, Sánchez had been informal rector, on March 9, 1574, the collegial cabildo duly nominated and elected the first official rector, Licentiate Gerónimo López Ponce. He had held the office informally after Sánchez. His salary was 100 pesos a year. This selection of an administrative rector is likely to complicate the gubernatorial situation for the reader unless he is reminded that there was also a Jesuit rector (Díaz) over the group in spiritual and scholastic matters, who at the same time was superior of the Jesuits residing in an adjacent and rather poor dwelling.

Reserving for the next chapter the beginnings of the education of these seminary students and the opening of the classrooms of the Jesuits for secular students in Mexico City, which followed shortly upon the establishment of San

Pedro y San Pablo, we shall find it convenient to finish the history of the seminary; though for clarity's sake it is necessary to mention the establishment of three other colleges of a similar type, which will be described later in detail.[10] These were San Bernardo and San Miguel and San Gregorio. They were part of the center forming under the name of the Colegio Máximo, and like the seminary were steps toward the goal of the Jesuits. In presenting the forthcoming details, however, caution must be given against overemphasis of the importance of the seminary.

López Ponce, installed in March, 1574, ruled over the temporal destinies of San Pedro and San Pablo Seminary for three years. While the students were prospering, the governing board, ever increasing in numbers, began to grow unwieldy. Various pettinesses whose precise nature we do not know entered into its conferences. Furthermore, López entered the Society of Jesus in January, 1577. In consequence of his resignation, the *señores* of the governing chapter besought Sánchez to have the Jesuits take complete charge and direction of the seminary just as they were doing in many places in Europe.[11] Its house was now built.[12] The provincial, even though he was pleased with this manifestation of their confidence, replied that in an affair of such importance he would have to hold consultation with his superiors. He assured them they would not have long to wait, because a father visitor from Rome was on his way to Mexico, who would surely know the mind of the general and would be in a position to solve the question conveniently.

At the suggestion of Sánchez a provisional rector was chosen. He was Licentiate Felipe Osorio, who held the office with a salary of 150 pesos and the rental from one chapel until March 2, 1578. When the Jesuit visitor, Plaza, was detained in Peru, the governing chapter, again in trouble, came to Sánchez a second time and asked him to appoint one of his subjects as rector provisionally. The members wielded a potent argument in favor of the step, declaring that much was being lost to the students in virtue and letters under the existing system.[13] Evidently they had taken much of the control of the student body from the hands of the Society. Sánchez could not well refuse the request. He appointed Father Vincent Lanuchi as vice-rector.[14] The choice was unfortunate, because, while Lanuchi was a scholarly man, he was also a disturber. He betook himself to Italy in the following year at the request of the father visitor. From March 31, 1579, until October 13, 1580, the Jesuit Alonso Ruiz guided the destinies of the college.

A dramatic episode occurred a few months before the last date. Ruiz seemed to be doing well when for some unknown reason the cabildo presented itself before the father visitor, Plaza, and confronted him with a startling alternative. He was asked either to close the other seminaries which were in the charge of the Company, or abandon the care of San Pedro y San Pablo. The proposal was as amazing as his reply was firm. He called Ruiz into the room wherein the conference was taking place and announced to the cabildo that the Jesuits could not give up the other seminaries, from which such great good had come to the city, unless they had some reasons for the dissolution; and with respect to San Pedro y San Pablo—Plaza's answer consisted of simply placing the keys of the college on the table before them. Either the drama of it all or the sight of the keys caused the harassed cabildo to withdraw, leaving the government as it had been. Plaza became Provincial of the Jesuits and asked the cabildo to appoint its own rector of the college. Their choice fell upon the Licentiate Bernabé Sánchez de Betansos, who ruled from October 13, 1580, until August 18, 1581.

On the first day of the last-named month and year a junta was called to settle some diversity of opinion among the founders. Rumors of dissensions had reached the viceroy, who was bent upon establishing harmony. To avoid any evil consequences of the bickerings of which he had got wind, Enríquez had made pointed suggestions to the members of the cabildo, with whom he associated daily. Hence, when the meeting was called to order and the question of electing a new rector for the college came up, there was a burst of magnanimity. Under the circumstances it seems to have been quite sincere. The voters, led by Dr. Pedro López, passed a unanimous resolution to turn the college over to the Jesuits. They had the Royal Audiencia confirm their resolution with an *auto*.[15]

As an outcome of this edict, Pedro Díaz became rector over all the colleges which had been established thus far by the Jesuits in the city. Vice-rectors were named for the four collegial groups—Sánchez de Betansos for San Pedro y San Pablo. The latter was succeeded by three others until 1585, when a new Jesuit rector was appointed, Pedro Hortigoso. On June 15, 1586, Peláez took charge, and exactly a year later Báez; the last three named were Jesuits and each had appointed various vice-rectors for the seminary.

Father Juan de Loaisa took charge in 1587 after Báez had been in office for four months. Trouble began to brew again. San Miguel, San Bernardo, and San Gregorio colleges had been officially united into one student body, that of San Ildefonso. By 1589 the collegial seminary of San Pedro y San Pablo was laboring under conditions which it could not endure very long without a change in constitution and government.[16] Respect for the ordinance of the Royal Audiencia which had placed the college in the hands of the Jesuits, had waned. At least it was not sufficient to restrain the señores from proposing novelties to which the Jesuits could not condescend without impairing their prestige. The proposed changes concerned the seminary's temporal relations. When the general, Claude Aquaviva, was informed of them he sent peremptory orders to the provincial, Mendoza, in which he required that, if the board of trustees did not cede to the Company all the temporal administration of the seminary and at the same time keep within its rights of presentation of students according to the orders of the Audiencia and of the approved constitution, the Company was to give up entirely the direction of the college.

In consequence of this order the rector asked the cabildo to a conference with the fathers, at the end of July, 1588. The fathers indicated the pernicious effects which were likely to result from the founders' perpetual interference. The provincial exposed the instructions he had received from headquarters, fully conscious that the señores were in no frame of mind to accept the hard conditions. Nor did they; whereupon Loaisa, to their mild indignation, surrendered to them the keys of the building, and the college re-

verted to its original status with a rector, Núñez, chosen by
the cabildo for temporal affairs, and with the Jesuits giving
the group its education. From then until 1612 it was con-
trolled by the seculars,[17] who repeatedly endeavored to give
back its management into the hands of the Company.

In 1612, when the building of San Pedro y San Pablo began to crumble, the Jesuits brought its occupants up the
street a short distance towards the Cathedral and housed
them in their college of San Ildefonso.[18] That was the beginning of an incorporation which received royal sanction
in 1618 and became known as a Royal College.[19] In its incorporated state, San Pedro y San Pablo y San Ildefonso continued until its fiftieth Jesuit rector was expelled with his
subjects in 1767. The history of San Ildefonso, however, will
require another chapter, after we shall have considered the
beginnings and conduct of the Jesuit classes in Latin and
philosophy. The story of the San Pedro y San Pablo group
from its foundation in 1573 until its incorporation is important in that it led the Jesuits directly into education. Again,
its history has been a source of much confusion. Finally, it
serves as an illustration of the legalities and other difficulties
which attended collegiate foundations in early New Spain.

Chapter VII

HUMANISM IN MEXICO

IT MUST NOT BE SUPPOSED that the Jesuit fathers during their first few years in the capital remained impervious to the lure of the far cities. The mountains which loom about the valley of Mexico were inviting, and the bishops and the people in the lands beyond were beckoning. Hence this Jesuit could be found in Pátzcuaro, this one in Valladolid, that one in Vera Cruz; and another had the happiness of viewing the old volcanoes, Popocatepetl and the "Sleeping Lady," from the Puebla side. The provincial himself did not fear to wend his way north and west to the silver outpost of Zacatecas to consider its possibilities for a college site and missionary vantage point. His namesake, Father Juan Sánchez, had preceded him, and the people were anxious for both to remain.[1] They even offered him a house. He was keen enough to see that there was a floating population in the town, which was busy about many other things besides education. He excused himself on the ground that he had to hurry back to the distant metropolis to open a college which would require the services of nearly all his men. So, after promising the people some missionaries, he got back to Mexico City in the latter part of September, 1574.

A few days after his arrival in the city an important event took place in the halls of the Old University of Mexico. Father Bartolomé Ledesma, afterwards Bishop of Oaxaca, was presenting the theological viewpoints of the Dominicans in the presence of the notables and the faculty and

student body. It was a familiar episode to Europeans, this
defense in theology, and it had become an important manifestation of scholarship in Mexico. The Royal University
had invited the Jesuits to attend the disputation, and several
of them were there with the provincial. As in all such affairs, the discussion was thrown open to the house after the
learned Dominican had defended his theses and answered
the objections of the appointed antagonists. Then the Jesuits were asked to venture an opinion. This they did so ably
that after the applause had subsided their listeners concluded there was no sense in keeping such wisdom hidden.[2]
It should be utilized immediately in favor of the youth of
Mexico. The masters of theology, the *oidores,* and the inquisitor urged them to open their classes. They brought in
the viceroy and the archbishop to add pressure. The scene,
the applause, the exuberance were typically Latin. It seems
clear that this was only the occasion for pressing the school
question; the fathers would have opened the classes any-
way. Still, as events showed, there was a note of profound
sincerity in the demonstration. Why not begin? The good
will was assured, the two years' wait specified by Borgia
was up, the Old University had only one chair of Latin,
and Sánchez was bound by agreement to instruct the small
group of San Pedro y San Pablo seminarians. The Latin
classes which he would have to open for the latter might
just as well be thrown open to all.

About the first of October, then, the provincial appointed
Pedro Mercado and Juan Sánchez the first teachers of the
Jesuit *collegium inchoatum.*[3] The selection of the former
struck a pleasing chord in the hearts of the people, because

he was an American and a member of one of the distinguished families of the capital. There was no doubt about the scholarship of either teacher; from the story of his after life, Juan Sánchez must be rated as one of the foremost Jesuit humanists of colonial times.[4] These are the first of the many Jesuits who remained in the cities devoted to the drudgery of the classroom when "otro México" was calling and when their more famous brethren were out in the missionary fields. Juan particularly had to sacrifice his desire to evangelize the natives to the north and expend his zeal at home, where he stole some hours of his days for work among the Indians of Tlatelolco.

While they were preparing for their classwork and making up a roster of their first students, Sánchez was afflicted with the besetting worry of all Jesuit provincials—lack of subjects to satisfy the requests from other places. He breathed a sigh of relief a few days later when seven new Jesuits came in from Vera Cruz.[5] It seems that the new band of educators had had plenty of exercise on the voyage from Europe, for the craft on which they had sailed became so leaky when it was a few days out that every one aboard had to man the pumps. Tragedy hovered over it in the long, tempestuous trip; many voyagers fell sick and died; some reached port safely, but soon yielded to the fever contracted en route. A bit of the fine Mexican climate, however, restored the Jesuits.

The auspicious beginning of the study of Latin in the Jesuit fashion occurred October 18, 1574.[6] It was the opening class for the collegial Seminary of San Pedro y San Pablo; it might be called the same for the Colegio Máximo, whose building was to go up in 1576. So, too, one might say it was the start of several little colleges which developed into that of San Ildefonso; in a word, it was the opening of the Jesuit center of education both ecclesiastical and secular. There had convened for the inaugural function Viceroy Don Martín Enríquez, his *audiencia,* and some of the distinguished personages, as well as prebendaries and representatives of the other religious orders. The student body, some three hundred strong with externs, was of course present; the colorful garb of the San Pedro y San Pablo students stood out as conspicuously as the mounting golden tassels on the caps of the faculty members from the University,— which same caps must have had a great processional value, unless the specimens in the Museo Nacional misinform us.

The morning was not very old when the prayers had been said and Father Juan Sánchez was well launched in an eloquent Latin oration. Its purpose was to exhort the citizens to send their sons to school, where they might become proficient in letters, virtues, political and civil affairs. It was all flattering to the intelligences of the listeners; how intelligible it was, we have no way of ascertaining. The students were told in an energetic Ciceronian style to seize their opportunities and to make the best use of them by industry and application. They were given the reasons for the pursuit of Latin in particular; it was the door to the temple of knowledge and science, the way to truth, and the stepping stone to culture and virtue. We are left to wonder what impression it made upon the lads.

This inaugural address began a custom which called for a similar Latin oration the first school day of each year, and the custom persisted until the Jesuits were driven out of the colleges two centuries later. This for a time worked a hardship on the viceroy. Little did he think, as he listened to the novel introduction of the school year of 1574, that it would become an annual ceremony, and that very soon the other colleges would wish their opening day brightened by his presence. He and his successors were put in the predicament of attending each "Inicio"; even the viceroy had to go to school at least one day of the year. A halt was called later, when the number of schools increased. Maybe the Latin became poorer, but it is more likely that viceroys were in a better position to revolt than were students. The gownsmen generally were willing to listen to anything for half an hour, since there would be no classes for the remainder of the day.'

For the first part of the year there were only three divisions of the three hundred students. Two of the sections studied the fundamentals of Latin. The two Jesuit teachers were carefully picking out the brighter boys, according to the plan in vogue in Europe. In a comparatively short time the more apt pupils were put into the third section with those who had previously studied Latin at the University, so that they should not be retarded, while the others were given longer drills. Even in the same hall Juan Sánchez handled the other group, which he called the *minimos;* being beginners, they were forced to plod away at denominatives, tenses, and declensions. The upper division, or *menores,* progressed to the study of verbs, genders, syntax, and finally to the fashioning of little compositions. Mercado's class underwent similar permutations. When a few months' instruction had given the teachers sufficient data and various tests had been satisfactorily passed, the advanced pupils were put under the care of Mercado and were known as the *medianos*. After this adjustment, their schedule consisted of advanced syntax and composition, while those who remained with Sánchez continued to be *minimos*. Thus the student body was resolved into three grammar sections in a three-year course.

There was every reason in the world why the boys of Mexico should advance rapidly. They had good teachers and they were both apt and studious; if we may judge by the present-day Mexican boy of the cities, we might call them very bright boys, mentally alert, quick-witted, and vivacious.[8] In this judgment we should not be far wrong, for the European fathers and visitors repeatedly remark these qualities in the youngsters and have only one complaint against them, namely, their inclination to "temperamentalism," by which we mean they are inclined to take up a task readily and enthusiastically, and to drop it with equal readiness for another if the teacher's cajolery is missing; in other words, we seem to be saying they were like all boys, at one moment hopeful, at another dejected, now serious and now mischievous. This defect the Jesuits were quite capable of checking, because they came into immediate contact with the boys in their play and study. They handled each case individually, curbing the boisterous lad and arousing the diffident one. Nor was it difficult to get the students to study, for their extracurricular concerns were neither multiple nor distracting. The friendly rivalry between the boys in book lore extended to the parents, who were keen about the progress of their sons. Again, Latin itself was not as repugnant to the Spanish ear as it is to the present-day practical American. Finally, the climatic conditions, lacking extremes of any sort, were conducive to study, and the classes could readily be conducted in the open air close to the sunny patios, with no grating noises of a bustling city to intrude upon the quiet.

Small wonder is it, then, that the school year 1574–1575 saw remarkable improvement in the boys. Long before the end, the repetitions of the matter were made and examinations held, and there remained time for the teachers to begin the reading of the authors of Latin prose and poetry. This necessitated the appointment of a master of humanities and another class of students. Classes continued during the summer of 1575 and new adjustments were made according to the various stages of progress which had been attained by the student body. At the end of the summer there were three masters and three rooms, two for the *minimos* and *medianos* and one for the *mayores*. The last were advanced students under the care of Father Lanuchi, one of those seven whom we mentioned as having pumped their way across the Atlantic in the preceding summer.

We are informed that the classes were conducted as they were being conducted in Europe at the time.[9] The Ratio Studiorum, it will be recalled, was in the evolving in 1574; it had not taken definite shape. The class arrangement just described must have had some general application in Europe, but the teaching methods probably varied with the different teachers, depending upon the university from which each had been graduated. The course content was evi-

dently the same in both Europe and America, for the early
Jesuit teachers were trained in Europe in the particular
manner of the Jesuits, which was described in an earlier
chapter. The boys of America were in no wise of a mental
caliber inferior to that of the boys of Europe; and hence
they could assimilate the same matter. It becomes patent
now that the Jesuits were bringing to America their best
qualities as teachers and the full content of the European
Latin schools.

What were the arrangements of the Jesuit schools in Europe before the Ratio of 1586 and that of 1599? Fortunately
we have a document which comprises the complete scheme
in vogue in the Roman College. It was composed by the
Spanish Jesuit, Diego Ledesma, and therefore may be said
to indicate the line of his training in Spain as well as that
which he formulated and put into practice in Rome from
1560 to 1575.[10] Suffice it to say here that the dispositions of
classes, their contents, and the methods of procedure appear
to be the same roughly as those described for America up to
the year 1576, namely, the three grammar classes, humanities, and rhetoric.

All this was being carried on in the presence of a fearful
disaster. In the early months of 1575 an epidemic, particularly fatal, broke out in Zacatecas and soon appeared in the
whole of New Spain. The Indians were the chief sufferers. Juan Sánchez, who worked among the plague-stricken
during the moments he could spare from the classroom,
estimated that two-thirds of the natives of America died
during the scourge.[11] The church sepulchers were soon filled
or closed; trenches had to be dug for the dead; whole fami-

lies died, and their homes were sealed; villages were deserted except for the dead bodies which lay in the plazas; the entire native population was affected and found no medical means of combating the disease; children cried beside their dead mothers; death hovered over all. The officialdom of the realm tried in vain to aid the sufferers, while the priests were constantly busy with spiritual ministrations and with carrying the stricken into the hospitals and the homes which had been set aside for the sick. The scourge continued during the whole of the year 1575 and the greater part of 1576. The Jesuit rector at Pátzcuaro, Juan Curiel, was one of the victims.

Yet the classes of the Jesuits in Mexico remained in session and preparations for the fall term of 1575 went on apace. When it began, more than three hundred students were enrolled for the five classes.[12] Evidently the sight during the preceding year of so many progressive classmen, and the propaganda which they spread, had been a great stimulus. Word went about the city of the scholarship of Lanuchi, whose advent in America was hailed as a great boon to the province. Because of his preëminence in the classics he was assigned by Sánchez to the class in poetry and rhetoric, where his ability to inspire the students, coupled with his facility in interpreting and explaining Ovid, Vergil, Horace, Cicero, and Quintilian, were the occasions of his great success. Some moderns may be inclined to condemn the emphasis placed on the rhetoric and word mechanics of the Latin eloquence; but such was the practice of the times.

It is remarkable that the Creoles, by far the major element in the student personnel, were generally superior to the Spaniards or aristocrats. Great was the admiration in the city for the orations composed by the students and for the verse modeled after the ancients; greater still was the delight of parents whenever the Latin colloquies and comedies which the boys composed were presented in public, or whenever their sons were chosen as characters. Undoubtedly the masters had to do considerable polishing before the exhibitions; in fact, they themselves had at times to compose little dramas and comedies in whose showing the students took all the parts. There was even in that far-off day the prodigy child. At the age of twelve this boy, Agustín Cano, of the College of San Pedro y San Pablo, was so expert in Latin poetry and oratory that his master averred there could not be found a better in any of the schools of Europe.[13] There were others whose aptitude was matched only by their docility; for Pérez de Rivas, who by reason of his many contacts with European school conditions should have known, avouches at a little later date that the youth of the City of Mexico were more apt than any he had encountered in the Jesuit schools of Europe.[14]

What with the increase in numbers and the progress in Latin and the students demonstrating their ability in prose and poetry before the viceroy and citizens, the conviction grew day by day that the boys were an exceedingly intelligent lot and were quite ready for higher studies.[15] So Father Pedro López de Parra was told to prepare the lectures for a fundamental course in philosophy. This was instituted October 19, 1575, and marks a great step in the cultural advance in America. At the time it could serve for the older students, for the seminary group, and for the younger Jesuits.

The by-products of the teaching of Latin grammar and the humanities were many. What appears to the modern educators as a surfeit of one subject did not show itself in that light to the learned of those times. The principal idea was the training of the mind of the student and the disciplining of the memory. The imagination was to be stimulated by the production of the playlets and by the oratorical compositions. The ancients, to them, were great teachers and had much to communicate to any generation. The formalism which was bound to attend upon the slavish imitation of the classicists was lost sight of when the students set themselves to the task of imitating the stylists. Necessarily there was training in elocution and public speaking, even though these branches never appeared in the subject lists. Likewise ancient history and geography came in informally. While precision, mental and vocal, was attained in the Latin classes, it was absolutely necessary for success in philosophy. Over and above all this there was being engendered in the children of the land a love of learning and an inspiration to scholarly endeavors. It might be said truly that the humanism of Europe in its nonpagan aspects had taken hold in Mexico and that the rediscovered charm of the Latin classicists had begun to work its spell there.

I do not wish to imply, however, that the Jesuits were the originators of the trend toward humanistic studies. In an earlier chapter there was summarized the general state of education before they came to America and the interest which had been aroused before the establishment of the Old University. This pertained to education in general. Latin grammar, we know, was taught as early as 1536 in the College of Santa Cruz Tlaltelolco, and to the Indians. But a systematic program with emphasis upon the classics, such as the Company was inaugurating, was not the vogue before 1553, although there had been a number of individual scholars in the country who were outstanding in their devotion to human letters rather than to natural or divine science. The general tendency during the thirty years following the taking of Tenochtitlán was to emphasize the importance of Castilian more than of Latin, and to study the native languages.[16] There was no concerted effort to establish the ideas of the ancients; there was rather an effort to spread Iberian and particularly Castilian thought. The Castilian and native tongues were used in many of the pageants, plays, orations, and poems produced in the sixteenth century. The bibliographies of books printed in Mexico reveal preponderance of grammars in Castilian and in the native languages. Still, since the men of culture who came from Europe were imbued with classical traditions and Renaissance inclinations, these cropped out in the art and literature of Mexico.[17] One Latin grammar printed in 1559 for the Indians remains.

No exception to this was Fray Julián Garcés[18] (1447–1542), the first bishop of Tlaxcala, a contemporary of Erasmus, More, and Luther, who was interested not only in contemporary history but also in psychology and sociology. He was a humanist at heart, but at the same time his sermons and orations were classical in form and allusion. Another humanist of great importance was the Augustinian friar Alonzo Gutiérrez,[19] who landed in Vera Cruz in 1536 and became the principal agitator for the founding of a university in Mexico; he is better known as Fray Alonzo de la Vera Cruz, the founder and regent of the Augustinian Colegio de San Pablo. He it was who went to Spain in 1560 and brought back the seventy boxes of books which formed the nucleus of the famous library of San Agustín. He labored fifty years in America, a true patron of letters.

It will be a surprise to many to know that Francisco Cervantes de Salazar,[20] who carried with him from the Peninsula in 1546 a profound knowledge and love of Latin, translated into that tongue the *Dialogues* of Luis Vives about the time he took the chair of literature in the University of Mexico. He applied his extraordinary genius to lecturing on many humanistic subjects and prefaced his literary course for the year 1554 with his own Dialogues, which we know as *México en 1554*. His was the task of upholding almost single-handed the merits of the study of letters during the next ten years. His successor, Frias de Albórnoz, carried on in the chair of rhetoric from 1564 until the Jesuits arrived, hampered, like Cervantes, by lack of financial remuneration, for the annual salary was less than a hundred pesos. Besides these outstanding humanists as distinguished from those who taught Latin for purposes of clerical study, there were only a few others. The Jesuits, therefore, were in a position to fill a great need.

Father Juan Sánchez Vaquero[21] was, as we have said, a true lover of the classics in literature, painting, and sculpture. He and Pedro Mercado were the first Jesuit teachers of secondary Latin classes in the metropolis. Each was an undoubted success. It was left for the third of the Jesuit humanists to desert the cause. Lanuchi went in for causing trouble on a large scale. The occasion was his lecture course on the old authors, but the cause went far deeper. We left him and the other Jesuits in the classrooms at the beginning of 1575. Lanuchi continued his work throughout this and the following year, when he complained that the teaching of the pagan authors was not a fit occupation for a priest and Jesuit. He asked to be removed. The provincial, thinking it was a passing whim, told him to remain in the lecture hall, since his work was precisely in harmony with that of the Order.

Lanuchi had something else in his head, which had been put there, and for that matter, into the heads of the younger Jesuits, by Father Alonzo Sánchez.[22] This latter, austere beyond the rules of the Society, had arrived lately from Europe. He was victim to the spirit of those few members in Spain who were causing trouble, not by laxity, but by following the opinion that the Jesuits were a contemplative more than an active order. For all his fervor, Alonzo Sánchez proved a veritable stormy petrel when he took up his abode in Mexico. There he lived the life of a quasi hermit. Since he had been a rector of some note in Spain, his example had a great influence. He urged all to prayer and penance; as a consequence some few began to neglect studies for holier things, while some few others hearing his words chose to spend their time praying rather than in preaching, confessing, or teaching.[23] Lanuchi, carried away by these ideas, which were altogether foreign to the Jesuit Institute, finally told the provincial of his desire to enter the Carthusian monastery, there to devote himself to prayer. He had lost all interest in teaching the classics and had strayed far from the Jesuit ideal of combining the active with the contemplative life. Alonzo Sánchez, too, had withdrawn to his cell. The result was the arrival in the province of a *visitador,* Father Juan de la Plaza, who sent Lanuchi back to Italy and Alonzo Sánchez to practice the apostolic life in the Philippines. Father Alonzo later changed his ideas and did notable work, but Father Vincent is heard of no more in the pages of history.

All this happened by 1579. It serves as an illustration of the position of the Jesuits with respect to the humanities which had been flourishing in their colleges in Mexico City from 1575. Definitely they were bent upon making a stout effort to install humanistic education as a permanent colonial institution, just as they were in Europe. Furthermore, a glance at the arrangements of courses and course contents obtaining in the Latin schools of Europe will reveal little substantial difference between them and the schools we shall have to consider in sixteenth-century Mexico.[24] We must leave such an interesting comparison, however, in order to see the developments taking place in the Jesuit center of education.

Chapter VIII

SEVERAL LITTLE COLLEGES AND THE ROYAL COLLEGE OF SAN ILDEFONSO

MEXICO CITY IS DIVIDED roughly into two parts. The old colonial portion with its many historic sites and monuments lies to the eastward in the form of a circle, the center of which is the Plaza.[1] The newer part encircles this and spreads particularly south and southwest. There is a fine colonial building in the old part of the city, which at present is pointed out to tourists as the Preparatory School of the National University and even as the National University itself, yet it has not lost the familiar name of the Colegio de San Ildefonso.

It has much to recommend it besides a wine-red façade of *tezontle* and massive foundations covering almost an entire square. Walking along the cool Calle de Ildefonso, one is struck by the baroque style of the building, by its great carved medieval doors, its quaint windows, and its marble gargoyles mounted aloft. On entering one of the two portals, one sees through the large columns an Aztecan patio, one of the three wherein until recently the youth of Mexico might be observed at their military drills and wherein collegians now loll between lectures or study on the shaded side. The rooms on all three floors of the building attract one. Some of them are halls worthy of the Vallejo paintings which grace their walls; others are classrooms; yet others are the offices or living quarters. Then there is the library, and the former hall of the disputations around whose walls are likenesses of famous rectors and alumni; while beneath the paintings are the choir stalls, damaged by neglect though still revealing the beauty and grace of free Renaissance and Gothic carvings. Beyond all this, the edifice recommends itself because of the hallowed memories lingering within it of the days when its walls echoed to the footsteps and voices of generations of students who had dedicated their lives to the intellectual and spiritual welfare of the kingdom that was New Spain. The building, heavy with the weight of years, was reared in 1749 at a cost of 400,000 pesos. Its history reaches back to 1574, when, with the opening of the first classes of the Jesuits, there were no portents foreshadowing the great development of the future.

Like all sturdy growths, that of San Ildefonso was slow. To all official intents and purposes an older building than the one we have described opened its doors in 1588 on the same site, as a plaque informs us. It is to our purpose to trace its origins even beyond this date, principally because of the manifest confusion surrounding them. The rise of the one college of San Ildefonso from an organization of several little colleges is an involved story. There is a strong academic motive for undertaking the task, since the study pertains intimately to the educational developments of the Company in New Spain and has to do with a source of colonial intellectual activity. The reader forewarned about the complexities is forearmed against magnifying the importance of many of the details which follow.

SAN GREGORIO, SAN BERNARDO, AND SAN MIGUEL

To link things up chronologically, then, the house of the seminarians of San Pedro y San Pablo was finished by July, 1574.[2] The sight of this group of maroon- and purple-clad gownsmen and that of the flashy scarlet and gray habits of the collegians of Santa María de Todos Santos led to an increasing desire on the part of some of the citizens to have their sons educated.[3] Both of the colleges were limited in numbers by their constitutions and in no wise endowed sufficiently to care for boarders even up to the small number of three hundred. Students were gathering to this number from Mexico and other cities.[4] Consequently the residents began to negotiate for the erection of new colleges, or halls, and carried their appeals before the viceroy and the archbishop with such fervor that these officials began soliciting alms from the rich and powerful for a beginning. What they desired was a building or two near the Jesuit house where students could live and study.

Of course the provincial, Sánchez, was familiar with this European type of *convictorio,* or college.[5] It was what we might call a hall after the English plan. If this was supervised, as was desired, by a Jesuit prefect, and if its hours of study and recreation were carefully arranged, it was ideal for the educational purposes of the Jesuits. It was a time-saver by reason of its proximity to lecture halls, and it afforded poor students a more comfortable place for study and one that was possibly less congested. Besides, tutorial help from the Jesuits in charge was available, and for advanced students repetitions and quizzes were conducted by the prefects after the lectures. Then, too, attendance at a boarding college curtailed the tendency of the wealthier boys to squander their off hours in amusements. Furthermore, it would produce a community of interests, bring about regular habits of life, and forestall moral difficulties. Perhaps immorality on the part of the boarders was a dread specter which haunted the minds of the fathers; it was to be avoided by more ample leisure for letters and by perpetual contact with bettering influences.

So with this background Sánchez established the first of the strictly Jesuit collegial seminaries, with the title of San Gregorio, and shortly afterwards added two others called San Bernardo and San Miguel.[6] This was evidently before the opening of the Jesuit classes on October 18, 1574, for Alegre states that all four groups of collegians began to follow the Jesuit courses on that day.[7] The establishment of San Gregorio attracted the attention of the king, so much so that he approved and confirmed its constitutions with his royal pen, meanwhile reserving the patronage to himself.[8] He gave power to the viceroy for the correction of anything which might appear amiss, and at the same time held him responsible for the taking and rendering of the accounts of San Gregorio. This gave rise naturally to a lot of bookkeeping, as a glance into the Archivo General will make patent.

There is little of accurate data about the San Bernardo and San Miguel establishments. Alegre, Florencia, and Rivas say that they were established separately, while Osores says there was a single college with the double name.[9] This leads us to a surmise that they may have been two halls of one building. Florencia informs us that the three colleges were begun "in the two following years 35 and 36," which means that the printer entered into the conspiracy of confusion.[10] Alegre and Rivas, on the other hand, aver that the students of these colleges were present on the opening day of class in 1574;—and we prefer this latter opinion.

The three establishments apparently were soon crowded with boarders, some of whom paid for their own support and some of whom were supported by the alms of kindly Mexicans.[11] Where were they situated? The query brings us to a note from Veytia's *Apuntes:*

Father Pedro Sánchez in the following years of 1575 and 1576 founded two other colleges with the title of Seminaries for boarders, the one in a house contiguous to his Church of San Gregorio under the name of San Bernardo in the house which until then had been that of San Pedro y San Bernardo in the house which until then had been that of San Pedro y San Pablo and at the beginning served as I have said for some students who were pupils, who until this time did not have the name of a college, and is known today by that of Rosario . . .[12]

A curious person might desire much to behold a house which bore so many titles. There is no mention of a San Miguel, but Osores enlightens us with the statement that San Bernardo y San Miguel was established in April of 1576 and was given an official license by the viceroy on November 28 of the same year.[13] If these had been large foundations, the Jesuits would have perpetuated the memory of benefactors; moreover, there would have been records of legal transactions. An obvious reason for the lack of records is that the house or houses were already constructed and the officials, who were urging the fathers to open schools, granted some verbal permissions that eliminated rubrics and seals.

Evidently, all four of the colleges were rated as seminaries, but the terms college and seminary should not be taken according to the modern usage. Although the students in a school so classified had to observe regulations and wear a distinctive garb, the great majority were not studying for the priesthood. They studied neither philosophy nor theology at that time; after their Latin training with the Jesuits, many heard lectures in the University. From the viewpoint of the Jesuits there was just one student body to teach, numbering three hundred with extern students in 1575, and six hundred in 1576. And this student body was to the Jesuits their Colegio Máximo even though the building which went under that name was not yet completed.

It may be noted here that the students were Spanish and Creole boys. At a later date the question of establishing a college of this type for Indians came to the fore. From evidence shown in succeeding quotations it will become clear that the Indians were to be given opportunities similar to those of the favored classes. There had been considerable debate during preceding generations over the question of elevating natives to the priesthood.[14] The Jesuits arrived at the fag end of the discussions involving this racial prejudice. After the preliminary attempts of Sahagún and his confreres in the faculty of Santa Cruz Tlaltelolco had aroused opposition, the first provincial council, held in Mexico in 1555, forbade the ordination of natives, because being of a lower state they would not have influence among all peoples.[15] This edict was rectified by episcopal legislation in 1585, though tacitly the practice had been permitted for some years previously.[16] The Franciscans feared at first to admit Indians into their convents because of their inclination to drink, but once they and the other orders accepted them into their ranks "the Indian priests were extremely sober and exemplary."[17] At any rate, in 1586, the Jesuits opened a college for Indians which was called San Gregorio. Why the fathers in the presence of a whole catalogue of heavenly patrons again selected San Gregorio is a puzzle which becomes clear only if we understand that the "old" San Gregorio for whites was dropped before the beginning of the "new" San Gregorio for Indians.[18]

Apparently no Jesuits lived in the rooms of these three seminaries during the first years of their existence, at least, even though the buildings were rented or owned by the fathers.[19] The major-domos were of the laity, while the spiritual direction of the boys was given by the Jesuits along with student counsel.[20] We gather, more from tradition than from documents, that the discipline in the halls was a constant source of worry to the fathers, what with a crowd of lads living together, and what with lack of facilities for sports and games.

THE UNION OF THE SMALL COLLEGES—SAN ILDEFONSO

Our narrative of the story of these colleges would come to a happy termination at this point if we were to follow the advice of Father Florencia when he remarks tersely: "No more about these colleges; they were separate, and as time went on were reduced to San Ildefonso."[21] Yet we must interest ourselves in their evolutionary process, which Florencia avoided so neatly, in order to understand the development of San Ildefonso. There is much disputing over the question of the origin of the famed institution. Strangely enough, three of the main disputants whom we quote were its old graduates:

Speaking of San Gregorio [says Veytia], it lasted until 1582, when the Jesuit provincial received orders from his general to give it up together with another college they had founded under the title of San Bernardo, and to reduce them both to one; this was done; the collegians of San Gregorio were transferred to San Bernardo, which was close to the colleges then called San Pedro y San Pablo; and of San Bernardo and San Gregorio they made one, but under a changed name, for from then on the college was called San Ildefonso.[22]

This would appear to establish the first date for the name of San Ildefonso, and all would be well if the *Carta Anua* for 1590 did not mention the individuality of San Gregorio, and if that of 1599 did not favor us with the statement:

San Gregorio ... for Indians, the sons of caciques ... was united to the Colegio Máximo ... its students being used for the instruction of Indians of Mexico. ...

Whence the conclusion that San Gregorio survived as a name beyond 1582, but that its Creole students were transferred to the house of San Ildefonso about that time. But San Bernardo surely existed as a college beyond 1582, for a letter from the general, Aquaviva, dated August 7, 1587, states:

Regarding the government of the colleges of San Pedro and San Bernardo, supposing that it is not convenient either to give them to the seculars or to allow that of San Bernardo to lapse, it seems that if the Company cannot be excused from assuming this great trust, it should be undertaken in such wise as to attain the end desired and with all exaction.

The general goes on to the conclusion that there should be only one college governed by the fathers in Mexico City, and San Ildefonso is not mentioned.

There is more, however, because Osores holds stubbornly to 1588 as the year of the origin of San Ildefonso:

In spite of the already founded colleges of San Pedro y San Pablo, San Gregorio, San Bernardo, and San Miguel, the Provincial ... found it necessary to establish another in 1588....To this effect he obtained a license from Viceroy Alvaro Manrique de Lara, dated July 29, 1588, by which was founded the Colegio de San Ildefonso y San Bernardo, on August 1, uniting on the same day the College of San Bernardo, in which had been incorporated San Miguel, if it ever had been distinct from San Bernardo, and San Gregorio.[23]

Thoroughly complicated becomes the situation when Alegre, referring to the year 1583, says:

The province being short of subjects, it seemed better to reduce the collegians of San Miguel, San Gregorio, and San Bernardo to one, to which the name San Ildefonso seems to have been given. They applied the name San Miguel to a newly organized group of Indians in the College of Puebla, and that of San Gregorio was reserved to the seminary for the same nation in Mexico.[24]

He adds for the year 1588:

The two seminaries of San Bernardo and San Miguel were happily united under the name of San Ildefonso.[25]

What really happened? The student body was composed of four distinct collegial groups to the year 1582. There was over each a Jesuit prefect or vice-rector. In 1583 the provincial, being short of subjects, put them under one head and called the whole body San Ildefonso, thus freeing two fathers for other work. I say two, because San Pedro y San Pablo had a separate vice-rector. The living quarters remained distinct except for San Miguel Hall, which probably was in the San Bernardo building and hence took the latter name. This was done with tacit permission of the viceroy. So things went until 1588, when the San Pedro y San Pablo patrons grew obstreperous and the Jesuit rector turned over to them the keys. At the same time *official* license was given by the viceroy for the foundation of San Ildefonso, so named unofficially since 1582. A new building was constructed, other constitutions drawn up, and thirty of the collegians were enrolled as the San Ildefonso seminary group as distinct from many other students.[26] More color was introduced, for all the San Ildefonsans from whatever group had to wear gold and black, except the San Pedro y San Pablo boys. The latter still appeared publicly in the purple and maroon. All had the same constitution to obey. The physical aspect of the college had changed; most probably San Miguel and San Gregorio halls were vacated.

San Ildefonso, then, had two birthdays; officially it began August 1, 1588, and unofficially in the school term of 1582–1583. Its component parts originated earlier. With it San Pedro y San Pablo almost succeeded in merging in 1590, when our old friends the patrons lost part of their foundation principal and cut down on the allotments for scholarships. The attempt at incorporation of the two, or, better, the attempt to turn over the financial liabilities and assets of San Pedro y San Pablo to the Jesuits, failed again in 1597.[27] In 1612, however, the royal cedula[28] gave complete administration of the college to the Company, the patronage to the king, and the rights of appointment of collegians to the viceroy, who also was to provide the burses; and thus the patrons were finally eliminated.[29] So far as the physical setup was concerned, we may add that about 1618 the old building of San Pedro y San Pablo was dismantled; San Gregorio

Hall was conserved under the name of San Pedro; San Bernardo Hall was lost, but its name was conserved on another building; San Miguel Hall remained for ministrations to the Indians of the city.[30]

CRISTO

Almost parenthetically must the little college called Cristo be discussed. It was a collegial group founded March 23, 1612. Four poor students were allotted scholarships and tuition; they went to classes with the San Ildefonso students and after completing their law or theology courses were rated as graduates of the larger institution after 1618. In that year Cristo was merged with San Ildefonso, maintaining none the less its distinctive colors and financial accounts.[31]

THE ROYAL COLLEGE OF SAN ILDEFONSO

It was on January 17, 1618, that San Ildefonso became a Royal College according to a cedula issued by Philip III. His dispositions called for the fixture of the coat of arms of Castile and León to the main portals. The king gave a hacienda, to go toward maintaining twelve scholarships; the beneficiaries of these were to wear the garb which had obtained, but to the black capes and golden gowns a dash of green was added in the form of a large border to the cape. The capes and gowns went with the scholarships. The fellowships ran for six years and the recipients were to study philosophy and theology during that time without leave of absence. At the end they were graduated as bachelors, yet they were not left homeless whilst making a decision regarding their future. The alumni were sheltered in the college without expense for a year after the degree was conferred, during which time they decided to continue at the university, to take orders, or to practice law or politics.[32]

While in attendance at the college the twelve recipients of scholarships were no privileged characters. They had to obey the common statutes and their own particular rules like the rest of the students. The Jesuit rector had power to expel any one of them for misconduct. The viceroy was bound to see that only those of studious habits and strength of character received appointments. The rector informed him whenever there was a vacancy. These royal students led all processions, even to the common refectory and halls of disputation, not through distinction in the ranks so much as for observation; if they were out in front any absence could be easily detected.[33] Once a week there was a special convocation for them at which some chosen one delivered an oration before the rector. The rector was also obligated in many ways by the king, since he had the details of the entire administrative, spiritual, and educational program to carry out and to account for to the viceroy. He had to record all expenditures and receipts and anything touching the hacienda which was to ballast the college financially as the king's foundation. His duty it was to enforce the new constitutions modeled after those of San Martín College of Lima. Thus finally did San Pedro y San Pablo come to rest in 1618 and San Ildefonso to fare forth on a long journey as a Royal College.[34]

We must distinguish between the San Ildefonso group of twelve and the physical edifice known as San Ildefonso in which were housed others besides the twelve and wherein they had some recitations and made their studies. It must also be noted that the students, particularly those in the lower divisions, attended lectures a short distance away in the halls of the Colegio Máximo, or at the university. When, though, we arrive at a point where we must give an esti-mate of the products of San Ildefonso, we are referring to students of the college *in globo,* whether they spent their time as members of the San Pedro y San Pablo group or of that of San Ildefonso, or unattached. The last classi-fication is put in advisedly, for the total number in the whole group in 1582 was 150. This number remained about the same until 1599, when it dropped to "more than 110," according to the *Carta Anua* of that year. It must be remem-bered that the collegians constituted part of the larger student body of the Colegio Máximo. In 1599 there were among the graduates thirteen San Ildefonsans in belles-let-tres, while fourteen others entered religious orders, six be-coming Jesuits.

During this time the only masters of Latin, philosophy, and theology for these students were the Jesuits, who gave their lectures in the halls of the Colegio Máximo soon to be described. Some Jesuits lived in the San Ildefonso quarters and acted as rectors in a directive capacity or as tutors and "readers." In the following centuries the college was able to sustain chairs for lecturers in jurisprudence whose occu-pants presided as *presidentes* at the examinations and pub-lic acts in law and arts, and presided at the two academies (seminars) held each week in those branches of learning. In academies of moral theology the Jesuits presided. The groundwork for much of the development in graduate studies was laid in the sixteenth century, and it included (besides the academies) literary acts, sabbatical defenses, and forensics for some particular student to worry about and for all to attend.[35]

The student body of San Ildefonso lived on without any break during the succeeding two centuries of Jesuit control and yielded a fruitful harvest of distinguished alumni. There were many who entered religion; the available records reveal that between the years:

1633 and	1755	16 became	Dominicans	
1620 "	1753	40 "	Franciscan observants	
1639 "	1754	28 "	" discalced	
1713 "	1757	14 "	Missionaries *de Propaganda*	
1666 "	1724	10 "	Augustinians	
1623 "	1754	12 "	Mercedarians	
1635 "	1763	13 "	Carmelites	
	1735	1 "	Belemite	
	1725	1 "	Hipólito	
	1693	1 "	San Juan de Diós	
1618 "	1767	293 "	Jesuits	

429 total religious[36]

Among the historians who were trained in San Ildefonso were Fathers Florencia and Alegre of the Company of Jesus, Osores de Sotomayor, Dr. José Ignacio Bartolache, Licentiate José María Bocanegra, Bishops Juan M. Castoreña y Ursua, Eguiara y Eguren, Juan Gómez de Parada, Father Julián Gutiérrez Dávila, Fray Alonzo de la Rea. There were the journalist Licentiate Juan Barquera, the literary fathers Jose Antonio Alzate and Juan Corral, the orator Vade los Rios, and numerous philosophers, theologians, and lawyers. There were architects and poets and scientists, such as Don Antonio León y Gama and José López Castrejón; foremost of the doctors of medicine was José Escobar y Morales; foremost among the public servants was Licentiate José M. Fagoaga. Many were the benefactors who aided their alma mater in its needs, many the philanthropists who gave to the city and country: Dr. Eustaquio Fernández, the charitable medic, Fr. Manuel Bolea, the founder of the Colegio de Niñas, Fr. Francisco Pérez Aragón, the founder of San Luís College of Zacatecas, Bishop Gómez de Parada y Mendoza, the founder of the public library. There were at least eight bishops, one of whom we recall as Fray Pedro de la Concepción, the companion of Margil. Besides the diplomats, Fr. Diego José Abad y García, Tomás González Calderón, and Barrientos y Padilla, many patriots went forth from those halls, such men as Don Ignacio Alas, illustrious insurgent; Licentiate Don Ignacio Aldama, a general of the insurgent army and royalist victim; Dr. Pedro de la Llave, and insurgent Don Melchor Muzquiz; and there were missionaries, too, among whom we remember Juan de Ugarte and Pedro Velasco, and martyrs, Father Luís Álvarez among the Tepehuanes and Felipe de Jesús, the Mexican saint slain in Japan.[37]

Many were the benefactions which facilitated such a development.[38] Donations were given for buildings and repairs; premiums were offered for the encouragement of both students and professors;[39] chairs were established,[40] and bursaries presented.[41] The library was begun by the first founders shortly after 1573, when each of the thirty gave 2400 pesos for that purpose.[42] Other gifts followed and books were brought from Europe. Most lamentably, the suppression of the Society was occasion for pilfering the library, and for the loss or destruction of the indices so that we are without trace of the records of the numbers and descriptions of the tomes, if they ever were made.

In conclusion, many aspects of the development we have been tracing are sources of surprise. It happened in America and before the United States came into being. All the famous alumni just mentioned were native-born Americans from among the many who trekked in a constant stream to the capital and then carried back with them to their home cities as fine an education as even Europe could give. Each became a center of influence for the furthering of culture and in the affairs of his community. Certainly, therefore, a commendable exploitation of talents was in progress at San Ildefonso. Teachers went out into the far cities and missionaries into the wildernesses. The arts of painting, music, drama, oratory, and poetry were appreciated; native writing was encouraged and European productions translated.[43] The whole resolves itself into an instance of the magnificent effort at elevating the intellectual life of Spain's North American colony, for which praise must go to the Spaniards who were instruments in the enterprise, and to the Mexicans and Indians who rejoiced in their opportunities and developed them to a point where they could truly aver: "This is our culture."

Chapter IX

THE COLEGIO MÁXIMO

S AN ILDEFONSO WAS ONLY ONE PART of the center of Jesuit educational influence, which was to send forth radiations to other parts of New Spain, to Central America, to South America, and to the faraway Philippines. It is time to turn to another institution, which antedated and which stood as the educational force behind San Ildefonso and the other seminaries incorporated within it. I refer to the Colegio Máximo, situated a stone's throw down the avenue from San Ildefonso. This was the hub of all of the activities of the Company in New Spain. Any product of the colleges described thus far might be referred to the venerable institution. In it the Jesuits themselves were trained for their various works. Here during the colonial period the famous missionaries found surcease from their labors in the north and south of New Spain; here for them and for all the Jesuits was—home.

It will be appropriate, after having extended the account of San Ildefonso into the centuries beyond the sixteenth, to gather up a few threads pertaining to the infancy of the Colegio Máximo, even at the risk of repetitions.

The wealthy old caballero Alonzo Villaseca was interested in having the sons of his compatriots educated.[1] He invited the Jesuits from Europe and promised them financial assistance. Then toward the end of 1572 he gave them some lots and those old burro sheds; the fathers built some slightly better accommodation which was home to them for several years while they were constructing the small colleges in 1575 and 1576. Classes were opened in 1574, and kindness allows the assumption that these caused joy to the heart of the gruff old man. Students flocked to the classes up to and beyond the number of six hundred; they kept Juan Sánchez, Mercado, and Lanuchi very busy even during the days of the harrowing plague. The numbers began to be a chief concern of the rector and the provincial, because something would have to be done about a college building for them, as well as for the novices, juniors, philosophers, and theologians of the Society, all of whom were living on the premises in the old buildings. These and many other architectural and administrative worries agitated the mind particularly of Pedro Sánchez; but what was most mysterious to him was the prolonged silence of Don Alonzo. The dear old man had withdrawn to his hacienda during the year 1575, and, as far as appearances went, seemed to have lost interest in both the Jesuits and education.[2]

Why should he be interested in education? A mining man with whom the world had dealt well should have had no qualms about the educational status of the masses, according to all our preconceived notions of miners, especially in those early days of a remote, post-Conquest colony. It may have been that he was shocked by the moral ineptitude of some of his fellow Spaniards and wished by educational and missionary activities to promote a better concept of Christian conduct.[3] Was he depressed by the lack of more abundant educational facilities than those afforded at the University and existing schools?[4] Did he consider the clergy poorly trained, and therefore decide to start a quasi reform by means of the much heralded European Jesuits?[5] Perhaps he was far-visioned beyond all our comprehension and foresaw, as a consequence of getting teachers to America, his land peopled with schools and scholars, or perhaps he was just one of those stout, public-spirited citizens who see a need and an opportunity to supply it, and who in a businesslike way unostentatiously put through a great program, neither debating all the reasons for or against it, nor anticipating happy results. He would seem to have been the latter type of man, and one motivated, like so many other Spanish miners, by the desire to give something toward glorifying "the Lord for the largess he had received from His hand."[6] And give he did.

Villaseca's benevolences are well followed in an old manuscript tome resting at present in the Archivo General.[7] He opened his purse first on November 6, 1572, with a large donation of 26,500 pesos. Periodically he made additions until August 22, 1574. Then there is silence for over a year in the account book. This may have caused the provincial his anxiety about the prospective founders. The man's total gifts to that time amounted to 88,930 pesos. Some had been used by Sánchez for construction purposes; some had purchased a few extra lots; what the balance sheet showed in 1575 we do not know. Sánchez, however, was convinced there would not be enough for the building he had in mind, a great project in which all the Jesuits were interested, their Colegio Máximo. When Villaseca seemed to have deserted them in 1575, the provincial's policy could be questioned. Why had they not accepted the offers of money for this foundation, which had been made by others than Villa-seca? Why had they waived other suitable sites for their college?[8] The man had given magnificently, but could they be reasonably assured of his giving much more? As a matter of fact, they had really no positive assurance from Alonzo that he ever intended to endow a college for them. If he had any such intentions, he had not manifested them openly in the past three years. The only basis for their hopes was a statement of his, made while the Indians were putting up that early church for the fathers, to the effect that some day he would do something for them in a large way. Some opined he had already done what he intended to do and had cautiously retired.

The provincial's estimate of Alonzo may have fluctuated with each of these new considerations, but he gave up none of his hopes; in fact, he drew up plans and decided in 1575 to lay the foundations of his building.[9] News of this move undoubtedly reached the ears of Villaseca, who must have felt gratified to know the college was to be on the site he had donated; otherwise we cannot account for his gift of 36,200 pesos[10] on September 3, 1575, dispatched on two mules. Still, the peculiar twist of his character caused him once more to surround himself with an aloofness as far as the Jesuits were concerned, and his silence caused the fathers to wonder. We must recall the point at issue for them. They had enough to start the building, but hardly enough to complete it. Moreover, they wished to charge no tuition. Hence, only a solid endowment could free them from financial burdens. Now at the critical moment their great prospect for this help seemed fading. Sánchez, nevertheless, pushed forward boldly with his work on the building, and revealed to the full what the present generation might call his unbounded optimism, but what his fellows called his trust in God.[11] They were probably more correct, for it took faith in the face of the plague which was killing off people by the thousands, including the Jesuit rector, and in the face of many difficulties besetting his projects in the other cities, to tide Sánchez over the trying period. He believed in making a start. The future would be well cared for when it arrived.

One day in the spring of 1576, he received an invitation from Señor Villaseca to meet him in the mines of Ixmiquilpán. It was then that Villaseca revealed his true intentions.[12] He declared that he had written some years previously to the king through his viceroy, offering to bring the Jesuits to America at his own expense. The king did not at the time make use of his wealth for the furtherance of his glory, but sent the fathers with greater honor and expediency than his subject could have done. He himself had given what seemed suitable, with the intention all along of giving more at an opportune time. That time had come. It was his desire to found in Mexico the college which would be the mother institution of the whole province, if the provincial were gracious enough to accept it.

Sánchez was gracious and profoundly grateful in his acceptance. He hastened to the capital, informed the fathers, and hastened back with the notary Villaseca had requested. And thus the notary was able to write:

In the mines of Ixmiquilpán ... Alonzo de Villaseca ... on the 29th day of August [sic], 1576 ... before me ... declares: that ... having offered ... 2000 ducats ... to bring the fathers to this New Spain ... , and that His Majesty for just reasons ... having chosen to send them ... to New Spain ... where they arrived ... ; and that now ... having acquainted the Provincial ... of his intention to found the said college ... , seeking to repay in some measure our Lord for the largess he has received from His hand ..., he asks Sr. Dr. Pedro Sánchez to accept him as a founder of the college, whose ... will is to give for that work and for the support of the religious who are and will be engaged in it ... 4000 gold pesos in silver tithes ... etc.[13]

The deed thus witnessed made the Colegio Máximo independent of the royal patronage, even though in 1583 a royal grant of 1000 ducats a year for ten years came to the college. The deed likewise freed the College from untoward litigation. Villaseca's wish to have the institution named after the Apostles Peter and Paul was fulfilled, whence arose the later confusion between the collegial seminary of San Pedro y San Pablo and the Colegio Máximo de San Pedro y San Pablo.[14]

Perhaps the distinction between these two is sharp. The student body of both comprised a unit; the Jesuits taught both groups as a unit; but the foundations were separate. Few there are who date the foundation of the Colegio Máximo as far back as November 6, 1572, when Villaseca made his first bequest.[15] This could be done, if consideration is given to the fact that there was a Jesuit rector and community come to establish a college,—which would be a *collegium inchoatum*. Others might say that the opening of the classes for beginners marked the birthday of the Colegio Máximo; others could hold that the first stones laid for the building in 1575 should mark the date of origin; there would be added reason for this in that the first college course, namely, philosophy, was added to the curriculum in this year. Yet the preference seems to lie with the date of Villaseca's legal document.

Sánchez in his optimism had not undervalued the generosity of Villaseca nor that of the other citizens. Once lumber and stone began to pile up about the site of the college, many became otherwise than the crowd of interested bystanders which is wont to gather through civic pride around the earthworks of a construction going on in the heart of their town. The Jesuits were going to give education gratuitously; therefore, presumably with the graciousness that still characterizes the people of Mexico, there flowed a steady stream of contributions to the work, contributions of time, labor, materials for building, money, a house here and there, and ranches.[16] Since there were no banks of credit in those days, the houses and ranches served as capital; the sale of the produce from them, and the rents coming in, met running expenses of the college. The largest farm was the one given by Lorenzo López, valued at 14,000 pesos, which Sánchez named Jesús del Monte. Its cattle numbered five hundred head. Besides producing wheat, it yielded loads of timber for the college building. All these donations added to the sum of about 150,000 pesos given by Villaseca in furniture, ornaments, buildings, haciendas, and money, shaped up into a very substantial foundation.

Of course there were plans for the construction of what Sánchez wished to be the greatest Jesuit college in New Spain. If the usual custom of the Society was followed, these had to be sent to the general at Rome for inspection and approval. Probably Sánchez had been instructed to put up this building and those in other cities in which he was then interested, just as he saw fit. At any rate, we may suppose that this was so from the letter of approval and gratitude which the general, Everard Mercurian, sent to Sánchez and Villaseca two years later.[17]

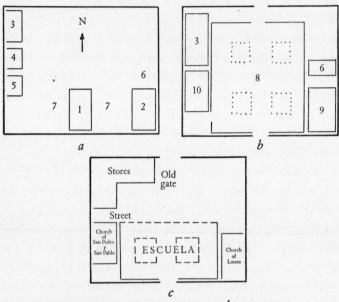

GROUND PLAN OF THE COLEGIO MÁXIMO GROUP

[a] 1, first chapel, 1572; 2, church built by Indians, 1573; 3, San Pedro y San Pablo Seminary, 1574; 4, San Gregorio College, 1575; 5, San Bernardo College, 1576; 6, San Miguel College (?), 1576; 7, residences (?). [b] 8, Colegio Máximo, 1576; 9, San Gregorio College, 1588; 10, Church of San Pedro y San Pablo. [c] The group as at present.

The whole plot of land on which the Jesuits had been settled was somewhat oblong, measuring about 650 feet on the street now called San Ildefonso, its southern boundary, and a little less than that on the Calle de la Merced, its boundary on the west. In the center of the plot, near the southern street and facing south, was the first little chapel which the Jesuits used; clustered around this were the several houses for the members, fathers, students, and novices. In the far southeast corner was the church built by the Indians of Tacuba, called Jacalteopán. In between the church and the old chapel, probably, was San Miguel. The building which the San Pedro y San Pablo seminarians utilized at first cannot be indicated, but their new one, on the Calle del Carmen, faced west. Beside it were the old buildings sheltering San Gregorio and San Miguel.[18]

The Colegio Máximo was put in the center.[19] It was square, 110 varas, or 308 feet, on each side, and about 40 feet high.[20] The main door looked south, opening on Calle de San Ildefonso. This necessitated tearing down the little chapel, whose plot thereafter supported the main door. Inside the door was a large lobby. Straight forward were the marble steps leading to the second floor. To the left and to the right were a few steps leading down into the first two south patios. There were two more patios directly north of these, which may no more be traced, for a street is being cut through precisely where they began. The first-mentioned patio to the left of the main entrance is, as it was originally, about 90 feet long by 80 feet wide; it is flagged and encompassed by stone pillars and arches 12 feet in height, and within them is an ambulatory. In the center of the patio is a stone monument whose four sides bear the inscriptions of the Colegio Máximo, the Colegio de San Gregorio, the Universidad de México, and the Escuela National Preparatoria. The second patio is similarly constructed, but is a little smaller in its dimensions at present, probably because of recent remodeling. Some of the pillars are newer and never felt the shoulder of a tired sixteenth-century student.

The large building lay around these four patios and divided them one from another; its center therefore was cruci-

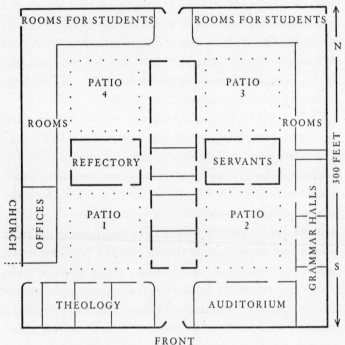

FRONT

GROUND PLAN OF THE COLEGIO MÁXIMO

form. If the patios be taken one by one, we get a fair impression of the distribution of rooms and halls. In the first patio to the southwest were two or three lecture halls of the theologians;[21] on the east that for philosophy; on the north the refectory, and on the west the porter's lodge and some office rooms. Putting the porter's lodge in that locality indicates that there was an entrance door there, probably the one used by the fathers. On the second floor were the rooms for the lecturers, administrators, and guests, except on the north, where the large library was placed. The second patio, to the right as you enter the main entrance, was surrounded by the large assembly hall on the south, grammar classrooms on the east, servants' quarters on the north, and philosophers' hall on the west; the second floor had rooms for the teachers of grammar and philosophy, except on the north, where there was the fine chapel of St. Ignatius. The other two patios in the north end of the building were surrounded by the living quarters of the students, the dispensary, infirmary, and sacristy.

There must have been a high stone wall enclosing a yard to the north of the building, for the high arch of its gate was standing in 1934 amid the heaps of dust and debris dumped about it by the wrecking crew. Massive stones, in all likelihood the very ones hewn for the building in the sixteenth century, littered the spaces once called the north patios. The remnants of a cobblestone roadway lead into the north gate.[22] Outside the wall there was a walk of the same rounded stones, going east and around the far corner toward the south. The northern half of the old Colegio Máximo, then, which was a glory of the fathers for two centuries, returned to inglorious dust in 1935; thus one of the few remaining buildings of the early century went the way of all things. At present a spacious market place occupies the site of the rooms and patios that were once the scene of devoted educational labor.

The entire square of the Jesuit property underwent many

changes in the course of the years.[23] Unfortunately we do not know the exact sites of the first residences of the fathers, but we are safe in assuming that they were near the chapel. They had to make way for the new building, except for one, which was most probably on the southwest corner. Then too, the site of San Bernardo is doubtful; it is located by Veytia as "close to the church of San Gregorio" in the sixteenth century. In 1756, Veytia's time, however, the Church of San Gregorio was that one first built by the Tacuban Indians.[24] In this time, too, San Gregorio for Indians was situated in the southeast section of the Jesuit plot and was still under Jesuit direction. The old Indian church was torn down in the late eighteenth century and gave place to the present leaning towers of the church of Loreto. At the west end of the land, the church of San Pedro y San Pablo still remains as a national monument. It had been a school for San Gregorio seminarians at one time; at another it housed the first national congress of the Mexican Republic. Afterwards it was closed. In late years it has been opened as a forum for free speech, and lastly as a school for little girls.

What became of the remains of Alonzo Villaseca, buried in a magnificent vault in this church, is hard to tell. The old man did not survive long enough to see the effects of his foundation upon education in Mexico. He was called away September 6, 1580, but not before he had willed a large sum for the building of the college church, which was completed in 1603. He was generous to the end. He sent smaller sums to the fathers from time to time after 1576; and in his last days he had a larger sum of 24,000 pesos hoisted on the

backs of four burros for transport to the College and hospital,[25]—the hospital to receive one-third of this silver. The
Jesuits, the citizens, and the clergy and all the dignitaries
of the city paid full honor to the memory of Alonzo, "the
common father of all the colleges."[26]

The importance of the Colegio Máximo to the Jesuit cause
of education can hardly be overestimated. In every province
of the Society there is supposed to be a *colegio máximo*.
Sometimes it is not the largest in student numbers, but it is
always the mother college of the rest. It is a sort of Jesuit
university wherein courses of theology and philosophy are
given to the scholastic Jesuits, and to others who may wish
them. It is at the same time a university, or at least an
arts college, for extern students. It is an essential part, therefore, of every province. It is designated as the educational
center by the general, and is capable with papal permission
of conferring the same theological degrees as the pontifical
universities.

This institution was transferred very early to Mexico by
the Jesuits. The Colegio Máximo de San Pedro y San Pablo
became the center not only of Jesuit education, training, and
administration, but of all public education in New Spain.[27]
In the Colegio lived the provincial until 1592 (when the
Casa Profesa was built); and there he held the provincial
congregations. It was the novitiate, the juniorate, or normal
school until 1585, when Tepotzotlán was opened for the
younger members. Likewise during that time it was the tertianship, or house of third probation, wherein the final
touches were put to the training and education of the newly
ordained Jesuits. For fifty years it was the only residence of

the student theologians and philosophers, and the only college designated for lectures to the younger Jesuits in those subjects; for after 1626 some scholastics were taking philosophy and theology at Puebla. Furthermore, it was the residence of all of the Jesuit professors and regents, those who were engaged in teaching and lecturing in the Colegio itself as well as those who were occupied in San Ildefonso and the various seminaries discussed in the last chapter. Besides this, its halls were open to extern students, who could receive gratis a full course in the liberal arts with what would be now a preparatory training. It was high school, college, and university combined.

Ultimately, before the suppression of the Society, the Colegio Máximo supplied teaching faculties to twenty-eight Jesuit colleges of New Spain, and to a number of seminaries. It was indeed an intellectual center. Its import in the missionary work which was undertaken by the Jesuits, its import as a center of spiritual ministries, needs no description, and we have already given some inkling of its influence upon the Colegio Real de San Ildefonso. And so, having considered the Colegio Máximo under its natural aspects with an indication of its educational force, we are ready to see the educational side more in detail.

Chapter X

DEVELOPMENTS IN THE COLEGIO MÁXIMO

THE MATERIAL STRUCTURE of the Colegio Máximo was some years in the completing. It was not easy in those times to finish the decorations, prepare the furniture, and collect the art works and school materials, in a year. Neither was it advisable to endeavor to round out the educational program in so short a time. More customary was it in the ways of the Jesuits to proceed slowly and to evolve plans to meet the special requirements of time and place. Consequently, it may be affirmed in general that years[1] were required to polish the new college to a degree where it might be termed a finished product comparable to its models at Alcalá and Salamanca in both physical and cultural aspects. About their intentions in this regard there seems to be no doubt, for Florencia, speaking of the years 1575 and 1576 concerning the Jesuit center, mentions[2] it as "building up like Salamanca." More man power would be required in order to make it function like a smooth machine. Adjustments in the machinery of the province would have to be made during the first few years after 1576, with definite designations of fathers to missionary work, definite plans of study, assignments of teachers and courses, and apportionments of men to the other cities.

Since the superiors in Spain and Rome were bent upon transmitting the Jesuit institutions and Constitutions to America, together with their plans of studies, pedagogics, and lecture courses, we may say with assurance that Sánchez was having no fears over his inadequate supply of subjects. If he was impatient to complete the educational structure at which he was toiling, his peace of mind must have been somewhat restored when eight fathers and four scholastics from Spain put in an appearance in September, 1576. With these, Sedeño, Rogel, and three lay brothers joined up at Havana where they had just closed the residence.[3] Although this augmented the total number in the province to seventy-five,[4] nevertheless not all of these Jesuits were available for teaching, since seventeen students and novices and thirty lay brothers were included. Moreover, not all could be applied to the teaching work in the capital, for some were already scattering for work in Pátzcuaro, Valladolid, and Oaxaca. Still, more would come, Sánchez was certain; and come they did during the rest of the century. Calls for helpers went back time and again to the old country, and the Spanish provinces continued to send their subjects to the new foundation; but it seemed the more they sent, the more men were demanded, owing to the new establishments of missions and schools. To illustrate how steady was the stream of newcomers, it may be noted that the total membership of the province in 1580 was 107,[5] in 1592 it was 216,[6] and at the end of the century it was 314.[7] Thus persistently were Sánchez and his successors backed in their plans,[8] and thus was the worry over man power settled.

There can be no question about the qualities of those who were flung into the work of building and consolidation of the province. The eight fathers who came in 1576 had some very illustrious professors in their midst. Dr. Pedro Hortigosa was one. He was a happy choice, for his attainments along scholarly lines were almost universal. Besides being a man of erudition, he was an educator of the first rank, capable of projecting and carrying out a plan of education as full and as enduring as any in vogue in the Jesuit colleges of Spain.[9] He was a philosopher and he was particularly a theologian; he had therefore a complete grasp of the Jesuit scheme of studies which he was so instrumental in reproducing in his adopted province during the next half-century of his life.[10] The particular fame which he enjoyed was derived from his lecture courses in the University of Alcalá, where he had succeeded "with no inferior light"[11] the renowned Father Juan Azor in the chair of moral theology. As time went on, most of the clergy of Mexico could say that they had had a course under Hortigosa,[12] for he lectured both at the Jesuit institution and at the University of Mexico. In fact, he was the first and foremost connecting link between the two. Truly he could be called "the master."[13]

With him came also the new superior, Alonzo Ruiz, and another doctor of note, Pedro Morales. The latter had renounced his practice of law in the city of Granada, Spain, to enter the Society. In Puebla he really established the colleges of the Company and governed several until his death in 1614.[14] Probably more famous at the time was Dr. Antonio Rubio, who sailed to Mexico with a reputation kindred to that of Hortigosa, and lectured there for twenty-one years. After that he took time out to write a book, and—unfortunately for teaching in America—he was sent to Rome as procurator of the province, thereafter tarrying in Spain to have it published.[15] Both Rubio and Hortigosa had been

sent to open the courses of theology in the Colegio Máximo.
There was only one difficulty in the way of their executing
the commission immediately—they had no classes.[16]

The Jesuits could not have been expected in their two
years of teaching to have brought their pupils along to such
altitudes of learning. Only a few of the student Jesuits who
had come over recently were so far advanced in study. The
six hundred scholars were arranged, by the time Hortigosa
came, into three classes of grammar under Juan Sánchez
and Pedro Mercado, while advanced students were under
Lanuchi studying poetry and rhetoric. To these courses had
been added an introductory one in philosophy, in October,
1575.[17] This was the curricular material which the newcomers found. On it they began to enlarge. It was patent to all
that the liberal-arts program would have to be completed
with the philosophy courses leading to the bachelor's degree; consequently the knowledge of Hortigosa and Rubio
was not permitted to remain inert. They gave up temporarily the idea of lecturing in theology and went into the
classes of philosophy and letters, which meant rhetoric and
poetry.

Perhaps there is, somewhere, a full account of the educational program which the Jesuits evolved and used during
the rest of the century in Mexico before the final *Ratio* of
1599 went into practice. If so, we may continue to hope that
it will be found. For the present, however, it will be well to
repose a little confidence in three statements of Florencia,
namely: "the center was building up like Salamanca"; "the
work gained esteem comparable to that of Alcalá"; "in
Mexico they taught the same as they did in Europe."[18] Alcalá

and Salamanca, therefore, were ideals which the Jesuits were following.

The University of Alcalá can be traced back to the thirteenth century. Its foundation was laid firmly by the Franciscan prime minister of Spain, Cardinal Ximénez de Cisneros, in 1500.[19] Cisneros named it the College of San Ildefonso after his predecessor in the bishopric. San Ildefonso was intended to be the main college of the university. Ten other colleges were founded about it for various groups of students, and one of them was named San Pedro y San Pablo.[20] In 1508, the University was functioning as the "eighth wonder of the world."[21] Its privileges regarding degrees, professors, and students were the same as those of Salamanca.[22] In 1526 Ignatius of Loyola was enrolled at Alcalá, and in 1527 at Salamanca. Later, Hortigosa and Rubio were lecturers there.

Salamanca, "the old," whose doctors had encouraged Columbus, had roots deep in the centuries. It was "the glory of Spain," and in 1500 the most outstanding of the twelve universities of the land.[23] Here is not the place to bring in the debate about Isabella the Catholic as being an alumna of the University; it is pertinent, rather, to state that in 1580 it had students to the number of some six thousand who were divided up, as at Alcalá, into different colleges, called *colegios mayores* and *colegios menores*.[24] It was universities such as Salamanca and Alcalá which gave Spain a long tradition of culture. It was such as these that the Jesuits were endeavoring to bring to the outposts of civilization in the West. Hence the names of Pedro Sánchez, Juan Sánchez, Mercado, Hortigosa, Rubio, and Morales should live long in the pages of the history of American education. In Mexico they built their *colegios menores,* San Pedro y San Pablo, San Gregorio for the Indians, San Bernardo, San Miguel, and now the Colegio Máximo. Soon would come San Ildefonso. The best that Europe had to offer was being transmitted to America.

Hortigosa came from Alcalá; so did Rubio. Many of the Jesuits had been trained there. Hence we may suppose that they were saturated with the pedagogical methods existing there, and were familiar with the courses.[25] Now Father Diego Ledesma also attended the University of Alcalá during his student days and later became a lecturer there, when the Jesuits established a college called San Gerónimo in the university. He was then drafted into the service of the Roman College of the Jesuits, where he became prefect of studies, or dean. He was well fitted by reason of his teaching experience to draw up a plan of studies and courses for the Roman College. If the Jesuits in America "taught as they do in Europe," his was the plan they followed. Therefore as a conclusion to the discussion about Alcalá and Salamanca we may give briefly the *Ratio Studiorum* of Ledesma, as promised in an earlier chapter.[26]

The purpose of the different kinds of literary schools was, first, to train youths in the ways of good government and just law-making; secondly, to bring about their intellectual perfection; and, thirdly, to fit them to practice, defend, and propagate their religion. The classes of liberal-arts schools, as opposed to the mechanical schools, according to Ledesma, should include in their courses the best writings of the ancients in Latin, Greek, Hebrew, and Arabic. Students should begin with the Latin, because it is more used; therefore there should be Latin-grammar classes. The culmination of these is rhetoric, or ornate Latin. With the foundations well laid, the students could progress to dialectics, philosophy, mathematics, theology, medicine, civil and canon law. Those studying dialectics would form one college, those studying philosophy another college, and so forth.

Colleges were of different types. A particular college was one in which only the grammar and rhetoric were taught in several sections. The ones in Mexico City in 1576 were of this classification. A general college was one in which all subjects were taught. In the first type of college the grammar, syntax, declensions, genders, parts of speech, preceded the rhetoric and metric art. Textbooks were specified.[27] These were Cicero, Quintilian, and Aristotle for rhetoric; for reading, all of Cicero was prescribed, with Quintilian, Seneca, and Livy; and this was called the oratory class. History was taught from Sallust, Caesar, Livy, Suetonius, Nepos, Justin, and Valerius Maximus. The texts in natural history were the writings of the Plinys. The poetry studied by the higher class was Vergil, Horace, Martial, and some of Plautus. In Mexico, Lanuchi was beginning to object to some of these pagan authors. According to this plan, Greek was to be introduced, but if Homer and Demosthenes formally got into the curricula of sixteenth-century Mexican colleges there is no evidence of the fact.

If the Jesuits organized their classes in the colonies as they organized them in Europe, we may make a reasonable reconstruction of the arrangement for Mexico City from the standpoint of a boy. On first entering the school he was assigned to a chair in the patio, his study hall. He was really at the bottom of things intellectual. There were a number of sections in the same patio. He had to wait for the teacher, in this case Juan Sánchez, to come to his group to drill him in the alphabet. In a few days he found himself on words; after these were mastered, he had to puzzle out small sentences in a Spanish book. Then came writing, and he was over halfway through his beginner's trials. Then came a larger book, then memory lessons and arithmetic. Grammar in the vernacular was his next worry. Thus was the smallest boy trained in preparation for a seat in a classroom with the other boys within the building.

When the boy became possessor of the coveted seat in the lowest grammar class, a precise daily order was mapped out for him. Regularity was essential to successful Jesuit pedagogics. If the students were trained in orderly fashion, there would be order in the classrooms; this would be a material aid to attentiveness on the part of the boys and efficiency on the part of the teacher; and so, when classes were assembled in the morning for the first session of an hour and a half, a prayer was said. The collegians, or seminarians, had already attended Mass. Then while one of the divisions of the class was reciting the memory lesson assigned on the preceding day, the others studied or wrote until their turn came. Ten methods were specified for the recitation of this memory lesson, the last of which was the *decurian*. In this manner one boy heard the other, or others, and submitted his report to the teacher. There followed, after a few moments, an oral repetition of the grammar lesson which the teacher had explained and exemplified the day before. Then came the quiz, usually by the teacher, but sometimes in the form of a game or debate between chosen sides. At the end of the week there was a general quiz about the matter studied. Repetition played a most important part in the drilling. The rest of the morning period was given over to catechism, to outlining the new rules, or to dictation of grammar and theme.

In the afternoon, the boys were first quizzed before suffering through the correction of their themes. Methods of various sorts were to be used by the teacher to keep up interest in this arduous process[28] and to avoid dryness. Then new grammar points were gone over and another theme assigned, with a few cautions against errors. Thus the Latin program was carried out in the seventh class or grade. In the closing weeks of the term, there was a general repetition in preparation for the examinations.

The sixth class carried the students from the declensions and rules of Codretus to the higher precepts and advanced themes. The fifth, fourth, and third continued the Latin work, and prepared the students for more ornate compositions and little orations; the compositions were converted from the vernacular to Latin, and Latin writings were converted from the active to the passive voice and vice versa. According to the Constitutions,[29] the master had to give very personal attention to each of his students, and the capacity of the class should not be so great as to prevent this. He was supposed to train the students to speak Latin in class, using the method of question and answer, and have the boys ask each other questions. When these lower classes of grammar, which might be three or five, depending upon the ability and progress of the students, were completed, the authors and rhetoric were taken. The students were spurred on by public and private declamations to write prose and poetry; these were composed in Latin and Spanish; dialogues were a common form of composition, but comedies, tragedies, and pageants could be given only once in a year.

The Jesuits supposed that during this time there would be sufficient instruction in the vernacular; so too, there is mention of mathematics only incidentally. These were taken for granted; what was emphasized was the Latin course. We may by no means infer, however, that there was any such complete curriculum for the boys as that which obtains today in the grade and high schools, nor was there a variety of subjects in the primary class. Things were simpler then and fundamentals insisted upon.[30] And all the authors cited above were probably not studied completely by the extern students. The Jesuit students of humanities received additional courses and additional reading after they had finished their novitiate. There is a remarkable example of one of the Jesuits who was done with grammar, poetry, rhetoric, philosophy, and theology, at the age of twenty-one.[31] Evidently he had begun studying with the fathers long before his tenth birthday, like Oviedo in the seventeenth century, who began at seven in the minims class, finished grammar at ten, and was a bachelor of arts at thirteen.[32] These are exceptional cases, otherwise they would not have been mentioned. Most startling to educators will it be to know that, soon after the foundation of the Colegio, Greek was taught; but Greek appears only here and there during colonial times, like a fugitive star.[33]

The Jesuit system, then, had developed to the point of rhetoric and classical studies under Lanuchi. Hortigosa and the others had to complete the picture, particularly the arts course. It was at the petition of a number of the collegians and secular students who had taken the rhetoric course, that Pedro López de Parra began his preliminary course in philosophy in 1575.[34] In the following year the junior members of the Society had completed their rhetoric. Evidently Father López had not been able to give a complete course, so Hortigosa was given the philosophy section. Hortigosa, in 1576, was the first of the Jesuits to give a complete course in major studies to a class composed of seminarians, seculars, and young Jesuits. The college lost the services of Mercado, who was sent to Oaxaca to teach grammar and rhetoric.[35] College classes opened on October 19, 1576. On November 2, a law was passed prohibiting the college from granting any literary degrees.[36]

It took some time for knowledge of that law to come to the ears of the persons most concerned. Meantime the archbishop, Doctor Moya y Contreras, having decided that the theological lore of the Jesuits should be utilized to the full, asked the provincial to conduct some conferences at his episcopal residence. All the secular clergy had to be present on stated days when Sánchez discussed moral theology. Fictitious cases of conscience were proposed and the Jesuit, after explaining the principles involved, solved them. These meetings had been going on for some time with great success. The Archbishop, aware of the obligations imposed upon his office by the Council of Trent and knowing of the repute of Hortigosa, wished him to give privately a lecture course in scholastic theology or philosophy. This was difficult to refuse, for Moya was a frequent visitor at the classes of the college, and at the villa where the Jesuit students held their literary academies on vacation days.[37]

At about the same time the viceroy at somebody's suggestion asked Hortigosa and Rubio to give their philosophy lectures at the Royal University of Mexico. This, he argued, would be a help to religion in New Spain; in the second place, it would preclude the possibility of wrangling in future over theological opinions, for some of the professors at the University might hold to one interpretation of a mooted point while those at the Jesuit institution would be clinging to another. These were very similar to the reasons advanced to the Jesuits when they had been asked a few years previously to take chairs in the University of Salamanca.[38] Modesty, according to Alegre, prevented them from accepting such an honor.[39] There was undoubtedly another reason, namely, that the Jesuits did not want to tie themselves up with another institution with so few subjects available for the work. They wished to develop their own college independently, and avoid the discord which could easily arise if they became important in a royal foundation. However, they did want to work in harmony with the older institution, since one of their purposes was to train students who could later present themselves there for higher studies. The viceroy, nevertheless, did not give up his intentions, and forced in an opening wedge when he had the doctors of the University confer doctorates on Hortigosa and Rubio.[40]

For the Jesuits there was clearly question of an adjustment. They would not only have to obtain some guaranties for their own college relative to the conferring of degrees, but they would have to obtain for it legally a status regarding its relation to the University. There would have to be a compromise. Consequently, during the very period in which Drake was raiding the Pacific Coast, the procurator of the province (Pedro Díaz) was in Spain and Rome armed with instructions pertaining to this agreement with the University.[41] The result was a cedula from Philip II, drawn up at the request of the procurator-general of the Company:

The King: D. Martín Enríquez—Father Francisco de Parras, procurator-general of the Company of Jesus, has made us a report that the religious of the said Company ... have opened some colleges in those places, and particularly one in that city, in which they have been, and are, reaping great fruit; and that the sons of the inhabitants ... are employing the time they used to waste idly, in laudable exercises, learning Latin, rhetoric, arts, theology, and morality. They have discovered some very likely students and are of a mind to continue their lecture courses in those faculties. Since there is founded in that city a University, it is possible some doubts may arise between it and the religious, concerning the lectures some students are attending in the colleges, and graduation ... wherefore some discord might arise to hinder the benefits accruing to the state from the education and doctrine of the same religious. Being petitioned that this work be not obstructed and that it go on, we order, that, since the religious of said Company are teaching gratis in their colleges, without any stipend, Latin, rhetoric, arts, and theology, in the form of a seminary to the University, all those students matriculating at the University and following its courses ... be able to hear the lectures which are given in those faculties in the said colleges ... and you should take care that the persons engaged in the said teaching and education be ever favored and helped. Done in San Lorenzo, April 14, 1579. *Yo el Rey.*[42]

This cedula was presented to Enríquez and with it the papal bulls by which the sovereign pontiffs had permitted the Society to confer university and college degrees.[43] Moreover, by the same declarations, the popes had conceded to the Company the right to establish chairs for the faculties in question, even in places where there was a university. Obviously, the Jesuits had learned from their European experiences to have all grants to the order firmly fixed on paper in documentary form. Obviously too, the previous law against their granting degrees and establishing courses was done away with by papal and kingly pens. The humorous note in the affair was that the doctors of the University, backed by the viceroy, had drawn up plans to have Hortigosa assigned to their faculty, and had determined to get a cedula to this effect from the king which would permit them to dispose of the teachers "as kings were wont to do in Spain." From the aftermath, we judge the doctors took their defeat in good grace. It was now a question of compromise and adjustment in order that the harmonious spirit might continue between the two faculties.

The agreement guaranteeing concord for all time between the University of Mexico and the Colegio Máximo and actually maintaining it until the suppression of the Society, was drawn up by the viceroy in accordance with the instructions of the cedula. First of all, the students could transfer without loss of standing from one to the other if they so wished." Although this was clearly a boon to the younger college, a certain provision put both institutions substantially on parallel footings scholastically, and at the same time gave the students an opportunity the like of which we have not come across in any other North American university; it was a provision that the classes at the Colegio and those at the University be conducted at different hours. As a result of the stipulation, if the University did not offer a particular course its students could attend the same at the Colegio, a short distance away; and the students of the Colegio could likewise attend courses at the University.[45] Great numbers of the students took advantage of this privilege; and probably an equally great number took advantage of another arrangement. Some of the classes were identical at both institutions; for instance, first-year theology, and some philosophy courses. These were given at the University from six to eight o'clock in the morning and from two to three o'clock in the afternoon; if, as is quite conceivable, the students missed those early morning lectures, they could get them at the Colegio Máximo at other hours.

The happiest part about the agreement was that it made no difference in which place students finally completed their courses. There is no available information concerning the arrangements for sheepskins, except that they were granted at the University. All enjoyed their rights to a university education. The poorer students could complete their arts course at the Colegio and then continue with their higher studies of law or medicine at the University. Theologians at the University could have the benefit of the Jesuits' opinions on their chosen subject at any time. The University profited both in these and in other ways. At the same time that it utilized Colegio courses as supplementary to its own curriculum, and professors who gave their services without cost, it was receiving a greater number of students into its halls who had been advantaged by a fine preparatory training. Then, too, the University was relieved of the financial strain of paying salaries to preceptors of grammar, for it had had to do this ever since the law of 1572, which stated: "No salary is to be paid to preceptors of grammar from the Royal Treasury either by viceroys or by governors."[46] So the viceroy was happy, the University was content, the Jesuits were satisfied, and the students prospered.

The inauguration of this program of reciprocity, however, marks the date of another event, inevitable in the ways followed by the Jesuits. Father Pedro Sánchez was relieved of his duties as provincial at his own request and the former *visitador,* Father Juan de la Plaza, took over that office.[47] Yet Sánchez was by no means finished with his work, nor was he called from it, and the various important offices he subsequently held, until 1609. He lived on to see the complete development of his Colegio Máximo and the rise of other colleges, even other provinces, upon the foundations his untiring zeal and optimism had laid.

Hortigosa began his first course in philosophy in 1576. Rubio took up the second year in 1577 and also gave preliminary lectures in theology, for which some of the Jesuit students who had come from Spain were ready. From then on it was merely a question of adding the other year of philosophy and the other three years of theology. The students were being pushed ahead by the many newcomers entering the lower sections. The new arrivals were probably Creoles for the greater part, since this class was rapidly increasing in numbers in New Spain, while the Spanish population was static and small[48] and the natives had suffered tremendous losses in the late plague and were to suffer again in the plagues of 1594 and 1595. The provincial congregation, when it convened at the Colegio Máximo toward the end of 1577, was able to subscribe truthfully to the statement Sánchez made to the general:[49] "Everywhere we have established our Constitutions and rules as well as possible."

By 1582, when the unofficial amalgamation of San Gregorio College, San Bernardo, and San Miguel took place and the Seminary of San Ildefonso had its rise, the Colegio Máximo could be said to have completed its adjustments and to have given final form to its curriculum. From the lowest class, through what would be equivalent to our high school and two years of college work, and into university studies, it was as follows:

1. Reading and writing—a preliminary year
2. First grammar......(several divisions)..... *Minimos*
3. Second grammar....(genders, preterites)... *Menores*
4. Third grammar.....(syntax, etc.)..........*Medianos*
5. Poetry............(humanities)
6. Rhetoric...........(humanities)
7. Logic and mathematics
8. Physics
9. Philosophy.........(first and second year)
10. Theology..........(three years)
11. Moral theology and canon law
12. Scripture

Chairs were established ultimately in each of these[50] courses.[51] Study in Mexican languages was taken care of at this time in Tepotzotlán. Canon law was given at the University. Thus the college of the Jesuits had really grown to be like Salamanca, and Archbishop Moya testified to its excellence in that same year, 1582, before the Audiencia.

The fathers are most exemplary and of great erudition and learning . . . aiding in general and in particular persons of all ages in this city and in other parts where they have founded colleges, with their studies and doctrine, . . . and I have witnessed their teaching of Latin and rhetoric arts and theology, and their public and particular acts in arts and theology . . . and have been amazed to see the singular and solid doctrine of the masters and the progress of the students . . . and those who are the good students at the University are the disciples of the Company. . . .[52]

In 1599 there were more than 700 students at the Colegio Máximo.[53] There were twelve lecturers, and we suppose they were for the upper classes. The better students were acting as teachers in primary sections. Some collegians were out in the parishes instructing the children in religion, or aiding the sick in the hospitals. Four acts had been held that year in theology and three in arts, at which the other religious of the city and the doctors of the University were in attendance. At San Ildefonso there were three other masters and more than 110 students. How many received the bachelor's degree at the Colegio is not stated, but thirteen were graduated from San Ildefonso.[54]

We must leave the Colegio Máximo at this point from whence it went on sending forth its notable alumni to teach in the other Jesuit institutions and to the missions of the north. It continued to be *the* college of the Jesuits" until the time of the Suppression. Through the foundation and development of this center, the Company had charge practically of all secondary public education in New Spain, and of the greater part of higher education, except civil law, medicine, mining, and architecture.[55] Later we may tarry a bit over its graduates, its book producers, and its printing press.

Chapter XI

OUT WEST

Pátzcuaro is important for several reasons. It was from the bishop of Michoacán presiding there that the first practical invitation to venture to Mexico came to the Jesuits in Spain. There was established the first episcopal seminary in America. There and not in the capital was held the first Latin grammar class taught by the Company in the new lands. There the first Jesuit to be ordained in the New World received his orders. Pátzcuaro might also claim to have had the first school fire in America.[1] It was the first place to which the Jesuits sallied after their coming to Mexico City. Since that hub of their educational endeavors in the sixteenth century has been taken care of, we may begin the discussion of the spokes and rim of their efforts with the schools of Pátzcuaro and the adjacent town of Valladolid, the present Morelia, capital of the state of Michoacán, lying about twenty-five miles to the northeast.

Pátzcuaro, "the place of delights,"[2] and Morelia are situated, according to their respective citizens and many travelers, in the most beautiful region of all Mexico. They enjoy a seven-thousand-foot altitude. Lakes and rivers, springs of various kinds of waters, mountains and gorges abound in the whole province of Michoacán. Its early peoples, who spoke the Tarascan, Otomí, and various Chichimec languages, were healthy and vigorous. They were famous for their artistic featherwork, and were known to the skirmishing missionary fathers for their primitive simplicity of soul, their sweet disposition, and their deep native religious traits.[3]

When the conquerors came to the region of the lakes and fishes, they found the last of the ancient line of kings in the populous city of Tzintzuntzán, on the east shore of the lake of Pátzcuaro and about ten miles north of the present city of that name. The king, his lands and people, became a phase of the conquest of Nueva Galicia. Nuño de Guzmán swooped down upon the city in 1529 and left there a reputation for cruelty on his way to Guadalajara and Sinaloa.[4] In 1534, Michoacán was designated as one of the four bishoprics of New Spain.[5] In 1538 the erstwhile *oidor,* Vasco de Quiroga, became first Bishop of Michoacán, and from then until 1565 spent the last years of his beautiful life straining every effort to atone to the natives for the injustices of the conquest.[6] He became the Gante of the West, the kind pastor to the peoples of his vast diocese, keenly appreciative of their social needs and intent upon their progress through the education both of their new ministers and of their children. His first see was at Tzintzuntzán. In 1544 he moved the cathedral site to Pátzcuaro.[7]

Quiroga introduced more Franciscan and Augustinian friars and soon had schools of the lower grades operating in a goodly number of the towns of his diocese. The natives were taught to read and write the Spanish language, and were instructed in manual arts, catechism, music, and the Latin prayers.[8] The schools were like those of the metropolis, and therefore were close to the churches. Teaching was carried on in the patios. The better students from among the Indians were allowed to continue with the Latin classes held in the Seminary of San Nicolás Obispo, near the cathedral. This collegial seminary was opened in 1540,[9] and appears to have been progressing so well by 1543 that Charles V declared: "The college of Spaniards, mestizos, and Indians, where grammar is studied, and the hospital for the infirm poor of the city of Michoacán, pertain to our royal patronage."[10] The college referred to was not at the time a full-blown seminary nor was it solely for those who intended to become priests. Any students with inclinations to the clerical state had to wear a distinctive black cassock and obey the strict seminary regulations, which, it may be added, antedated by thirty years those we have described for San Pedro y San Pablo. Native languages also were taught to the students in anticipation of future work among the Indians. With the office of rector went the task of teaching Latin and moral theology. A library was collected. The king turned over the revenues of several haciendas as a means of supporting the college and the boys (for whom everything was gratis). Quiroga provided for the Indians in the following clause: "In recompense and satisfaction for what the Indians of this City of Michoacán and the towns around the lake have suffered . . . their sons may be perpetually taught in it . . . in whatsoever is taught or studied there, and that gratis."[11]

Bishop Quiroga decided to get all the assistance possible for his flock. Wherefore, when the illustrious prelate sent his precentor, Don Diego Negrón, to Europe to discharge some important business, he included letters to the king, the pope, and the general of the Jesuits, with pleas to each to procure the services of some of the Company for his land.[12]

Ignatius died (1556) soon after the arrival of the emissary, who could not wait for the election of Laínez. Quiroga bided his time. Several years later he himself was in Cádiz, and with four Jesuits, all ready to sail west.[13] The hour of their going to America had not arrived, evidently, for the fathers took sick, and Quiroga had to carry home his disappointment unaccompanied by the four. It was only natural, then, that when the group of Jesuits arrived in Mexico in 1572 they should recall the invitations to Pátzcuaro.

Now, by the springtime of 1573 Juan Curiel, one of the three Jesuits who were still studying theology with the Dominicans in Mexico City, had finished his course and was ready for his ordination. Moya, bishop-elect of Mexico but not yet consecrated, could not confer the orders. So Sánchez sent Curiel out west to Bishop Antonio Morales of Michoacán for the ceremony. He was warmly welcomed by the bishop and given a room in the college of San Nicolás.[14] While waiting for the separate orders, the young scholastic dedicated his hours to the teaching of grammar in the Latin class.[15] After his ordination he returned to Mexico, and Bishop Morales was changed to Puebla. The see being vacant, the ecclesiastical *cabildo* of Pátzcuaro, remembering the energy of the young teacher who was the first Jesuit to be ordained in New Spain, dispatched a prebendary of the diocese to Sánchez with an invitation and an offer. The spirit which animated Quiroga still hovered over the *cabildo,* for the members expressed a wish to found a college for the Jesuits.

The chapter was willing to give 800 pesos a year for the support of the fathers and 300 for a chair of Latin.[16] The fathers were told they could have the old cathedral for a college church. This had been erected by Quiroga, was sumptuous and still in good repair; next door to it was a smaller oratory. The ground plot for the college building would be that on which of old had rested the temple of the Tarascans. Moreover, the fathers were asked to take charge of the Seminary of San Nicolás. An offer of this kind brought the provincial posthaste to the western lakeside. He realized the importance of a foundation, not so much because of the possibilities for students from the Spanish families, which numbered less than one hundred in Pátzcuaro, but rather because of opportunities for working among the thirty thousand natives.[17] He told the *cabildo* he could accept the church, the grounds, the house, and the 800 pesos for support of his subjects and the management of the seminary, but he could not accept the 300 pesos for the teaching or the 100 pesos for pulpit work, since these ministries were what the Jesuits gave without stipend. Moreover, he deemed it an honor for the Jesuits to exercise themselves in these offices in the diocese.[18]

The *cabildo* was satisfied with the answer. Sánchez returned to Mexico and legally admitted the grants in the name of the general, from whom he had received authority to act under such circumstances. The *cabildo* had petitioned him to send back Father Curiel; Sánchez appointed him superior of the new house. Juan Sánchez was to be rector of the Seminary of San Nicolás, Pedro Rodríguez, a scholastic, recently arrived from Spain, was to conduct the Latin class, and the coadjutor, Brother Pedro Ruiz de Salvatierra, was to have charge of the school for boys. One may wonder why it was that Juan Sánchez and Curiel did not go into the classrooms. The former answers the question himself.[19] They had begun their tertianship, or third year of probation, immediately after their ordination, and therefore according to the rules of the Society were not supposed to teach but rather to devote themselves to preaching and spiritual works. Thus Pátzcuaro became the first tertianship of the Jesuits in New Spain.

The four Jesuits arrived in Pátzcuaro in the autumn of 1573. They were warmly greeted. Their quarters near the church were not at all commodious. What they worried about was their temporary college,[20] for they had not the wherewithal to lay any foundations, and it would be a year before the promised sums could be paid by the *cabildo;* yet, in spite of handicap, they carried on two classes of grammar for a large number of boys,[21] supposedly in the same fashion as those which were open the next year in Mexico City, and which have already been described. If anything notable happened during the school term of 1573–1574 in Pátzcuaro, we have no record of it. At the end of the period Juan Sánchez was recalled to the capital to teach the first class opened there. Obviously his work at Pátzcuaro was temporary. Juan Curiel, remaining, became rector of the Seminary and of the Jesuit *collegium inchoatum.* Nevertheless, the school for smaller boys conducted by Brother Salvatierra made great progress and had 120 pupils in 1575.[22]

Then came the plague of 1575 and 1576. Fortunately it did not take so many lives in Michoacán as elsewhere, thanks to the hospitals established by Quiroga and the friars.[23] Strangely, the first Jesuit to die of it was Pedro Caltzontzín, the ninth and last King of Michoacán.[24] Despite all early repulses to his entrance made purposely by Curiel to test his vocation, Pedro had persistently demanded admission. He was admitted to probation and became a schoolmaster. When the plague struck he was sent to help the sick. He contracted the smallpox and died shortly. Within a few months he was followed to the grave by the rector, Father Juan Curiel: "humble, happy, charitable Juan Curiel," as Juan Sánchez aptly characterized him.[25]

It was not only the poverty of the city, the plague, the need of men in Mexico, and the death of the rector, that prevented the rapid development of the Jesuit college of Pátzcuaro. There were other factors. The emphasis was being put for the time on the missionary phase. The boys and men trained in the college of San Nicolás, in the grammar classes, and in the grade school, were utilized during their spare time in helping to spread the gospel. The first care of the fathers was to translate dogmas, precepts, and little orations into Tarascan. Sometimes these were put into the form of songs and chants. The boys, over and above serving as guides for the priests on missionary excursions, instructed other natives in the outlying barrios. There were waverings at first among the new converts, owing to the usual source of trouble to the missionaries—the pagan priests, and pulque; but the work gradually progressed.[26] A remarkable thing about the Seminary of San Nicolás is that from the time of its foundation until 1576 it had in its student body more than two hundred clerical students.[27]

Another drawback to the educational program, strictly speaking, was indeed serious. The school burned in 1578.

The building which had been the old cathedral was of wood; being very dry, it was a fine morsel for the lapping flames fanned by a strong breeze.[28] When the fire broke out, the few Jesuits were helpless; but the Tarascans divided themselves into three fire battalions under the leadership of three caciques. One group ran in and out of the church with movables; the second got out the altar and adornments; the third acted as a well-drilled fire department, knocking out boards and pouring water. The church was mostly saved; the school, however, went to ashes. Within a few days five hundred volunteers went to work raising new edifices on the ruins. The Indians undertook the labor of rebuilding for the fathers in their customary manner, which was striking, for they went to work in the mornings festooned with garlands of flowers and accompanied by the flutes and songs of the womenfolk.

The last of the more serious difficulties which beset the paths of the Jesuit educators and the citizenry of Pátzcuaro occurred when the civil powers decreed that the population was to be moved to Valladolid and the ecclesiastical powers decreed the same for the cathedral of Michoacán. A story similar to "Evangeline" was about to be told in Pátzcuaro long before Acadia was settled.[29] The Indians to the number of almost thirty thousand had been moved in 1554 from Tzintzuntzán to Pátzcuaro. Now the majority of them, with all the Spaniards, were to be moved from the lake city to the rapidly growing Valladolid. The transfer of population was begun at the end of 1578. The movables of the cathedral, pictures, ornaments, relics, and gifts of the people were put on carts. The Indians stood by in resentful silence, until they realized fully the trend of events, by which time the officials had come to taking down the bell from the church tower. This was the last of the intolerable acts in the eyes of the Indians. They rushed to arms and surrounded the tower. The officials branded the movement as an open mutiny, and it would have been treated as such had not the Jesuits intervened, explaining to the officers that it was the act of a simplehearted people guarding their most treasured possessions. They told the authorities the Tarascans should have been prepared for the move.

Now if the cathedral and its belongings were transferred, the college also would have to go. This was specified in Quiroga's constitution. If San Nicolás went, the Jesuits would likewise go. Wind of such a possible exodus got to the Indians, who came to beg the fathers to remain. Although the Jesuits promised they would do so, the Indians, still distrustful of the government, would not be convinced that the fathers were to stay. A new rebellion appeared imminent. Again the childlike warriors armed themselves with bows and arrows. With Tarascan sentinels perpetually on guard around their church, the Jesuits' residence, and the tomb of their beloved Don Vasco, nothing could be touched. The *cabildo,* recognizing its defeat, had to leave the relics and the college at Pátzcuaro. The moving faith of the people left Sánchez no other course of action except that of committing the charge of the college to several of the fathers and to open another at Valladolid. Since the Spanish families had moved out of Pátzcuaro, San Nicolás College building and the primary school were left for the remaining natives. Most of the Indians were transferred.[30] The situation becomes a bit involved at this point, since we now have to explain the affairs of the Jesuit schools in each of the two cities and since there was the old San Nicolás College of Pátzcuaro and the new one of Valladolid.

Juan Sánchez was taken from the classrooms of Mexico City to become superior of the new residence at Valladolid. Pedro Gutiérrez went with him to teach the grammar classes, and a brother was added to the little community for the purpose of conducting the primary grades. The *cabildo,* now at Valladolid, had promised them much. They had to sustain themselves none the less upon the baskets of food sent by the other religious communities. The *regidores,* seeing the lamentable condition of their dwelling and school, went out begging; the results of their tours were negligible. Yet in spite of hardships instruction in the school was somehow carried on during 1578–1579.

In view of the dire financial straits to which the Valladolid college had been reduced, it became necessary for the provincial to come to some agreement about the 800 pesos promised by the *cabildo* and capitularies of Pátzcuaro. These founders were now living in the newer city, and the support money was going to the older place where a new building for the Indians was in the process of construction. Sánchez split the sum equally between the two. At the same time he made the two groups of teachers one community, as a temporary measure. The two colleges, though miles apart, quite anomalously were recognized as one. Perhaps it was a mistake for the fathers so to divide their energies and resources, but no other way lay open. Even when forced to drop some of the students at Valladolid for lack of funds, they were loath to desert either place because of the good will of the Spaniards and Indians. Moreover, they reasoned, was not the future promising? Had not the aged licentiate Juan de Arbolancha promised to make the college of Pátzcuaro heir to all his possessions? The interested viceroy evidently realized that the transfer of the site had involved the state in a minor injustice to the natives and to the Company. He likewise recognized the fathers' power for peace maintenance, and so he ordered the slaughterhouses to contribute 1000 pesos a year toward the expenses of the Valladolid college.[31]

Just how faithfully the odd revenue was paid we do not know; the Arbolancha heritage later sustained the Pátzcuaro institution, while gifts from the viceroy Enríquez, and from Don Rodrigo Vásquez, aided Valladolid until 1581. The Jesuit school in the new city, as distinct from the seminary, carried on for several years, but it appears to have been closed temporarily just before 1585. Father Mojano, the superior of that time, wrote to the general of the poverty of their dwelling place, and at the end of his letter made mention of opening a primary school and Latin class for the boys.[32] Probably the lads were being instructed during this time with the seminarians of San Nicolás College. The idea of a college with one foot in Valladolid and the other in Pátzcuaro did not sit well with the Jesuit general, Aquaviva. In 1589 he separated the two, making them distinct units. Pátzcuaro was to be for the Indians.[33]

Meantime, what had happened to the collegial group of San Nicolás which had been moved with the episcopal see in 1579? The Jesuits, busy with their own classes and missions, had come to no agreement over the conduct of this seminary. To it had been added the Seminary of San Miguel, founded in Valladolid in 1566 by the Franciscans. For the first year or so, the Company had taken over the teaching and the management of the combined seminary.[34] In 1581 they gave up the charge and also ceased for the time being to instruct the seminarians.[35] These latter gradually drifted away from their customs and studies. The anxious *cabildo* petitioned (1582) the provincial, Plaza, to take over the seminary completely. This was done by the Jesuits on several conditions: first, the 300 pesos, which the *cabildo* had been allotting to the rector, was to be given to support poor collegians; second, a major-domo responsible to the patrons was to be appointed by the *cabildo* to manage the temporal affairs; third, a papal bull was to be obtained, confirming the agreement and eliminating the possibility of any interference on the part of the *cabildo* in the ecclesiastical concerns.[36] These items agreed to, Juan Sánchez returned again as superior of the diocesan Seminary of San Nicolás,[37] which was open to both Spaniards and Creoles. In that same year the building of the church of the Company was begun; next to it, later, went up the residence and school of the fathers;— these were both just south of the college of San Nicolás.

To conclude, then, with these institutions about which there are few pedagogical data, we may say that Pátzcuaro maintained its status as an Indian school, with the aid of several bequests. In 1592 there were four priests and five lay brothers attending to the classes and the missionary program.[38] In 1599 the schoolrooms were full and great progress was being made.[39] We may suppose that the Latin grammar and the primary grades were conducted in a manner similar to that of Jesuit schools of the capital whence the teachers were appointed. It was more important to the Company, however, as a center for the training and dispatch of missionaries. For this reason, grammars in the Tarascan and Otomí languages were prepared there and at Tepotzotlán, and Jesuits were trained in them and in the native customs at both places.[40] This procedure did not stop at the end of the century, but continued until the Suppression.

In the middle of the next century, an old catalogue of the province tells us, there were still eight Jesuits in Pátzcuaro and seven at Valladolid, and that they were hampered in their work by lack of necessaries.[41] Things must have gone better in the eighteenth century, for twice at Pátzcuaro did the students develop to a point where philosophy courses could be introduced with one in moral theology; each time, however, the chairs had to be removed to Valladolid because the supply of students for the higher studies ran low.[42] In 1751 there was founded the new Seminary of San Ignacio. In Valladolid, chairs of Latin, physics, and rhetoric were established in the seventeenth and eighteenth centuries in the Jesuit arts college.[43] Of these we know little, probably because both schools were small compared to the other colleges in the vice-royalty, and because writers after the foundations just took for granted their presence and work. Yet it cannot be gainsaid that they were important missionary centers during the next two centuries and were necessary adjuncts to the drive by land up the coast, for they held the back country peaceful by means of the new civilization which they spread, and they kept the natives even to Acapulco occupied with assimilating the new culture. Progress overland by stages ultimately got the Spanish arms to California, but progress by cultural stages lay behind the move.

At present in the scenic city of Morelia, formerly Valladolid, formerly Guayangareo, folk are wont to point out the ruins of the tower of the old Jesuit church and the convent and school beside it. The latter building dates from 1681. There a boy named Miguel Hidalgo y Costilla was taught by the Jesuits just before they were cast out of the land.[44] Down the street a few paces is the old Colegio de San Nicolás de Hidalgo.[45] Here Miguel Hidalgo y Costilla studied for the priesthood before going to the University of Mexico for his final preparations for orders. Here also he became rector of the Colegio and a lecturer in theology. One of his pupils was Don José María Morelos.[46] The efforts of these two men from the schools of Valladolid enkindled the flames of revolution. Indeed, they have been compared to Washington and have been allotted credit for a share in the establishment of the present Mexican national independence. Valladolid, before it was renamed Morelia in honor of the latter priest, was the center of revolutionary activities; all the larger cities of Mexico have come to have their Hidalgo Street and their Morelia Street, just as our cities have their Washington Street. But it must be admitted that colonial times furnish happier examples of constructive social and cultural workers than those of the revolutionary padres of the "land of delights."

Chapter XII

PUEBLA

A FEELING OF GREAT EXHILARATION may have come over the Jesuits when they paused in September, 1572, at Puebla, the city of the angels. Worn by the long sea voyage to Vera Cruz, which had been made during the hot months of the summer, they probably had found the heat of the low coastal region unbearable. With Sedeño guiding them they had pushed up into the plateau and soon were in the valley in which Puebla de Los Ángeles lies. Pedro Sánchez, Juan Sánchez, Juan Curiel, and the others saw for the first time the interesting landmarks as they followed the road of the conquerors. There was the old volcano Orizaba towering on the horizon to the left, the white tops of Popocatepetl and Iztaccihuatl ever looming larger before them, and finally on their right, when they drew nearer the city, lay somber Malinche.

The night of their arrival they put up gratefully at the public inn,[1] and so ruined certain plans of the archdeacon of the cathedral, Alonzo Pacheco. Some time previously this man had erected a house with the intention of giving it to the fathers when they should have come to his city. They were informed of this generous gesture the following day on their way from the inn to the house.[2] Discovering to his disappointment that the fathers had to hasten to the capital, he put in his application for their services at the earliest date possible and extracted from Sánchez the promise of a few subjects for Puebla. Father Pedro did not fulfill the promise until after the time of the erection of the Colegio Máximo and until Pátzcuaro had already had its school fire.

Sánchez turned his eyes once more toward Puebla in 1578, because Pacheco would not forget the word of the Jesuit.

PUEBLA DE LOS ÁNGELES

PUEBLA DE LOS ÁNGELES: SITES OF THE JESUIT COLLEGES

The archdeacon, who was something of a literary person, had meanwhile fallen heir to the cares of the diocese, for Bishop Morales, the same who had ordained Curiel at Pátz-cuaro, had died in 1576; and now, rejoicing in a plentitude of authority until the seat was filled, Señor Pacheco pressed

his former invitation.[3] Father Hernando Suárez de la Concha, a veteran missionary by reason of his journeyings in
Nueva Galicia and Nueva Vizcaya, was finally sent to the
environs of the city to evangelize the natives; though probably he had visited Puebla some time before he went there
formally to preach. Being a man high in the estimation of
his townsmen, Pacheco had no difficulty in convincing the
other members of the civil and ecclesiastical *cabildos* of the
urgent need of a Jesuit college in their city. Concha's sermons delivered in a masterful style allayed any misgivings
the city fathers may have had about the advisability of such
a step.[4] In fact, they held a meeting and proposed to Concha
that he stay with them and open a college. As a subject he
could do nothing but send word to his provincial.

The news brought Sánchez over the mountains to complete the negotiations. It happened that Pacheco had been
forced to sell the house which at one time had sheltered
the fathers and which he had intended for their use, but
he did the best he could for them under the changed circumstances. He sold them property and houses for a minimum price of 9000 pesos, payable in installments. The
signatures were affixed to the deed on May 9, 1578.[5] The site
was about five hundred feet east of the cathedral plaza, just
where the Jesuit college is at present under different management. This was a meager Jesuit beginning of the College of Espíritu Santo and of a great center of education.
Because of the greater progress in Puebla we are considering it before we do the somewhat older College of Oaxaca.

Puebla in 1578 was the second city of New Spain, principally by reason of its Spanish population numbering close

to a thousand families.⁶ Into the fertile valleys which surround it, the missionaries of the other religious orders had come long before the Jesuits. The Franciscans began their labors soon after the Conquest and by 1530 were rather firmly established. Noteworthy it is, that they had their usual little schools for natives, their novitiate, and a college for the study of philosophy for their own subjects.⁷ The Dominicans, appearing in 1535, made the fourth of July a day of celebration some two hundred years before we other Americans did; for on that date in 1558 their Colegio de San Luís Rey de Francia was established as a seminary for their own students, with courses in arts and theology.⁸ The other precursors of the Company were the Augustinians, whose preaching was first heard in 1546.

In the early struggle of the Jesuits to keep a footing in Puebla the good will of the citizens was manifested by donations of small alms which sufficiently sustained them. A rich *caballero,* Mateo de Maulión, contributed almost a thousand pesos.⁹ The Jesuits, however, with a certain independence of spirit, were anxious to satisfy the installment collector; the rector, therefore, courageously sallied forth on a begging tour of the neighboring towns and haciendas. He proved somewhat of a mendicant, for he returned with 500 pesos. No great joy awaited his return. An unnamed father, who like the others had been exercising his ministries in the prisons and plazas, had inveighed against some abuses prevalent in the city. The truth should not have come out in such an ill-advised manner. Several of his hearers started a whispering campaign, saying he had spoken critically of the other religious orders. The sermon grew more

distorted as it was bandied about from lip to lip, and the
resultant coolness toward the Jesuits increased by bounds.

It seemed the Jesuit projects at Puebla were about to crash
in untimely ruin. No more alms were forthcoming. Still,
in the midst of the murmurs and tribulations a ray of light
suddenly shone. Diego Romano, the new bishop, arrived in
1579; and Diego Romano had already founded a college
for the Society in his native Old Castile. He reopened the
gates of the good graces of the citizens to the fathers by
abetting them in the task of winning the hearts of the
younger generation; for with his protection assured they
did not hesitate to commence their grammar classes. The
boys did the rest. They praised Father Rincón, who was in
charge of the classes, and told of the affability of the other
priests. By the end of 1579, Pueblans had rekindled their
liking for the Company.[10] But if Scylla had been grazed,
Charybdis lay ahead.

The Bishop all the while was maturing some plans of his
own. He wanted a diocesan seminary, and he had the Jesuits teaching. With these premises, what might be done
about his seminary was obvious; nevertheless the financial
means for following his logical course of action were lacking. The gap was bridged by Don Juan Barranco, who produced from his large fortune a gift ample for a working
basis. Death prevented his giving more. After the customary preliminaries, the school was begun under the name of
San Gerónimo. It was categorized as a collegial seminary;
consequently it was of the usual type. There were more than
thirty boys in the seminary group on the opening day, and
the number soon increased. Some scholars were boarded

free. From among those who wore the caps and gowns and followed the rules of San Gerónimo in the years following, a steady stream of notable alumni shed luster on the city's name in *audiencias,* assemblies, cloisters, and episcopal sees.[11] Reinforcements of Jesuits came to Puebla for the college and seminary in 1580. The faculty residence housed five priests, two scholastics who taught grammar classes, and six lay brothers some of whom instructed the smaller boys in the rudimentary grades.[12] Things scholastic were moving well, for Rincón[13] proved a capable rector for the guidance of the seminary group and a good prefect of studies for the direction of the scholars and teachers. Besides this, he was meeting his own section of Latin and instructing the natives, with whose dialect he was fluently familiar.[14] (He composed a grammar of the Mexican language, which was used generally as a text.[15]) Not finding this a sufficient teaching load, he spread the rest of his energies over a program of social service which he instituted among the prisoners in the jails for his Sundays; for the terrible condition of the inmates of these "schools of inquity" had deeply touched the indefatigable padre's heart. Certainly it was through no fault of his that the educational beginning in Puebla nearly "died a-borning."

But those murmurs began to be heard again; and a darksome calumny, which touched the honor of the Company in a vital spot, aroused Rincón to a point where he was all for shutting up the school and shaking the dust of Puebla forever from his feet. It was bruited among the slandering group that the fathers were taking privately some of the rentals coming in for the support of the seminary and scholars and were maintaining themselves on this money, which therefore constituted just such a salary as the fathers in public hypocritically refused.[16] The fact was, the rentals were coming in so uncertainly that the provincial was about to close the place for fear his men were a burden on the city.[17] With this course in mind he had even refused a gift of 14,000 pesos from Melchor de Covarrubias, to the deep chagrin of the worthy *caballero*.[18] Melchor was soothed only by an explanation from the new rector, Father Morales, and Rincón was mollified by an edict against the calumniators issued by Bishop Romano, who effectively took up cudgels on behalf of the fathers and prevented any stain from tarnishing the escutcheon of Loyola.

San Gerónimo from that time increased in the estimation of the people, not only because of the episcopal protection but also because of the scholastic products. The boys worked diligently, and public literary *actas* were held which were attended by the prelate and prebendaries and citizens. Gifts came in which enabled the Jesuits to put down the foundations, material and educational, of a structure which was to rival the Colegio Máximo of the metropolis.[19] In 1581 the lots adjacent to the several buildings which they already owned, were purchased. Debts were paid off during the ensuing few years. In 1584 Morales, according to a letter he wrote to the general,[20] was told to represent to the people the difficulties under which he and his faculty were laboring without a foundation, and to explain to them the need of a library. The students on their part were ready for their higher studies. He preached in the cathedral on the feast of Espíritu Santo and within a month gifts from the bishop, *cabildo,* and citizens amounted to 8000 pesos.[21] In the following year Melchor de Covarrubias gave 2000 pesos and asked to be the founder of the college. The general (Aquaviva), being appraised of his request, admitted him to honors like those held by Villaseca.[22] The nine years of famine in Puebla were over.

They treasure an old manuscript volume in the present State College of Puebla. It is entitled *Títulos y Méritos de los Señores Covarrubias.* It contains in the opening pages pictures of the various members of the illustrious family and their coats of arms, done in colors and traced in gold. Then follows the history of Melchor, whose parents were among the first settlers and who himself was a native-born Pueblan. He rose to places of trust in the government of New Spain and was appointed to throw up defenses around San Juan de Ulúa against the attacks of the swarming pirates. His benevolences to Church and State were well known and merited a cedula of commendation from Philip II, which also rests in the archives of the secretary of the State College. Deeds of his bequests conclude the cherished volume. Precious as it is to the present owners, it was probably more so to the students or fathers who guided its fashioning as a mark of esteem to the founder of El Colegio del Espíritu Santo. Covarrubias signed the deed of foundation April 15, 1587, in the presence of the latest Jesuit provincial, Antonio de Mendoza, and then handed over to him the money.[23] The amount was 28,000 pesos in cash for the college and 13,000 pesos in bonds. Because he had a singular devotion to the Third Person of the Trinity, he asked that the name of the institution be that of Espíritu Santo. What the Jesuits had called this college during the years preceding this foundation gift, is hard to tell; San Gerónimo remained the title of the little seminary foundation. Like the Colegio Máximo, Espíritu Santo was open to seculars, and no tuition was required. According to Veytia, it was even greater than the Mexican seat of wisdom; "it was the best the Jesuits had in the Kingdom."[24] This manifestation of civic pride, made almost two centuries later than the foundation, is pardonable, and perhaps justified.

The material structure was intended to be beautiful, but how long a time was required to complete it cannot be estimated from the documents. The square of property owned by the Jesuits was situated about six hundred feet from the center of the main plaza,—in which, by the way, Colonel Childs barricaded himself with his American contingent for a month in 1847. The ground area for the college was more than two and one-half acres.[25] In the northwest corner facing the plaza was the college church, called now, in its second edition, *La Compañía.* The architect of this structure was the same Basque lay brother of the Society, Juan López de Arbaísa, who was rearing a college church similar to that near the Colegio Máximo. It was completed and dedicated at the beginning of the next century, and the remains of the founder rest there.[26]

The college itself occupied the rest of the square. It was constructed solidly around three large patios, and in the past century, four.[27] The façade with its balconies and windows was adjacent to the church. Inside the large door was a double vestibule. To the right was an arch leading to the first patio and beside this a stairway to the second floor.

Rooms of the fathers and students were around the patios. In the center of the building between the first two patios were the refectory and the chapel. Upstairs where now are the science laboratories and lecture halls, were the library and classrooms of the Jesuits. The marble staircases, the balustrades, cornices, fountains in the patio, the hallways and art works, would attract all our attention were it not for the artistically carved chairs and tribunal of the "*salón de actos publicos*."

We may suppose the class arrangement to have been similar to that obtaining at the Colegio Máximo during its first few years. In the patios the smaller boys would have been divided up for the teaching of reading and writing in the vernacular, arithmetic, singing, and catechism. These would move on to the classes of Latin grammar and composition. There is no mention of the number of boys in attendance except the indefinite statements in the *cartas anuas* to this effect: "great progress is being made in the Latin school," or, "the numbers of students is increasing," or, "full days at Puebla College of Espíritu Santo, where there is the novitiate, the tertianship, five teachers of grammar, and a great increase of students."[28] The students were sent through the grammar classes and on to humanities and rhetoric.

Just when the Company completed the curriculum by adding the arts courses of philosophy, cannot be stated with certainty. The *Anua* of 1592 does not mention philosophy, neither does that of 1599; but the latter gives the equivalent when it says there were literary exercises of rhetoric and philosophy during the year mentioned. Alegre verifies this, even though he gives no further information.[29] The students who finished their courses before 1592 had to go over to Mexico if they desired to receive from the University there a bachelor's or a master's degree in arts or theology.[30] Although there can be no doubt about the younger Jesuits' going to Mexico for studies, we have only one mention recorded in the earlier history of education in Puebla of a secular student who pursued his higher studies in Mexico. He was the extraordinary young man who returned home for his vacation and so electrified the people by his display of literary skill in a "public act" that they wished the Jesuits to institute higher studies.[31] That was in 1582. It is reasonable to suppose, however, that others garnered the fruits of wisdom in the capital.

Why the Jesuits moved the novices of the Company to Puebla in 1592, and some of the tertians before that time, will be told later. Neither of these groups did any lecturing. In that year there were nine priests and nine lay brothers and scholastics to do the teaching and missionary work.[32] The lay brothers, as was usual, taught the lowest grades of boys. Besides these there were seven Jesuits conducting the College of San Gerónimo, five of whom were scholastics who had finished their teaching preparation in Mexico. The collegians at this seminary were following the rules similar to those of the seminarians at San Ildefonso in the metropolis, and in the year mentioned four of them entered the Society. In 1599 there were twelve priests in Puebla college, and twelve secular students entered the various religious communities.[33] In this last year of the century the collegial group of San Gerónimo was united to that of Espíritu Santo, a union which consisted probably in nothing but putting both places under one rector, for the seminarians remained in their former building, and the Jesuits still directed and taught them in the classrooms of Espíritu Santo. Possibly they took all higher courses at Espíritu Santo and heard the lectures in moral theology, which were not listed in the catalogue of studies. It appears no distinction was being made in the Colegio between the races, because Indians and Spaniards alike were admitted. The younger natives, however, had a room set apart for their instruction, somewhere in the college building.[34]

Melchor de Covarrubias was through with life in 1592. Just before his death he signed his last will and testament in favor of the College of Puebla and thus brought the sum of his bequests, with the 28,000 and 13,000 pesos previously mentioned, up to 88,869 pesos.[35] His haciendas and the rents therefrom were to be used for the perpetual support and increase of the college and church of the Company and for the sustenance of the fathers, after some few debts of his family had been discharged. In case there were any students who had not the means of obtaining an education in the Colegio de San Gerónimo, the Colegio del Espíritu Santo, "his heir," was bound to keep and educate them up to the number of four, so long as they made good their opportunity for virtue and letters.

One of the haciendas enumerated in his bequests happens to be very interesting. Among certain older citizens of Puebla there are vague recollections of an agricultural college carried on by Jesuits somewhere in the countryside. One is struck by the suitability of the land for such a project;

it was a logical thing to undertake. Other well-informed
gentlemen know nothing of the institution. Tracking down
the idea, one may go to the branch of the National Bank of
Mexico in Puebla and find in the vaults two old volumes of
manuscripts. They are entitled *Títulos de San Gerónimo,
de Puebla.* In these are maps, pictures, and plans of a rancheria located about an hour and a half of driving out of
Puebla on the road to Oaxaca. The Jesuits bought the land
in 1596 and got a clear title to the whole in 1612, according
to one of the first documents in the book. Other papers are
of gifts and purchases of the Colegio del Espíritu Santo, to
which the volumes belonged formerly. In the plans and pictures of the rancheria are seen clearly the church and buildings, very similar to a small collegial establishment. Because
of the church, we readily conclude there was instruction
in catechism. Because it was a hacienda managed by the
Jesuits, we can suppose there were some lay brothers to
work the land. Because there were native and Negro workmen on the premises, it is clear they were told how to culti-
vate the crops. But was there a regular form of instruction
in agricultural affairs?

The only other hints we have of such an establishment
come from Alegre, who is concerned with the great missionary labors of the fathers of Puebla in the various towns.
In one place they had put up a straw-roofed church called
San Miguel.[36] This was in the early 'nineties. The second
lead comes from Carlos Pereyra, who quotes a work of
Ricardo Cappa, S.J., on the farming and herding indus-
tries brought to New Spain by the Spaniards,[37] a work not
listed by Sommervogel. Though it pertains at large to seeds,

plants, and vines imported from Spain, and to livestock betterment, in all likelihood it at least alludes to the Jesuits' efforts along farming lines. Perhaps precursors of Kino can be found in sixteenth-century Puebla.

The haciendas otherwise were a source of worry and almost of despair to the fathers. As supporters of the colleges generally throughout Mexico they may not be called a decided success. If we are curious to discover how the finances of the Province of New Spain stood, or about education as a paying proposition, or what the fathers did with the donations they received, let us take a glance at the catalogue of the goods of the Society in the middle of the next century.[38]

To the Colegio Máximo, annual rentals coming in amounted to 30,000 silver pesos; the debt on the college was 292,000 pesos, against which 13,000 pesos was being paid annually. To the Seminary of San Gregorio nothing was coming in; to San Pedro y San Pablo, 850 pesos, for the support of the *colegiales*. To San Ildefonso in Mexico came 8000 pesos each year, while its debt was 6500 pesos. The rents at Espíritu Santo amounted to 20,000 pesos a year and its debt to 29,000. San Gerónimo had a 1500-peso debt. The rents at Pátzcuaro and Valladolid were 21,000 pesos and the debts were 24,000. Oaxaca received 4000 as against a 33,000-peso debt. Guadalajara had a 4000-peso income and an 8000-peso debt. In brief, we may say that the total income of the above-mentioned colleges coupled with that of the foundations of the first half of the next century—Mérida, Guatemala, Querétaro, San Ildefonso of Puebla, San Luis Potosí, Zacatecas, and Guadiana—was 127,600 pesos, and the debts were 581,450.

The story of the Puebla developments cannot be told completely unless we go somewhat beyond the sixteenth-century period, since the full course of higher studies was not added until another college was erected. The College of Espíritu Santo and the Seminary of San Gerónimo continued to function after the fashion described, carrying studies in Latin grammar, the humanities, rhetoric, preliminary philosophy, and moral theology, with a single student body and faculty. Motives and an occasion for filling out the program of higher courses were not lacking.[39] It was expensive for the citizens to send their sons to Mexico, and it was expensive for the bishop to send his seminarians thither for the completion of their training. Bishop Alonzo de la Mota y Escobar had not only wanted long to have his own diocesan seminary, but besides he was very friendly with the Company, so friendly that he was keen to found a college for it.

The bishop had some property on the west side of the city which he had destined for the site of a hospital for the Indians. Actually he had drawn up a contract, involving 40,000 pesos, to that purpose in 1622.[40] This sum had been left at his disposal by will. After long consultation with the important men of the town, he decided to alter his plans in favor of an educational building, instead of a hospital for forty sick Indians who could be cared for in existing hospitals.[41] (Singularly, the building is now a hospital.) The viceroy Cerralvo and the Jesuit provincial Laurencio were consulted and gave their approval; consequently the deed of foundation of the College of San Ildefonso was signed January 23, 1625.

The prelate donated the church on the northwest corner of the plot, and the building, both being already under construction. He gave some money for the continuance of the work, and a hacienda for the support of the fathers. Afterwards, by gifts and by his will, the total of bequests mounted beyond 200,000 pesos; the Colegio de San Ildefonso cost some 130,000 of this sum, hence it is a fine structure.[42] The Jesuits began immediately to fulfill their part of the agreement by opening the lecture courses in philosophy, moral theology, dogma, and Scripture. Father Andrés de Valencia was the first notable lecturer; he had been giving a course in moral theology at Espíritu Santo. The halls were soon full, some two hundred students taking advantage of their facilities. Nor were the young men by any means all clerical students, for the college was open to all, irrespective of class.[43] By an agreement with the University of Mexico, a student could continue at the older institution, or study in Puebla and receive a degree in Mexico. The staff consisted of five lecturers, and we are left to suppose the courses were arranged like those of the Jesuit institutions in the capital. Besides the teachers there was the Jesuit dean of studies and a director for the seminarians.

At its silver jubilee there were sixteen Jesuits at San Ildefonso, four of whom were lay brothers, and the whole establishment was doing so well that there was question of dividing the province of New Spain, making Puebla the head of one province and Mexico the head of the other.[44] This was nearly effected some years later, for Puebla considered it had as great a college in the combined chairs of Espíritu Santo and San Ildefonso as Mexico had in its Colegio Máximo. The civilians were proud of their colleges and of their education, with thirteen chairs of learning established.[45] Various lawsuits and the famous Palafox incident did not affect the school program, even though accounts of them took many pages of history which might have preserved details of college life and of the progress in letters which undoubtedly was being made. However, in spite of the roughness of the way, in 1702 a collegial seminary called San Ignacio was erected and opened across the street from San Ildefonso, and in 1751 another fine building went up for the instruction of Indians in the lower grades. It was known as San Javier. Its chapel at present is a fire-engine house; and the college that was, is a penitentiary and barracks. Strife was a characteristic of the ingress and maintenance of education in Puebla de los Ángeles.

Chapter XIII

OUTPOSTS

A<small>T A TIME WHEN</small> Shakespeare was ten years old and Elizabethan England had no system of elementary schools,[1] one might not reasonably be expecting sane men to be hastening to Oaxaca from Mexico City, bent upon starting a Latin school in an outpost of civilization. Two Jesuits went, nonetheless, harbingers of the coming of education to the southern country and of the extension of the Jesuit system of colleges. The year 1574 fell within the limits of the activities in Germany of the famous schoolmaster Johann Sturm (1536–1582), and was just a bit anterior to the rise of the Württemberg state school system.[2] It was a little over one hundred years after the educational results of humanism began to be felt in Europe and long before the new learning had developed into what has been termed "Ciceronianism," or formalism. England in those times was in the throes of producing an inquisitorial policy with regard to schoolmasters, and the content of their teaching, which is to our minds intolerable and limited.

The city of Oaxaca lay in the valley of that name about eighty leagues from the capital of New Spain. It was called by the Spaniards Antequera, and was commonly known as the center of the Province of the Marqués del Valle, Hernando Cortés. Spaniards to the number of five hundred had settled within its limits. By the time the Jesuits came, it gloried in the title of the "third city of the land."[3] Fertile were the fields of the whole province because of the plentiful rainfall. Untold mineral wealth, particularly in gold and silver, lay in the earth—at least until parts of it were discovered. Antequera was not only a mining and agricultural center, it was important as a key station in the overland route of the caravans and pack trains moving perpetually back and forth over the plateau between Aguatulco on the south coast and Vera Cruz on the Gulf of Mexico. It was a link in the commercial chain between Peru and Spain.

The languages spoken in the city were many, and the Zapotec and Mixtec peoples who spoke them struck the Spanish fathers as being vivacious. Though there never was a care over fruits, grain, fish, and gold, earthquakes have always worried the Oaxacans. In the presence of the jarring temblors, the method of conquering the land for habitation was to build low dwellings of monumental proportions; thus only could it remain a great center of colonial affairs. As early as 1535 its first bishop was named, and the Dominican fathers were the early teachers. There was still plenty of work for missionaries fifty years later among the four hundred thousand natives of the Valley of Oaxaca, to say nothing of the three or four thousand Spaniards and Creoles.

A few days before the provincial of the Jesuits had returned to Mexico from his trip to Pátzcuaro, where he admitted the foundation grants for the college in the western city, Canon Antonio de Santa Cruz made a journey to the capital from Oaxaca,—to negotiate for the services of the Jesuits for the bishopric whose interests he had at heart. He went to the Jesuit residence and there outlined his plans to the rector, Diego López, and to Father Díaz. His ambition was to present to the Company a foundation in Oaxaca which would be as large as the one they were expecting from Alonzo Villaseca. Then he returned south.

Pedro Sánchez, coming home, went into a conference over the matter. When it was concluded that Oaxaca was a suitable place for a new establishment, he deputed Diego López and Juan Rogel to visit the city in order to verify the conclusion. (Rogel, it will be remembered, had lately terminated a disastrous stay in the Floridas.) They were instructed to consider the land and peoples from all angles, and especially to find out if the Jesuits were sincerely invited and wanted. It is a noteworthy fact, this care of the fathers to appear in places only after invitations had been extended. The point with them was delicate, for other orders of religious were involved, and secular bishops and clergy, and the rulers of the cities. The invitations became to them a kind of contract whereby their presence was established and recognized by parties to whom they were willing to concede priorities of rights. Again, once civilly and ecclesiastically invited, they considered certain rights were theirs, until such time as bishop, governor, and people should no longer want them.

In the beginning of December, 1574, Rogel and López mounted for the exploratory journey to Oaxaca. Ten days later they were at the outskirts of the city. Canon Antonio likely had been warned of their coming. He must have known that the two men were particularly desirous of avoiding any demonstration; nevertheless, he decided to publish the event, and to the consternation of the fathers was no mean publicity agent. The result of his propaganda was that the quiet Jesuits found themselves engulfed, even

at some distance from the city, in a concourse of ecclesias-
tics, civilians, and Indians who tendered them a reception
which outdid that of any other city of the land. The exchange of greetings and blushes continued on into the city,
where the two Black Robes presented their obedience to the
illustrious Bishop Bernardo de Alburquerque, of the Order
of St. Dominic.[7]

Canon de Santa Cruz, true to his promise, gave them
some houses for residences, and the contiguous lots whereon
they might erect a college. While they went about the town
preaching, he scoured Oaxaca and the neighboring cities
for donations for the school. The burden of his many
discourses was the need of education and the budding possibilities of the same in Oaxaca.

Fretful souls in the cloister of Santo Domingo had meanwhile developed a scruple about the location of the houses
and property of the Jesuits.[8] Did it not lie within the *cannas*
of the Dominicans? Were not the Jesuits rather ignorant of
the law prohibiting them from settling within the bound-
aries of their convent? What had come over the bishop,
himself a Dominican, to permit such a thing? The earnest
ones went to his lordship. Whether they presented their case
most forcefully, or whether he merely acted impetuously,
we are not privileged to know, but his action was drastic.
He ordered the two fathers to cease preaching and to give
up the houses and the site for the school. Furthermore, he
actually excommunicated them, as far as his diocese was
concerned. The fathers were serenely surprised—serene because they knew his edict of excommunication lacked force
in this instance, and surprised at its suddenness. The con-

fusion was complete when someone gave wings to a wild rumor that the bishop intended to eject them physically from their dwelling. On the day appointed by the rumor for the untoward event an armed band of the citizenry surrounded the place to prevent it. Of course nothing happened.

Why his lordship refused to see their credentials and disdained to admit any communication with them, remains a mystery. López went to Mexico. He notified Viceroy Enríquez, Archbishop Moya, and the Audiencia of the unhappiness of the excommunicate fathers. An official letter from each was soon on the way to Bishop Alburquerque. The total contents of the writing left the bishop in a position to declare that he was now fully informed in the matter.[9] Why had not somebody notified him of the privilege the Jesuits had of going anywhere? Who had branded them as transgressors? The mistake was rectified, and all was well; faculties and fathers were restored to greater favor. Old Father López, however, was wearied with the travel; age and chronic illness demanded a penalty for hasty jaunts about those mountains. Father Pedro Díaz was sent to Oaxaca in his stead.[10]

While the affair was in progress, Canon de Santa Cruz had repented him of his donation of the houses and lots, probably fearing the bishop's displeasure. López had freed him from his promise, and the Jesuits were without a home. Alburquerque became aware of this, and proceeded to forget the tiff. He offered Rogel and Díaz some better houses, larger lots, and a finer site, about five hundred feet southwest of the cathedral; and on this site arose the Jesuit college of the future. The deed was signed. The bishop wrote to

Sánchez for more Jesuits and especially for López. But López stayed in Mexico and died in the plague of 1576.

A certain Don Juan Luis Martínez died in the city a short time after this, and his testament revealed a bequest for the foundation of a collegial seminary which was to be under the supervision of the newly arrived Company.[11] With the bulk of the estate in money and buildings was a rental of 300 pesos from a hacienda. This was the seminary which went under the title of San Juan, and its first rector was Father Juan Rogel. It opened its gates in September, 1575, to a great portion of the Oaxacan youth of various ages. Since the old buildings of the estate were used for the school, the gates were not new; neither did they rejoice long in the voices of passing students.

The customary beginnings were made with a class in reading and writing. Simultaneously with the opening of San Juan Seminary occurred the opening of the Jesuit college, a procedure which should cause us no confusion now. One group of students was being supported on burses and followed a set daily order according to a special code of rules; the other part of the student body was comprised of day scholars only, who were taught free of charge. Turning our attention first to the seminary group, we find that as soon as the students had begun their grammar a course of moral theology was established. This certainly could not have been extensive, unless there were older boys in the school, and very likely was for local clergymen. How far the seminarians went toward their bachelor's degree we do not know, but some of them went to Mexico to continue their studies. Either because of the numbers of students who had to be supported or because of the lack of returns from the estates, it grew increasingly difficult to sustain the Colegio de San Juan on a separate basis. It appears to have been moribund financially about the time of its fifth anniversary, and was closed finally in 1580.[12] This means that the buildings were closed, but the student body of the seminary continued classwork in the new Jesuit college; and the few who went to live in the new seminary of San Bartolomé, founded by Bishop Ledesma,[13] also attended the Jesuit classes.

Meanwhile, back in 1575, donations were coming to the Jesuits for their college as soon as the citizens found them restored to the good graces of Bishop Alburquerque. He honored them publicly. Their new church was opened September 21, 1575, just about the time the first classes of their college were held in San Juan. Around the church went up the residence and school building. It was ready for Latin grammar classes in October of the following year. The donations[14] were ample enough to pay for a well-appointed college building on the site given by the bishop, who watched the work approvingly when he saw there would be advantages to his diocese in such an educational venture.[15] The structure surrounded a large quadrangle in which there was a beautiful garden; orange and fruit trees were planted, and all could be watered from a large pool and fountain. Pillars and arches graced the four interior sides. The classrooms opened into the quadrangle. Some of the students and teachers had their rooms on the first floor, others on the second along with the offices.[16]

Rogel at that time was in charge of the Seminary of San Juan, Díaz was rector of Oaxaca College. A number of

other Jesuits were sent out from Mexico, among them Pedro
Mercado, who was the first to occupy the chair of Latin. As
soon as he had trained his class to a point where they might
safely do so, he had the boys present literary pieces in the
vernacular and in Latin before, we may suppose, an over-
joyed audience of parents and citizens. The two successive
rectors who were also teachers, Pedro Díaz and Francisco
Báez, later became provincials. Progress in studies was the
keynote of the college for the next few years. Then in the
early 'eighties there was a slump, owing to the necessity of
dropping students because of crop failures on the estates.
We infer this from a letter of Father Plaza, the provincial,
to the general, April 6, 1584.[17] The latter is informed that
"the school for reading and writing continues, but there
are no students for grammar; with the new bishop [Le-
desma] interested in letters, I believe the studies will be
resumed here." Apparently this was done in the following
year. Furthermore, the general urged the provincial to open
a seminary of native languages.[18]

Peace seems to have descended upon the college for the
rest of the sixteenth century, except for the plague of 1595.
The students went to their classes of reading and writing,
grammar, poetry, and rhetoric. Surely, the picture of boys
studying Cicero, Caesar, Vergil, and Horace in Antequera
at that early date is almost without parallel. Sons of Indian
caciques mingled with sons of Creoles and of the *Peninsu-
lares*. It is supposed that the Creoles were the most numerous. A few of the boys, having negotiated the barriers of
Latin grammar and rhetoric, chose to follow the religious
life and entered the Dominican or Jesuit orders; others

elected to become secular priests and continued their studies in the Seminary of San Bartolomé in Oaxaca. Many more lengthened the span of their scholastic life by enrolling in the University of Mexico, or in the Colegio Máximo, becoming lawyers, doctors, and masters of arts.[19]

In 1592 there were sixteen Jesuits working at the College of Oaxaca, and in the little school for Indians outside the city, and as missionaries. In 1599 there was complaint that the student body had grown too large for the teachers. The Latin classes were flourishing and there was great good will and energy in studies. In the school for boys, that is, in the preliminary class of reading, writing, singing, and Christian doctrine, there were more than 170; besides whites, the Indians, Negroes, and mestizos were being taught.[20] And here at the turn of the century we must leave the college of Oaxaca. A violent temblor destroyed part of the building in 1604. This was followed by a flood in the same year. It required some time for the citizens to recover financially from these disasters, yet the school was repaired and carried on. It was heavily in debt by the middle of the seventeenth century, and both teaching staff and student body were diminished. In 1682 Captain Manuel Fiallo gave a foundation of 30,000 pesos, and chairs of arts and theology as well as more in Latin were established, six in all, exclusive of the assistant teachers and prefects.[21] The Jesuits worked continuously for 193 years in their College of Oaxaca.

Another outpost in the spread of the Jesuit educational system was Guadalajara. It did not become the western educational center of the Company until the seventeenth century; and so, as in the other cities outside of Mexico,

intimate details about its early school life are lacking;—
there were too many greater projects occupying the attention of the chroniclers. Jesuit writers were devoting more
space to the Casa Profesa, the novitiate, the missionary work,
Tapia's move into Sinaloa and subsequent martyrdom, and
to all the journeys the fathers were undertaking from Zacatecas to Guatemala and from Vera Cruz to Acapulco. Then,
too, they wrote at the end of the century of the move toward
Nueva Granada in South America. Other writers were concerned over the mines.

The invitation for the Jesuits to exercise their ministries
in Guadalajara came very soon after they had settled in
Mexico. The bishop of the capital of Nueva Galicia was
Señor Don Francisco de Mendíola, who had been elevated
to that dignity because of the esteem all people had for him
as *oidor*.[22] The king, observing his careful works as an *oidor*,
thought he would be an important aid to the government
in the holding of the new land, just as Quiroga had been
in Pátzcuaro. The Indians loved him and his work for them
was splendid both as an official and as bishop. He heard of
the arrival of the Jesuits and in 1574, just after Curiel had
been ordained in Pátzcuaro and Juan Sánchez and Pedro
Mercado in Mexico, he sent one of his chaplains to the
metropolis with orders not to return without some Jesuits.
The provincial sent Fathers Hernando Suárez and Juan
Sánchez to look over the site. They were received with every
manifestation of joy by the bishop and his flock. Mendíola
began to solicit funds for a school foundation, but the
fathers told him they had to move on to Zacatecas as soon
as their missions had been given in Guadalajara. Their work,

however, made him even keener to get the Company located in his diocese.[23]

Evidently the Jesuits could not consider Guadalajara in their plans for schools at this early date. It was only later, when the move by land bases to the north was more clearly defined, that they saw the importance of the city for educational purposes. By that time Mendíola had died and his successor was a Dominican friar, Bishop Domingo de Arzola. It is a coincidence that the Dominicans were instrumental in bringing the Jesuits to teach at Guadalajara just as at Oaxaca.

It was a full ten years before the Jesuits came to stay. Arzola had attended the synod in Mexico City, and during the time of his stay found out that some more of the Company had arrived from Spain. He asked for a few to start a house in Guadalajara. The provincial, Mendoza, complied by dispatching Pedro Díaz, Gerónimo López, and a lay brother, Mateo Illescas. They had been promised a residence. When they had arrived in Lent of 1586 they were housed in the bishop's residence, where they remained for nine months. The fathers preached in the cathedral and worked as missioners, while the bishop and his *cabildo* were trying to get money for the college foundation.[24]

The first offers of money to the Jesuits were held up because of certain conditions imposed by the donors. The *cabildo* wished to divert to the purposes of a school building 10,000 pesos of the rentals coming in to the hospital of their city, if papal and civil permission could be got. A hacienda was to be purchased with this sum and was to be tax free, while the upkeep of the establishment was to be managed for the time being on 500 pesos annually from the royal treasury. The condition was that the Society was to acquire no other tax-exempt hacienda. Mendoza answered that he did not wish to seem ungrateful, but he would have to refuse because the donation was too much involved and was open to complications. So the matter rested while the bishop and López went on a visitation of his diocese.

Brother Illescas had not been idle during the summer of 1586. He had gathered together a crowd of boys and had begun teaching them their reading and writing. Toward the end of the year the *cabildo* gave him a small house and the lads began their grammar. The response of the citizenry to this beginning of education was immediate. Two noble *caballeros,* Don Luis and Don Diego de los Ríos, seeing the need for better accommodations for the school, made a donation of a large plot of land in the very heart of the city, not more than six hundred feet from the main plaza. Melchor Gómez de Soria, the vicar-general of the bishopric, contributed 3000 pesos for the building, the foundations of which were laid in 1587. This was the origin of the Colegio de Santo Tomás.

The classes continued in better surroundings during the next years. After letters back and forth between the bishop, the *cabildo,* and both the provincial and the general of the Company, a final draft of the deed of gift of 10,000 pesos to the Company for its college was signed on April 30,1591.[25] The master of Latin and the brother in charge of the school of reading, writing, and singing were kept so busy that they could attend to nothing else.[26] Help evidently was given, since the teaching and missionary staff increased to ten in the following year, four priests, four brothers, and two scholastics. Hence there was an increase in the number of classes.[27] It was probably the same year of 1592 which saw the opening of a hall for boarders.[28] No records of the numbers of students or of the names of the teachers are available. In 1595 the new bishop, Francisco Santos,[29] instituted a lecture course in moral theology which was to be open to the public. All his clergy had to attend the meeting once a week. The lecturer was Father Diego Villegas, the Jesuit rector of the college.[30] By 1599 the classes in grammar, humanities, and rhetoric were flourishing.[31]

Thus we may conclude the discussion of education in Guadalajara in the sixteenth century under Jesuit auspices. The foundations were well laid. There is, however, a word to be said about the final development.[32] While historians find Guadalajara important in its relation to Pacific Coast history, educators may point to the material remains of colonial education surrounding the fine patios of the College of San Felipe, of the preparatory school, and of Santo Tomás, the arts college with six chairs established—of Latin, rhetoric, logic and philosophy, physics, and theology (moral and dogmatic).[33] In the church of the Colegio de Santo Tomás the mortal remains of Baja California's Father Salvatierra rested until a recent occasion, when unkind hands tossed them into a nameless grave.

There are two other outposts which are very significant in the spread of the Jesuit system of education: the Philippines, an extension into the Orient, and New Granada, an extension of the Mexican province into South America. These indicated that Mexico was no longer an outpost of

culture, but was rather a center from which culture radiated. The province had attained full stature. The Jesuits of
New Spain occupied a place in relation to these frontiers
similar to the one held by their precursors in relation to
Mexico. Manila and New Granada may only be touched
upon here, because they lie outside the territorial limits of
our discussion.

Another Dominican was involved in the advent of the
Company to Manila. Francisco Salazar of the Order of
Preachers chanced to be over in Spain receiving his appointment as the first bishop of the Philippines from Philip II.
He asked the king for a consignment of Jesuits to help him
in his work. The king put hand on the Mexican province
for the appointments. In consequence of the royal order
which followed, the Manila galleon sailing west became a
worry to a group of Jesuits, Fathers Alonzo Sánchez and
Antonio Sedeño, a scholastic named Gaspar de Toledo, and
a lay brother.[34] Gaspar died on the way. The others arrived
at Luzón and made their way slowly to Manila, arriving
there in September, 1581, with a box of books, and being
sheltered by the Franciscans. The box of books became important as the first table for the dining room of the house
in which they went to live.[35]

Sedeño learned the language, and for a few years the
fathers moved about the Islands getting their bearings. In
1585 three more priests and a lay brother arrived.[36] Alonzo
Sánchez returned through one tempest after another in January, 1587; his voyage to Acapulco lasted over six months.
A cedula from the king to the *presidente* of the Philippines
passed him en route. In this the king told his representative

to open a Jesuit college in Manila. The Jesuits had already done this in 1585, but their school was small and probably was attached to their residence or church.[37] Furthermore it was an unhealthy spot, for the rector, Hernán Suárez, contracted the fever and died a year after his arrival. The year 1585, then, was the beginning of education in Manila and likewise of the Colegio de San José. Latin grammar was begun probably in 1594. The Vice-Province of the Philippines had forty-two subjects in 1599, of whom twenty-eight were priests, twelve were brothers, and two were scholastics. There were two *colegios,* one at Manila going well and one at Zebú just beginning. Most of the Jesuits were employed in the thirteen mission stations.[38]

Just at this time the movement toward South America was under way. While Hurdaide and Father Santarén were out on the northern frontier of New Spain reducing the Guazaves, and while Vizcaíno, getting together his men for the voyage, was asking for Jesuit chaplains, two missionaries of the Company were rounding out the first year of their labors in New Granada. The archbishop of that empire, Bartolomé Lobo Guerrero, had received, on asking, the services of Fathers Alonzo Medrano and Francisco Figueroa. They left Vera Cruz the last day of April, 1598. Because of rumors of pirates and several frightful storms, the craft bearing them had to put in at Havana, and later at Jamaica. It was between Jamaica and Cartagena that they and the sailors were miraculously saved, first from the fury of the tempest and next from a sinister calm. It required a year for them to reach Santa Fé de Bogotá.[39]

Whilst they were adjusting themselves, they performed

the ordinary missionary work about the city. Toward the
end of 1599 they divided up some teaching work. Medrano
gave lectures in moral theology to the clergy, and Figueroa
taught grammar to the brighter Spanish boys and Christian
doctrine and singing to the little native Muiscas. This was
the beginning of Jesuit education in Santa Fé. A new troop
of Jesuits came in 1602, but it was not until 1696 that the
vice-province became the Province of Santa Fé. Meantime
by cedulas and donations the College of Santa Fé was
founded in 1604 and became a university in 1610; in 1611,
Tunja College was founded; in 1620, Honda; in 1622, Pamplona; in 1628, Mérida; in 1643, Santa Cruz de Mompox.[40]
Another book, however, will be required to tell of the labors
of the Mexican and Spanish Jesuits in this territory.

The last of the outposts were the rip-roaring mining town
of Zacatecas and the revolt-torn Durango, or Guadiana. Of
these I can give only the beginnings, and shall hold Durango over for the next chapter. Jesuits had been going
north at times to the silver city to give missions ever since
the time Concha first endeared himself to the people in
1579, but for years Zacatecas was not deemed a suitable place
in which to establish a college, because of its floating population. Repeated invitations to the Jesuits came until 1590,
when Avellaneda arrived as *visitador* to the province. To
this father belongs the credit of a definite and concerted
move on the part of the Jesuits into the northlands.[41]

Avellaneda, with powers of a provincial, sent Fathers
Juan Cagina and Agustín Cano to Zacatecas. The latter may
be recalled as the prodigy child of the first Latin class of the
Jesuits in Mexico City. The missionary successes of the two

were great, yet we must pass them over. The citizens gave them an old residence and erected a new chapel for them;[42] a school of reading and writing was opened, presumably for the Spanish, Creole, and Indian youths;—and these are all the available data upon the same, save that in 1592 a priest and a lay brother were added to the residence, as it was still termed.[43]

While preaching, the fathers seem to have leveled a few poignant shafts against exploitation of the Indians by certain Zacatecans. Many were the murmurs against the fathers. The accused citizens were all for banishing them, but the other class, wishing more and more the educational improvement of their sons, urged them to go ahead with their school plans.[44] After a number of reassurances and promises of support, a class in Latin grammar opened in 1593 and continued on through many successive generations. The story of this for the rest of the sixteenth century is brief. Two other subjects were added to the staff, the next classes of grammar followed, and finally the beginnings of philosophy.[45] At Zacatecas the Jesuits caught up with the advance forces of civilization.

Chapter XIV

TEPOTZOTLÁN

IN ORDER TO GIVE a complete picture of the Jesuit Province of New Spain as it was founded in the sixteenth century, it is necessary to say a word about two more institutions. In a way they too are outposts—religious outposts. These were the novitiate wherein the Jesuits began their religious lives, and the professed houses toward which the members tended.[1] Both pertained intimately to the system of training and spirituality brought by the Jesuits. The erection of buildings for these purposes reveals finally the province as a distinct unit. The Casa Profesa, housing the professed of three or four vows, is always given first place in the considerations of provincial historians, because it was the residence of the governing group of the province and because it was looked upon as the model house of all religious observance, an anchor as it were to Jesuit affairs. I shall let Father Pérez de Rivas, historian and twice rector of the professed house in Mexico City, speak of his abode:

Those are termed professed houses which are dedicated to the ministries generally professed by the Company with the exception of teaching letters. Those who ordinarily live in the professed houses are the professed of four vows. They are employed in preaching, hearing confessions, solving cases of conscience, visiting prisons and hospitals, and all other exercises which tend toward the spiritual progress of souls. Although it is true that in those places and towns where there is no professed house the fathers who reside in the colleges carry on these ministrations, still, where there is one, the fathers residing in it exercise these functions as their sole occupation. There is another difference between the colleges and the professed houses, namely, that in no case may the professed house have rentals or goods, either in common or in particular, not even for the sacristy, but it must be sustained solely by alms. Because of this the professed house is wont to be founded in populous cities. The same law applies to residences. The colleges, however, may have an income in common as do other mendicant orders, even stipends for masses, but not for any other ministry which the Company undertakes according to its institute. Finally, where a province has a professed house, this is the head of all the other houses.[2]

The plan of life to obtain in the professed house was one requiring a strict adherence to the original Constitutions of Ignatius. To carry it out meant that the house must be dependent upon alms. Under these circumstances there would be no sign of avarice, and services were rendered gratis. Anything obtained by bequest or otherwise had to be given to the poor, or to the province for the education of the younger members. Within the house there could be only what was absolutely necessary for habitation and use. The Casa Profesa was the ideal in the mind of Ignatius for the work he planned; other Jesuit houses were the outgrowths of necessities of education.

The Casa Profesa in Mexico and the famous old Church of La Profesa, now leaning so heavily in the heart of the downtown district, began existence with a will and a lawsuit. For twenty years after the arrival of the Jesuits in New Spain, the professed house, in an inchoate state, was the Colegio Máximo, for in that building the administrative personnel of the Mexican Province resided. Still, not all the professed were administrators. Some fathers lectured in the College; others devoted themselves only to missionary work and to parochial duties. Works multiplied and grew complex. Therefore the fathers wanted to make a definite separation of their respective duties, and to have those who were not engaged in teaching live in a separate residence.

A very honorable Mexican, Hernán Núñez de Obregón, died in 1584 and opened up possibilities for this division by willing a sum of 4000 pesos to the Company. Father Mendoza, the provincial, obtained a license from both Archbishop Moya and Viceroy Velasco to buy a residence for the Jesuits engaged solely in spiritual ministries. In 1591, Juan Luis de Rivera, the king's treasurer and a *regidor* of the city, and his wife, Doña Juana Gutiérrez, gave 50,000 pesos for a church and library. They added other donations and by a written deed became the founders of the Casa Profesa and its adjacent church, February 3, 1592. Followed then the lawsuits arising out of the objections of the other religious orders to infringement of the *cannas,* but these were settled happily (by 1595) and together with the history of La Profesa they must be passed over because they lack pertinence to the strictly educational program.[3] The professed fathers, now well rid of lawsuit worry, carried on their administrations in the cities, in the adjacent countrysides, and in the missions to the northwest.[4]

The conversion of the Indians had been a prime reason for the establishment of the Jesuits in New Spain. The urgent desire to get out among them was before the Jesuits from the time of their arrival, but while the material structure of their province was being erected it could not readily be achieved. Now that the colleges were in a sufficiently workable condition, the missionary objective again came to the fore and was of paramount importance to all the Jesuits by 1590.

Preparations for this work had been going on for many years. The languages were being studied and Jesuits were continuously exploring and reporting the likely sites for permanent missions. It was clear to Sánchez from the beginning as well as to his successors that men would have to be prepared from their early days in the Society for this work in the outer regions, hence his novitiate would have to form both missonaries and teachers. The best means for inspiring the younger members with a desire to labor among the poorer children of the kingdom was contact with their customs, languages, and necessities. And this was being done for the novices. The Jesuits had come to give themselves principally to the natives; but the Spaniards and Creoles, realizing what lay latent in the newly arrived organization for the intellectual betterment of their New Spain, had seized upon huge quantities of the Jesuit service for education in the cities. Education of the Spanish and Creole youth, then, was really an accident, though it became a necessary accident with the passing of a few years. To found some colleges was essential in order to make the province a unit. This was done; but at the same time the missionary program was ever in Sánchez' mind.

The novitiate existed from the year 1573 as a term of probation in one of the makeshift houses on the Villaseca property. We have already described the entrance of the first novices—Saldaña, a priest who had labored long years among the natives, Juan Tobar, who was later to evangelize the west coast, Canon Fernández, and the Indian of the

royalty of Texcoco, Antonio Rincón.[5] These and others went
through their exercises in the city. When the Colegio Máximo was erected, the incoming novices lived in one section of the building. There the novices had the two years
of probation until 1585, when the novitiate was moved
to Tepotzotlán. In 1591 the novices were in the Espíritu
Santo College of Puebla, where they remained until 1606.
Then they returned to the beautiful hillside whereon rests
Tepotzotlán.

Why all the movements and why Tepotzotlán? The little
Indian village is about twenty-five miles north of Mexico
City, and it seemed in 1585 a more quiet place for the
novices than the bustling Colegio Máximo.[6] There were
other reasons. Nobody had bothered much about Tepotzotlán until the Jesuits first went there. It had suffered the con-
tempt of city folk which is the lot of all suburbs. Cortés,
making his way around the lake after the Noche Triste,
might have cast an uninterested eye in its general direction.
Pedro Sánchez, on the other hand, became alert about the
possibilities of the place just before his term of office ex-
pired. He was interested in the Indians, both for what he
wished to do for them and for what he expected his subjects to learn from them of the aboriginal languages. There
were little human books out at Tepotzotlán which the
Jesuits might study.

Consequently, in 1579 when there was a parish vacant at
nearby Huizquiluca, Hernán Suárez got an appointment
as pastor. With him twelve Jesuits went to live.[7] Their purpose was to study the Otomí, just as others were out west
at Pátzcuaro learning the Tarascan language and the Chi-

chimec languages. One of the requirements for ordination in the Society was a fluent knowledge of at least one native tongue. A priest named Hernán Gómez, who had recently joined the Company, was to be the instructor. So, the younger members remained at Huizquiluca for eighteen months mastering the Otomí. During this time Tepotzotlán was within the radius of many missionary excursions. Indians were being forced by the Spaniards to make their homes in it. The parish there became vacant, and Gómez and Juan Tobar, both adepts in the Mexican, Otomí, and Masagua, fell heir to the parochial duties.

In 1580, the visitor, Plaza, decided that the seminary of languages at Huizquiluca could no longer subsist. He recalled his subjects. Hernán Gómez and Juan Tobar stayed among the Indians because they had received official appointment from Moya to act as pastors of Tepotzotlán.[8] Any young Jesuits who wished could go out to them to learn languages. Many took advantage of this opportunity. With a few scholastics teaching and learning among the Indians, a new vista was rather suddenly opened up to the Jesuits. A cacique, Don Martín Maldonado, governor of the pueblo mentioned, harbored a great idea for some time before he proposed it in 1582. The idea was no less than a seminary for sons of the native race of Tepotzotlán. The cacique was ready to back the idea with his wealth; he gave several houses and some property for the purpose. Thus the remarkable school was opened in 1584 under the patronage of San Martín.[9]

For the Jesuits, here was the germ of the mission as a frontier institution.[10] The concept was to grow and become an agency for civilization after the natives had been converted. San Martín was a decided step toward the cultural elevation of the tribes. For Jesuit missionaries it was the beginning of the larger opening which Bolton has graphically described with respect to the northern missions in New Spain. "If the Indian were to become either a worthy Christian or a desirable subject, he must be disciplined in the rudiments of civilized life. Missions were designed to be not only Christian seminaries, but in addition were outposts for the control and training schools for the civilization of the frontier." Indeed a broad vista had been opened at Tepotzotlán. Its missionary type of college was one of the most useful of the institutions founded by the Jesuits. The training of missionaries was just as important in the broadening field of colonial culture as was the establishment of the colleges. The Jesuits were quick to perceive the potentialities of places like Tepotzotlán for giving knowledge of all phases of the native character and of aiding in the problem of elevating the race. Hence the novices were sent in 1585.

We are not to think of the seminary of San Martín in the ecclesiastical meaning of the word; I prefer another characterization.[11] It was a school of Christian discipline "in which every act involved a lesson in the amenities of civilization." Nor was San Martín a college in any but the obsolete sense of the word. Thirty sons of caciques lived a boarding-school life in the houses, under the direction and instruction of two fathers and some scholastics and novices. The Indian boys were taught singing, church music, instruments, religion, ritual for the services, reading, writing, Spanish, and government.[12] Later on there were fifty of the

lads. The institution gained great favor. Its presence facilitated the bringing together of the scattered families into one
village. In fact, a great number of Indians moved from their
former homes to Tepotzotlán without either the violence
or the tears which usually attended such manipulations of
the Indians from the fields of their fathers. The boys of the
seminary became disseminators of knowledge.

In a way they were the teachers of the young Jesuits and
even of the older ones. From the Indians whom they were
instructing, the religious assimilated the native idiom.
When the boys went with the missionaries as guides and
interpreters, the fathers were not only put at their ease
but also had the opportunity of witnessing the manner in
which the youngsters conveyed ideas to the other Indians.
Thus they were valuable little assistants in many ways.
Short sermons were prepared for them, even as of old Pedro
de Gante had done, and they multiplied instruction possibilities for the fathers by repeating them in places to which
the fathers could not get. They helped about the altar, and
they sang. They became little missionaries to the far north.
Pérez de Rivas, our old friend of the footnotes, began just
such a school in Sinaloa and brought some of the Tepotzotlán "collegians" with him to show the boys on the frontier
how things should be done.[13] The attachment of the boys
to the fathers is one of the most charming incidents of mission history.[14]

Was there any higher education for these collegians who
lived in the old town of the Jesuit novitiate? Fortunately
there was. Some few of the brightest boys, having had a preliminary training at Tepotzotlán, passed on to the metropo-

lis to take the higher courses in Latin grammar, rhetoric, and the arts. Some took theology; at least one, Don Lorenzo, in the next century, completed all his studies, became a Master in Scripture, and lectured for forty years in that subject at Tepotzotlán and its big brother institution, San Gregorio in Mexico.[15]

During the sixteenth century in other parts of New Spain there were schools of a character similar to San Martín in operation under the auspices of the Jesuits. Some of these have already been noticed. The one at Pátzcuaro, for instance, was established prior to Tepotzotlán. Then just outside of Oaxaca a number of the younger Jesuits were studying the Mixtec, and they also, after 1587, had their elementary school for the Indian boys.[16] At Puebla there were two such, though the one called San Gerónimo, already referred to, was not so important as the other called San Miguel, which was begun by and was under the direction of the Mexican Father Rincón.[17] It was opened in 1583, and very soon afterwards Father Hernán Vásquez joined Rincón in the work. Vásquez died in 1592, but an Indian priest of the Company, native to the region, inherited his spirit and kept San Miguel flourishing. He was Father Diego Infante.[18]

These Indian schools were all in the already civilized areas, but in 1594 one was begun in the new pueblo of San Luís de la Paz. There the Chichimecas were being reduced. The best way to carry out the program seemed to be to introduce some Otomies and Jesuits, and so Fathers Francisco Zarfate and Diego Monsalve were sent to the work of evangelization. They chose as colaborers four of the Indian seminarists of San Martín, and by November an Indian school was doing well.[19] The Indian boys were taught how to sing, read, write. Even Latin classes were carried on.[20] Thus the youths on the borderland began to play their part in the spread of civilization, and later were to be the governors of the northern pueblos.

The little College of Durango was on the borderland in several ways. It was placed between the civilized and the uncivilized tribes. It was begun on the verge of the new century, and was begun as an Indian school wherein the natives were taught the usual primary matters. It was intended by Father Gonzalo de Tapia to be a central residence for priests and a seminary for neophytes going into the northern lands—Topia, Sinaloa, Sonora, the Laguna region, the Tepehuanes and the Tarahumares—in fine, a San Martín of the north. But Tapia's project did not materialize. After it opened in 1593, the Spaniards wished their sons to be educated and for this purpose gave a house on a hillside. Later this was moved toward the center of the town to conserve for better purposes the energy spent by the boys in climbing the hill. Latin grammar was taught, but beyond this we know nothing of the numbers in the classes nor of the school's affairs until the new building was constructed after 1616.[21]

The head of the Society did not at first grasp the broader significance of San Martín, nor of Tepotzotlán as a missionary college wherefrom civilizing agencies might emanate. In reality, he appears not to have been consulted about its establishment. At the first notification of its existence, he was not much taken with the idea of small quarry at a time when the men were needed so badly for the greater affairs of the province. Possibly he was somewhat chary about allowing his subjects to assist in the reduction processes as instigated by the government. His conversion to the idea is told in his letters to the provincials.

"It is not a convenient time for the Company to take charge of seminaries for the Indians," Aquaviva wrote on May 9, 1587, to Mendoza. "Those which have been commenced without license in Mexico and Tepotzotlán should be permitted to die out by degrees, lest any offense be given." But the archbishop had put the Jesuits to this task, and the government was all for its success; therefore explanatory letters had to go to Rome. August 11, 1587, the general again wrote to explain his stand. "These seminaries seem more inconvenient than useful . . . at a time when the province should employ its subjects otherwise than in governing seminaries for Indian boys." July 10, 1589, his attitude is, "If it is convenient to drop the seminaries, do so." June 8, 1592, he is much interested in the work being done for the Indians and in the acquirement of the languages, so much so that he thinks the tertian fathers ought to spend the last four months of their tertianship at Tepotzotlán, learning the tongues. And in January, 1594, Aquaviva wrote, "Let there be preserved in San Gregorio and Tepotzotlán the care of the Indian boys."[22] Was the general aware of the rapidly diminishing population from statistics of the native races, and did he fear their total extinction by plagues, when he first objected? We do not know. His conversion to the idea of training Indians was complete.

Tepotzotlán was another anchor of the province. To the

Company in Mexico it meant much more than the beautiful church with its Churriguerresque façades, the magnificently carved and gilded interior, the Cabrera and Juárez paintings along the corridors of the novitiate building, the sunny cloisters and patios, or the golden-toned chimes ringing out over the serene valley. Tepotzotlán stood for the beginning of things in the lives of the Jesuits. It was the symbol to the members of the Province of New Spain of their labors during the centuries which followed. The very word recalled to them their ideals, religious, missionary, and educational. It was a place where a Salvatierra could inculcate those aims which included in their scope the magnificent effort to elevate the white and Indian races of America to a higher level of culture. Paradoxically, this lowly village, this starting point and source of Jesuit activity and achievement, the novitiate, seems to be a fitting place at which to terminate the story of the Jesuit educational foundations of the sixteenth century.

Chapter XV

PRODUCTS

IT IS TIME TO MAKE a résumé of the educational and intellectual developments of the sixteenth century in New Spain as they were affected by the presence and efforts of the Jesuits, and thus to fit the Company into its proper niche in the complex colonial life. In general, the men who appeared in the rôle of founders of the Province of New Spain had done their work well. On the groundworks they laid, future generations were to build a wider educational structure. Many of the men who spent themselves as ordinary members in the ranks would have been called noteworthy educators and organizers in any community, but Pedro Sánchez, supervising the creation and organization of his province and laying the broad foundations for the future public education of Mexico in secondary and college studies, must be rated an outstanding figure.

When the century was drawing to a close, then, the Jesuits had molded their province into a complete unit. So firmly were they established that they were capable of offering their services in the variety of activities which aptly tended toward the betterment of Spaniards, Creoles, and Indians. They brought their own institutions—the Constitutions whereby they themselves were trained, the Spiritual Exercises which made for the religious improvement of all classes and which were the interior forces motivating their work, the Ratio Studiorum in its tentative form at first and in its final form in 1599. What they gave to Europe, they gave in like measure and quality to America. They grounded here the whole system.[1] With these institutions trained men were presented for a great task, and their numbers were rapidly multiplied. The founders were fifteen; by 1600, 272 subjects were in the strategic points of New Spain, and 42 in the Philippines. They were directing seminaries for the New World clergy, training the younger generations, establishing missions, lecturing in colleges and at the University, and teaching in the secondary and lower classrooms.

The results in material structure were great, if we consider the age and make a comparison with what was taking place in Europe. Besides the novitiate and Casa Profesa which appeared to pertain to Jesuits alone but which in reality affected culture considerably by reason of their products, there were first of all the various divisions of the university in which the Jesuits were trained. The juniorate and philosophate, comprising normal-school education, were at the Colegio Máximo in Mexico City. This building was also a college of arts for extern students to the number of seven hundred. Here too, university courses were given in theology. Hard by was the University of Mexico, with which a harmonious arrangement had been made for exchange of professors and for audition of lectures by students of both places. The boarding college of San Ildefonso, directed by the Jesuits, cared for above a hundred students, of whom some were to become priests of the diocese. Likewise San Gregorio, the college for Indians, was administered by the order. Thus a true center for the spread of humanistic education had been built in the capital.

Puebla was the second center of importance with an arts college, a preparatory, a seminary, and a primary school for Indians. In Oaxaca there was a primary school for Indians and a combination primary and Latin school, in the latter of which boys of both races could have courses up to rhetoric and could be assured of a suitable foundation for further studies if they wished to go to Mexico. A similar building was in operation in Guadalajara. In Pátzcuaro was a primary school having some Latin, and a seminary for Indians. Valladolid had a Latin school and a seminary under the Jesuits. The far Philippines had a Latin school, so did Zacatecas, and at Durango there were even some beginnings of philosophy. In Tepotzotlán and San Luís de la Paz were seminaries for Indians. In such wise was the Jesuit system established.

A brief glance into the future will reveal the superstructure of public education built by the Company before its inglorious ejection. We have already mentioned the spread of the program to New Granada at the dawn of the seventeenth century.[2] In New Spain a residence was opened in Guatemala (1608) and shortly afterwards the city had a college which began arts, or philosophy, in 1623 and theology in 1626. This same year Puebla got a new seminary. The Jesuits arrived in Mérida, Yucatán, in 1604; by 1611 they had a primary school which in 1620 was a college with classes of Latin, philosophy, and theology. In 1623 a Latin school was begun at San Luis Potosí, and two years later one at Querétaro. The fathers had resided in Vera Cruz since 1578, and Juan Rogel, of Florida fame, spent the last of his ninety years of life there, but owing to plagues, a fire, and the character of the population no college was established until 1639, and this did not prosper much beyond the primary-school status with some Latin grammar. At Chiapas a college was opened in 1684; and at Guadalajara, Salvatierra's seminary in 1696. Over and above these there were the Indian schools attached to missions.

Respecting the eighteenth century, when the membership of the province increased to more than five hundred, making it one of the largest in the world, I must be more brief. In 1702, another seminary was opened at Puebla; in 1714, a college at Monterrey and the following year a seminary; in 1716, a primary and Latin grammar school at Campeche; in 1718, another at Chihuahua; in 1720, one which later became a college began at Celaya; in 1722, a similar school at Havana, and in 1731 at León; the next year, the Latin school at Guanajuato was begun, and in 1744 a small school at Camagüey, Cuba. The last of the *colegios* founded by the Jesuits, at Puebla in 1751, was, like the first in Mexico, a seminary for Indians. Obviously another book will be required to account for all these foundations and to show how it was that the Jesuits came to have care of almost all the public instruction of New Spain.[3]

The products of culture should include books and libraries. The whole story of the progress of colonial education might be reviewed from the standpoint of the written pages. When the Franciscans came to America, Pedro de Gante and his fellow workers were confronted by the problem of languages. They went out to study these at Texcoco; there was founded the first primary school on the mainland and there the friars learned the languages from the Indians.

By a long, arduous process dictionaries of the Mexican language were written. They were of course on perishable material. Similarly, readers, primers, and catechisms were composed in Spanish and Mexican. Other friars came, other languages were encountered, and the study of philology began in earnest and continued during the remainder of the century. Grammars and textbooks had to be written. These necessarily were few in number, because of the time required to copy them when many other duties were calling. Picture books were made, but all have perished. Scores of primary schools attached to the convents dotted the central part of the viceroyalty.[4] Reading and writing were taught, and therefore manuals must have been used, especially in the Franciscan center of education at San Francisco for girls and boys.

On the foundations of primary education the College of Santa Cruz de Tlatelolco grew. In the year which witnessed its launching, 1536, a press was brought from Spain, for students had need of schoolbooks in Latin as well as in religion.[5] Several years after the college for Indians had got under way, Bishop Zumárraga set up the famous printing press.[6] An impetus was given to printing in 1553 when the University of Mexico opened its doors. If a copy of each book had been preserved as the stream flowed from the presses, we might be able to trace the story clearly. The catechisms, psalters, theological tracts, and manuals were augmented by texts on theology, canon and civil law, medicine, rhetoric, and the native languages. Many of the books could very easily have been reprints from European authors, but those on native languages had to be of American origin and publication, since nobody in Europe could proofread them. A glance at one of the bibliographies of sixteenth-century printing in Mexico reveals a surprising number of publications in the Spanish and Mexican tongues.[7] Besides these, histories were being written.

Meantime, libraries were being accumulated at many of the convents of Mexico City. Beyond the confines of the metropolis was a rather important collection at Tiripitío where as early as 1541 the Augustinians had a university for their own seminarians. There was another library at Tacámbaro. Collections of globes, maps, and scientific instruments were part of these libraries, whose contents, as far as the sixteenth century is concerned, have suffered the ravages of time.[8]

The Jesuits on their arrival gave a new impulse to practical printing. They, like the other orders, had their language difficulties. They began classes. The languages and their courses demanded the aid of a press; hence in 1578 a room of the Colegio Máximo was given over to a printer. He was Antonio Ricardo from Piedmont, and he brought his press. He went to Lima after two years, but the press continued and later was moved to the College of San Ildefonso. A general license was granted annually to the college to print what books seemed necessary for the students. The production seems to have been rather large.[9] Textbooks, however, are notoriously short-lived in the hands of students, and consequently few of those from the San Pedro y San Pablo press remain.

Of course, a number of laws governed the printing of books in Spain and in the colonies, and the sale and impor-

tation of books.[10] Happily a discussion of these has lately
come to hand, and I need not delay long upon the subject.[11]
Suffice it to say, lawmaking was one thing, enforcement was
quite another. Booksellers and printers and publishers were
in danger of severe penalties if they brought out or dis-
tributed books without license.[12] Censors were appointed in
Spain and in America, yet it seems clear that only certain
types of books, namely those pertaining to dogma and Scripture, were affected.[13] There was little trouble entailed in getting novels and comedies into the colonies, nor was there
much difficulty about getting a permission to publish works
in the colonies. The laws had lapsed before the seventeenth
century was very old.

Life in sixteenth-century Mexico was not drab. The Spaniards in their leisure after the Conquest enjoyed themselves
in hunting, falconry, horse racing, masquerades, and bull-
fights, and the Creole society which became preponderant
toward the end of the period imitated the aristocracy.[14] The
younger generations were in danger of being reared to idleness and play; the Jesuits, therefore, came with their educational system at a timely moment. Still, an inclination to
showiness remained. The affectation in customs which took
hold of the middle-class merchants was reflected in some of
the writings of the times. Ephemeral poetry became plentiful; but this I pretend neither to judge nor to discuss.[15] In
one poetry contest there were three hundred poets entered.
The Jesuits tried to turn the stream in a religious direction
and to give classical form and content to it in their classrooms. Several of the fathers became poets of some rank,
Juan Arista, for instance, and Pedro Flores, a native of Mex-

ico who held the chair of poetry at the Colegio for many years, and Bernardo Llanos. All three wrote poetic dialogues and eulogies.

Theologians and orators abounded, and there were many theological disputations in the halls of the universities and colleges. Theology, law, and oratory occupied a place in the educational scheme of things similar to that of science in our own day. Some of the Jesuit theologians have been noted. Sacred oratory received a new impetus from such Jesuits as Pedro Sánchez, Diego López, Concha, and others. Philosophers, occupying a very high place in that age, were common in and out of religious orders, and all rejoiced when the book on logic written by the Jesuit Rubio, in Mexico, became the exclusive text on the subject at the University of Alcalá in Spain. Medical books were published, but the Jesuits had small part in these and no part in the works on nautics, war, or horsemanship. A coadjutor brother, Alonzo López, who like Juan Rogel deserted the medical profession in order to enter the Society (in January, 1585), is responsible for the publication of the second edition of his quaint text on medicine in 1595. This work, in two hundred chapters, was entitled *Suma y recopilación de cirugía con un arte para sangrar y examinar barberos*. Joseph Steinheffer, lay brother in the College of Chihuahua in the eighteenth century, wrote in Spanish a *Medical Anthology* which was widely used in medical practice.[16]

The texts which the fathers of the Company arranged, or reprinted, or brought over from Europe covered the fields they were teaching. We have mentioned these fields often, except mathematics, whose presence we deduce from the treatise on that subject in Rubio's book.[17] Pageants and plays in Latin, and Spanish plays, were written regularly and produced. Cautions from the general in this regard were not lacking, lest they become more frequent than once a year. These plays, like the poems, were popular and hence were talked about and have led critics to overestimate their importance. Solider things were being done. What the Jesuits wrote in the way of enduring contributions are familiar by this time. The early fathers began the tradition of prolific writings of relations, letters, biographies, and descriptions, which have proved valuable sources for historical research. Mexico, its peoples, lands, and customs, were things about which one would wish to write.

If education is a process of producing, preventing, and directing changes in human beings,[18] the Jesuits did much to educate New Spain in the sixteenth century. The religious of all orders had encountered in the New World problems before unheard of, and these problems arose out of the complexities of race, customs, interests, and situations; in a word, out of contact with the products of the first American melting pot. No one will question the great change produced in the native races by the combined efforts of the religious churchmen. The Jesuits had a great part in directing the change, especially where education was concerned. Bringing the Indians and Creoles into contact with the European thought of the times, and that on a large scale and in a concrete manner, was a feat overshadowed only by their attempt to give to all classes the wisdom of the ancients. How much the thought of an intellectual Utopia may have addled these early colonial educators we are not prepared to say, but what was being striven for was knowledge sufficient to assure at least a modicum of intellectual happiness after college days. Hence there was a certain solidarity to the Jesuits' program—groundwork was emphasized, and the solid things as European educators then understood them, things which tended to make a student a good Christian and a good citizen, capable of enjoying art and study to the limits of his mentality.

A number of projects contributed toward the realization of this educational aim. The composite picture is striking. The physical aspects of city life had been changed for the better by the erection in the cities of school buildings. They were hints to the people of the value and necessity of education and they were a standing invitation to obtain it. The very presence of men engaged in learning and teaching, the presence of caps and gowns, the sight of boys trudging to school, the spectacle of the conferring of degrees, of literary acts, of disputations, of plays and pageants—all combined into a great lesson in culture. Libraries, presses, and books were indications to all that they were living in a civilized community. Art productions by the world's best workers in painting, sculpture, and architecture were lavished upon even the lowliest of peoples in the most out-of-the-way places; these, with the many churches, were decidedly uplifting. The Americans evidently liked all the details of the composite picture, for they went in for imitating the Europeans and for producing a similar picture of culture, substantially the same, but with new lights and shades. This was to be the canvas of Spanish-American culture.

To the more intellectually inclined, humanism came with

its broadening possibilities. Scholasticism, which was then the best system of mental discipline, was introduced. The study of languages inclined all toward a deeper sympathy between races. The travel from one city to another for college residence and the infiltration of college-bred men in outlying districts tended to break down provincialism. There was a lesson in social equality in the mingling of all classes and races in the college halls, and another in the coming of European priests and scholars who were not aloof in their attitude and dealings with the Americans. Teaching the native Americans of both races to be teachers of others was productive at once of a spirit of confidence, of individualism, and of personal enterprise.

The "Epic of Greater America" is in the making, as well as in the writing. An outline has been offered for historians of the present and future who will write the parts of the epic already completed by men on these two continents.[19] Long years will be required to fill in the outline. Meanwhile the epic continues; the complete development of greater America lies in the future. The first phases, discovery, colonization, the colonies waxing virile and breaking away from the European mothers, the formation of republics, are preliminaries to a longer history. Running through all this is the epic of American youth, of cultural development and education. Mexico of the sixteenth century occupies a favored place in the foundation of Spanish-American culture; under this broad heading comes the education which was offered to the rising generations. Similar developments were taking place in South America; they all form part of the epic of education in the Spanish colonies. We have necessarily confined ourselves to the progress which took place in one portion of one continent and to slightly more than a quarter of a century of the story and to the efforts of one group of educators. Other books, we may hope, will unfold the rest of the story of the pageant of American youth.

BIBLIOGRAPHY

ARCHIVES

THE ARCHIVES CONSULTED for materials for the story of Jesuit education in New Spain during the sixteenth century are as follows: the Bancroft Library at the University of California; the Jesuit Archives of Mexico City and of Ysleta, Texas, where part of the Mexican province of the Society of Jesus resides at present, and the smaller collections at Los Gatos and Santa Clara, California, containing some printed sources relating to the Institute, Constitutions, Spiritual Exercises, and Ratio Studiorum of the Society; the private collection of documents belonging to a Jesuit scholar in Mexico, whose name I am not at liberty to disclose; the Archivo General, the Museo Nacional, and the Biblioteca Nacional, in Mexico City; the old Palafox Library and that of El Colegio del Estado in Puebla; the Library of the Palace of Arts in Guadalajara, Jalisco; the Ayer Collection in the Newberry Library, Chicago. The loci of the manuscripts used in the text have been indicated. I am deeply grateful to the librarians in the above-named places for assistance.

MANUSCRIPTS

The bases for the study undertaken are, first, the *Cartas Anuas,* or annual letters. Each house, college, and mission was required to send a letter every year to the provincial, containing a formal account or status of the place. The provincial, from these and from information gathered during his visits, wrote a summary letter about his province to the general of the Society. We have used those of the *Cartas* for the period which still remain in the Jesuit Archives of Mexico; they are for the years 1579, 1582, 1585, 1591, 1592, 1593, 1595, 1596, 1597, 1598, 1599.

Besides these official letters there are others from the provincials to the general and from the general to the provincials regarding particular matters of various sorts. Some of these are published in Florencia, Alegre, Astrain, and Cuevas, and others appear in *Epistolae Generalium* in printed form and come under the more general heading of *Monumenta Historica Societatis Jesu,* which was described in Chapter I. The manuscript letters from the general, Claude Aquaviva, to the Jesuit provincials and visitors of New Spain for the period are as follows:

Aquaviva to Mendoza, March 15, 1584
Idem to idem, Feb. 24, 1586
Idem to idem, Sept. 9, 1586
Idem to idem, May 9, 1587
Idem to idem, Aug. 10, 1587
Idem to idem, Aug. 11, 1587
Idem to idem, July 10, 1589
Idem to idem, April 17, 1590
Idem to idem, April 18, 1590
Idem to idem, June 20, 1590
Idem to Pedro Díaz, Oct. 28, 1591
Idem to idem, March 15, 1593
Idem to the visitador Mendoza, Jan. 20, 1592
Idem to Avellaneda, June 8, 1592
Idem to Páez, March 15, 1595
Idem to idem, Nov. 21, 1595
Idem to idem, Aug. 4, 1597
Idem to idem, June 10, 1598
Idem to Báez, Dec. 13, 1599
Idem in reply to petitions, Jan. 1594
Idem in reply to petitions, May 9, 1594

Undoubtedly, other letters containing materials on the colleges will be discovered in time.

The third group of letters are those of the visitors of the province to the general in which an exact relation of provincial affairs is given. Astrain and Cuevas have published the ones used here, in their histories. The *Catalogues* of the provinces, made periodically, are unavailable in manuscript, but have been printed by J. Schmitt, *Synopsis Historiae Societatis Jesu* (Ratisbon, 1914). These have to do with statistics, and a copy of the work is at the University of Santa Clara.

While all these are rather concise relations, the *cartas* inscribed by different members are more detailed. A very fine manuscript source of this type is the one quoted under the title of *Carta de Juan Sánchez*. It is really a short history of the province for the first five years, written by a contemporary. Into this classification fall the biographical accounts of the members of the Company, many of which are contemporary and in manuscript in the Jesuit Archives of Mexico. These biographies are short, and may be divided into those which are edifying recitals of the virtues of the individual and those which narrate his activities. They are scattered through the histories of Florencia, Rivas, and Alegre.

Manuscripts pertaining to a particular college have each been noted in its particular place, those from the *Temporalidades* and *Jesuitas* of the Archivo General of Mexico, for instance. There are 247 *legajos* of *Temporalidades* in the same archive, of which number 42 bundles pertain to the temporal affairs of the colleges; these are de-

scribed in the *Boletín del Archivo General de la Nación,* Vol. III,
Oct.-Nov.-Dec. 1932, No. 4. The manuscript accounts, bills, inven-
tories, etc., contained in these materials cover the years 1686–1836, but
scattered all through the *legajos* are earlier accounts, deeds, and letters; for instance, Tomo 227 has papers from San Pedro y San Pablo
and Espíritu Santo from 1592, and 232 1.C some from 1576, while
234 1.F from 1572–1734 has Villaseca's gifts to the Jesuits. The *Jesuitas* are known by reason of Dr. Bolton's findings among the volumes.
The manuscript *Extracto de Títulos de San Gerónimo* of two volumes found in Puebla is described in the text of chap. xii *supra,* as
is that of the *Títulos y Méritos de los Señores Covarrubias.* Several
pages would be required to describe the volumes of Manuscrita Antigua in the Jesuit Archives.

PRINTED DOCUMENTS

The *Monumenta Historica Societatis Jesu* is a primary source. At
present it is being revised and amplified. There are plans afoot in
Rome for an edition of *Monumenta Mexicana* and *Monumenta Flo-
ridana* to be added to the many volumes. Cullings have been made
from the various collections of printed documents, such as those of
Cuevas, Cárdenas y Espejo, Corcoran, Foley, Genaro García, Caste-
ñeda, Osores, Veytia, García Icazbalceta. Source materials have been
indicated for the first three chapters in the notes.

Throughout the volumes of Florencia, Alegre, Astrain, and Cuevas
pertinent sources are published—letters of the visitors, cedulas, legal
deeds, gifts, bulls, and excerpts from manuscripts. Most important of
the large printed documents is Pérez de Rivas, *Crónica y Historia de
la Compañía de Jesús en Nueva España,* which was written between
1648 and 1655 and remained unpublished until 1896, when a limited
and private edition was printed in two volumes. We have used the
volumes in the Ysleta archives and those at the Newberry Library.
Although the work lacks forty-nine of the chapters, it is essential because of its almost contemporary character and because it narrates
the story of all the Jesuit foundations of the sixteenth century. It is
not detailed, and is almost utterly devoid of dates. Alegre certainly
used it, and so did Florencia. The author is better known for his history of the missions, *Historia de los Triunfos de Nuestra Santa Fé,* in
whose making he had passed his earlier years. The spelling of his

name as Rivas rather than Ribas was adopted in order to follow that used in the work cited.

With respect to the chapters on the Institute of the Society, the Constitutions, Spiritual Exercises, and Ratio, I feel that sufficient explanation and bibliography of the sources have been indicated.

SPECIAL AUTHORITIES

For the general setting H. H. Bancroft's *Native Races* and *History of Mexico* are still important as guides. H. I. Priestley's *The Mexican Nation,* while it is a shorter account, must also be rated as an important guide to the materials. For the history of the Church, Mariano Cuevas, *Historia de la Iglesia en México,* may be taken as the most comprehensive and authoritative; the five volumes contain excellent source bibliographies, many documents, and some good pictures mixed with others less good. For a survey history of the whole Spanish Assistancy of the Jesuits, the late Father Antonio Astrain's *Historia de la Compañía de Jesús en la Asistencia de España,* covering the work of the Spanish Jesuits all over the world to the time of the Suppression, is an outstanding work. His source lists are excellent. For the general history of the Mexican province, Father Francisco Alegre, *Historia de la Compañía de Jesús en Nueva España,* stands alone. He was one of the exiled Jesuits, a native of Vera Cruz who had been educated in the Jesuit colleges of Mexico. He wrote his three volumes in Italy, and they are a scholarly year-by-year narration. Gerardo Decorme has a compendium of the history of the province—*La Obra de los Jesuitas en México en la Época Colonial 1572–1767*—which is recently written and is in two typed volumes in Spanish; it may soon be translated and published. Based in the main upon Alegre, it indicates the use of sources for amplifications. A copy is in my possession and another is in the Bancroft collection. For the early history of the province, next to Rivas, Florencia is most important. The author of the *Historia de la Provincia de la Compañía de Jesús de Nueva España* was born in Florida in 1618 and educated at San Ildefonso and the Colegio Máximo in Mexico. He wrote many other books, held important offices in the Society, and was prefect of higher studies in his alma mater. He projected a very exhaustive history, but unfortunately did not get much beyond the provincialate of Pedro Sánchez in his one volume.

The general story of the activities of the Society in New Spain as told by the Jesuit writers is rather complete, and each account has a different flavor; Juan Sánchez wrote his *Carta* about 1582, Rivas his *Crónica* about 1650, Florencia his *Historia* in 1692, and Alegre his general history just after 1767. Supplementary data are taken from well-known writers, Mendieta, Vetancurt, Beaumont, Torquemada, González Dávila, Osores, Veytia, Icazbalceta, Engelhardt, and others. The works of particular value to this special topic have been described in the notes.

WORKS CITED

Acosta, José de, *Historia Natural y Moral de las Indias* (Barcelona, 1591); English version of 1604 is printed in Hakluyt Society works as Vols. LX and LXI.

Adamson, J. W., *Pioneers of Modern Education, 1600–1700* (Cambridge, 1905).

Ambruzzi, A., S.J., *A Companion to the Spiritual Exercises of St. Ignatius* (Magalore, India, 1928; 3d ed., London, 1930).

American Catholic Historical Researches, Vol. XXVI (Washington, 1909).

Anda, Ibarra de, *Geonomia Indígena Mexicana* (Mexico, 1932).

Archivum Historicum Societatis Jesu, published semiannually by the Jesuits at Rome, beginning in 1932. It contains documents and research articles pertaining to the Society.

Astrain, A., *Historia de la Compañía de Jesús en la Asistencia de España* (Madrid, 1902–1925).

—— *A Short Life of St. Ignatius Loyola,* English version by Robert Hull, S.J. (London, 1928).

Bancroft, H. H., *History of Mexico* (San Francisco, 1883–1888).

—— *Native Races* (San Francisco, 1882).

Barnard, H., *Memoirs of Eminent German Teachers and Educators* (Philadelphia, 1863).

Basalenque, Diego (1577–1651), *Historia de la Provincia de San Nicolás de Tolentino, de Michoacán* (Mexico, 1st ed. 1673, 2nd ed. 1886). The Augustinian foundations.

Bayle, Consantino, *España y la Educación Popular en América* (Vitoria, 1934).

Beaumont, Pablo, O.F.M., *Crónica de la Provincia de los Santos Apóstoles S. Pedro y S. Pablo de Michoacán* (Mexico, 1873–1874).

Benítez, José R., *Historia Gráfica de la Nueva España* (Mexico, 1929); has maps, charts, lists of kings, viceroys, university graduates, buildings.

Berganzo, Manuel, *Diccionario y Geografía* (Mexico, 1853).

Beristain y Sousa, José M., *Biblioteca Hispano-Americana Septentrional* (Amecameca, 1883).

Blount, C., *Leading Meditations of the Spiritual Exercises* (London, 1928).

Bolton, H. E., "The Black Robes of Spain," *Catholic Historical Review,* Oct., 1935.

—— "The Epic of Greater America," *American Historical Review,* April, 1933.

—— "The Mission as a Frontier Institution," *American Historical Review*, Oct., 1917.

—— *The Padre on Horseback* (San Francisco, 1932).

—— *Rim of Christendom* (New York, 1936).

—— *The Spanish Borderlands* (New Haven, 1921).

—— *Spanish Exploration of the Southwest* (New York, 1916).

—— and Marshall, T. M., *The Colonization of North America* (New York, 1920).

—— and Ross, Mary, *The Debatable Land* (Berkeley, 1925).

Bonavit, Julián, *Fragmentos de la Historia del Colegio Primitivo y Nacional de San Nicolás de Hidalgo* (Morelia, 1910).

Bourne, E. G., *Spain in America* (New York, 1904).

Burgoa, Francisco de, O.P., *Palestra Historial de Virtudes y Exemplares Apostólicos* (Mexico, 1670); and his second volume, *Geográfica Descripción,* for a brief history of the Dominicans.

Campbell, T. J., S.J., *The Jesuits* (New York, 1921).

Carrez, Louis, S.J., *Atlas Geographicus Societatis Jesu* (Paris, 1900).

Carriedo, Juan B., *Estudios Históricos y Stadísticos del Estado Oaxaqueño* (Oaxaca, 1850).

Catholic Encyclopedia.

Cavo, Andrés, S.J., *Los Tres Siglos de Méjico durante el Gobierno Español* (Mexico, 1836–1838).

Clavigero, F. X., S.J., *Storia Antica del Messico* (Cesena, 1780–1781); the English version is by Charles Cullen (London, 1807). Clavigero, like Cavo, was born in New Spain, like Alegre at Vera Cruz, and all three were products of the Jesuit education of Mexico.

Codina, Arturo, *Los Orígines de los Ejercicios Espirituales de San Ignacio de Loyola* (Barcelona, 1927).

Coester, Alfred, *A Literary History of Spanish America* (New York, 1916, 1928).

Compayré, Gabriel, *The History of Pedagogy,* English version by W. H. Payne (Boston, 1901).

Cubberley, E. P., *A Brief History of Education* (New York, 1922).

—— *The History of Education* (Boston, 1920).

—— *Readings in the History of Education* (Boston, 1920).

Cuevas, Mariano, S.J., *Historia de la Iglesia en México* (El Paso, Texas, 1928).

—— *Orígines del Humanismo en México* (Mexico, 1933).

Decorme, Gerardo, *La Obra de los Jesuitas en México en la Época Colonial,* still in manuscript.

Drane, Theodosia A., *Christian Schools and Scholars* (London, 1881).

Dugout, Ignace Henri, *Nos Martyrs* (Paris, 1900).

Duhr, Bernard, S.J., *Ratio Studiorum et Institutiones Scholasticae Societatis Jesu per Germaniam olim Vigentes* (Berlin, 1887–1894), four volumes of the *Monumenta Germaniae Paedagogica.*

Ecclesiastical Review, Volume LXIX.

Echeverría y Veytia. *See* Veytia.

Engelhardt, Fr. Z., "Friars Minor in America," *Catholic Encyclopedia,* Vol. VI.

—— *The Missions and Missionaries of California* (San Francisco, 1908–1915).

—— "The Earliest Books in the New World," in *Doctrina Breve,* published by United States Catholic Historical Society (New York, 1928).

Fernández, A. F. Alonzo, *Historia Eclesiástica de Nuestros Tiempos* (Toledo, 1611).

Fitzpatrick, E. A., *St. Ignatius and the Ratio Studiorum* (New York, 1933).

Florencia, Francisco de. *See* SPECIAL AUTHORITIES, *supra.*

Franciosi, Xavier, *The Spirit of St. Ignatius* (London, 1906).

Fuente, Vicente de la, *Historia de las Universidades, Colegios . . . en España* (Madrid, 1884–1889).

Fülöp-Miller, René, *The Power and Secret of the Jesuits* (New York, 1930).

Gann, T., and Thompson, J. E., *History of the Maya* (New York, 1931).

García Icazbalceta, Joaquín, *Obras* (Mexico, 1885).

—— *Bibliografía Mexicana del Siglo XVI* (Mexico, 1886).

—— "La Instrucción Pública en México," version in English by W. J. O'Donnell in *Historical Records and Studies,* Vol. XX (New York, 1931).

Garraghan, G. J., "George Washington, Man of Character," *Mid-America,* Vol. XVII, N. S. VI.

Goldt, John T., "Our Florida Martyr Priests," *Ecclesiastical Review,* Vol. LXIX.

Gómara, Francisco López de, *Crónica de la Nueva España* (Çaragoça, 1555).

González Dávila, Gil, *Teatro Eclesiástica* (Madrid, 1649–1655).

González Obregón, Luis, *México Viejo, 1521–1821* (new ed.; Mexico, 1900).

Goodier, Archbishop Alban, *The Jesuits* (New York, 1930).

Goodsell, Willystine, *The Conflict of Naturalism and Humanism* (New York, 1910).

Griffen, J. A., *The Contribution of Belgium to the Catholic Church in America* (Washington, 1932).

Grijalva, Juan de, *Crónica de la Orden de Nuestro Padre San Agustín en las Provincias de la Nueva España* (Mexico, 1624).

Hayes, C. J. H., *A Political and Social History of Modern Europe,* Vol. I (New York, 1933).

Herman, J. B., *La Pédagogie des Jésuites au XVIe Siecle* (Louvain, 1914).

Hispanic American Historical Review. Cited under Leonard.

Historical Records and Studies, Vols. XX and XXV.

Hughes, T., S.J., *History of the Society of Jesus in North America* (New York, 1917).

—— *Loyola and the Educational System of the Jesuits* (New York, 1892).

Hull, R., *A Short Life of Ignatius Loyola,* translated from Astrain.

Hyma, A., *The Christian Renaissance* (Grand Rapids, Michigan, 1924).

Inglis, A., *The Principles of Secondary Education* (New York, 1918).

Jouvency, Joseph, S.J., *Ratio discendi et docendi* (Paris, 1778).

Kane, W., *An Essay Toward a History of Education* (Chicago, 1935).

Kenny, M., *The Romance of the Floridas* (Milwaukee, 1934).

Laurie, S. S., *Institutes of Education* (3d ed.; New York, 1909).

—— *Studies in the History of Educational Opinions from the Renaissance* (Cambridge, 1903).

León, Nicolás, *Señor Don Vasco de Quiroga* (Mexico, no date, possibly 1904).

Leonard, Irving, "A Shipment of Comedias to the Indies," *Hispanic American Historical Review,* Jan., 1934.

Lowery, Woodbury, *Spanish Settlements Within the Present Limits of the United States* (New York; Vol. I, 1905; Vol. II, 1911).

McCormick, P. J., *History of Education* (Washington, 1915).

McGucken, W., *The Jesuits and Education* (New York, 1932).

Mecham, J. Lloyd, *Francisco de Ibarra and Nueva Vizcaya* (Duke University Press, 1927).

Medina, José Toribio, *La Imprenta en Mexico, Epitome 1539–1810* (Seville, 1893).

Mendieta, Gerónimo de, *Historia Eclesiástica Indiana* (Mexico, 1870).

Monroe, P., *A Cyclopedia of Education* (New York, 1911–1913).

O'Donnell, W. J., "Public Instruction in the City of Mexico in the Sixteenth Century," translation of García Icazbalceta's article, *q.v.*

Oswald, A., *Commentarius in Decem Partes Constitutionum Societatis Jesu* (Paris, 1845).

Pachtler, G. M., *Geschichte der Studienordnung der Gesellschaft,* Vol. XVI of *Monumenta Germaniae Paedagogica* (Berlin, 1887–1894).

Pastells, Pablo, *Historia General de Filipinas* (Barcelona, 1926).

Pastor, Ludwig von, *History of the Popes* (trans.; St. Louis, 1912–).

Paulsen, Friederich, *Geschichte des gelehrten Unterrichts auf den deutschen Schulen und Universitäten vom Ausgang des Mittelalters bis zur Gegenwart* (Leipzig, 1896–1897).

Peña, Alberto Pérez, *El Colegio del Estado de Puebla* (Puebla, 1931).

Pereyra, C., *La Obra de España en América* (Madrid, 1920).

Pérez de Ribas (Rivas), Andrés, *Historia de los Triúnfos de Nuestra Santa Fé* (Madrid, 1645). His *Crónica* is noted in the special bibliography above.

Pimentel, Francisco, *Obras Completas* (Mexico, 1903–1904).

Polanco, Juan de, *Vita Ignatii Loiolae,* in *Monumenta Historica S. J.*

Prat, J. M., *Histoire du P. Ribadeneira* (Paris, 1862).

Prescott, W. H., *History of the Conquest of Mexico* (New York, 1844).

Priestley, H. I., *The Coming of the White Man* (New York, 1929).

—— *The Mexican Nation, A History* (New York, 1930).

—— "The Old University of Mexico," *University of California Chronicle,* Vol. XXI, No. 4.

Quesada, Vicente G., *La Vida Intelectual en la América Española durante los Siglos XVI, XVII, XVIII* (Buenos Aires, 1910).

Quick, R. H., *Essays on Educational Reformers* (New York, 1890).

Rashdall, Hastings, *The Universities of Europe in the Middle Ages* (Oxford, 1895).

Raumer, Karl von, *Geschichte der Pädagogik vom Wiederaufblühen klassischer Studien bis auf unsere Zeit* (Stuttgart, 1857).

Ribadeneira, P., *Tratado del Gobierno de Nuestro P. Ignacio* (Madrid, 1594).

—— *Vida del Padre Francisco Borgia* (Madrid, 1592).

Ricard, Robert, *La conquête spirituelle du Mexique 1521–1572* (Paris, 1933).

Rippy, J. Fred, *Historical Evolution of Hispanic America* (New York, 1932).

Rose, Stewart (pseud. of Lady Buchan), *Ignatius Loyola and the Early Jesuits* (London, 1891).

Sahagún, Bernardino de, *Historia General de las Cosas de Nueva España* (Mexico ed., 1829–1830; Madrid, 1905); translation of one volume by Fanny Bandelier, *History of Ancient Mexico* (Fisk University Press, 1932).

Salazar, F. C., *México en 1554* (Mexico, 1875).

Schmitt, L., *Synopsis Historiae Societatis Jesu* (Ratisbon, 1914).

Schwickerath, R., *Jesuit Education* (St. Louis, 1904).

Shea, John Gilmary, *History of the Catholic Church in the United States* (Akron, 1886). Also his "Ancient Florida" *in* Winsor, Vol. II.

Shiels, W. E., *Gonzalo de Tapia* (New York, 1934).

Smith, Preserved, *History of Modern Culture* (New York, 1930).

Sommervogel, Carlos, *Bibliothèque de la Compagnie de Jésus* (Brussels, 1890). Sommervogel continued and reëdited the earlier bibliographies of Jesuit authors by de Backer and Carayon; Pedro Ribadeneira really inaugurated the work about 1600.

Spinden, H. J., *Ancient Civilizations of Mexico* (New York, 1928).

Suárez, Francisco, *Opera* (Paris, 1860). The "De Religione Societatis Jesu" is cited as Vol. XVI, Bk. IV.

Taylor, H. O., *Thought and Expression in the Sixteenth Century* (New York, 1930).

Torquemada, Juan de, *Monarquía Indiana* (Seville, 1615).

Ugarte, Rubén V., S.J., "The First Jesuit Mission in Florida," *Historical Records and Studies,* Vol. XXV (New York, 1935).

Valle, R. H., *El Convento de Tepotzotlán* (Mexico, 1924).

Van Ginneken, J., S.J., *De Navolging van Christus* (Louvain, 1930); unpublished translation by Joseph Malaise, S.J., San Francisco.

Veitia Linaje, José de, *Norte de la Contratación de las Indias Occidentales* (Seville, 1672).

Vera, González, *De los Primeros Misioneros en Nueva España* (Madrid, 1868).

Vetancurt, Augustín de, *Teatro Mexicano* (Mexico, 1870).

Veytia, Mariano F. Echeverría y, *Historia Antigua de Mexico* (published in Mexico, 1836, by C. F. Ortega).

——— *Historia de la Fundación de la Ciudad de Puebla de los Angeles en Nueva España* (published in Puebla, 1931, by Fidel Solis).

Watson, Foster, *Luis Vives* (Oxford, 1922).

Winsor, Justin, *Narrative and Critical History of America* (Boston, 1884–1889).

Zepeda Rincón, Tomás, *La Instrucción Pública en la Nueva España en el Siglo XVI* (Mexico, 1933).

NOTES TO CHAPTER I

[1] Carrez, Louis, *Atlas Geographicus Societatis Jesu* (Paris, 1900), has maps illustrating the extent of the activities of the Society, with enumerations of its establishments, etc.

[2] For a bibliography of lives of Ignatius from Jesuit pens see Sommervogel, Carlos, *Bibliothèque de la Compagnie de Jésus* (11 vols.; Brussels, 1890); Vol. V, pp. 59–124, lists 73 biographers. Astrain, A., *Historia de la Compañia de Jesús en la Asistencia de España* (Madrid, 1902–1925), Vol. I, has a source bibliography (this work will be cited hereafter as Astrain). Much has been printed in the 36 volumes entitled *Monumenta Historica Societatis Jesu* (Madrid, 1894), and the 9 volumes of *Monumenta Ignatiana. The Autobiography of St. Ignatius* is translated by E. M. Rix (London, 1900). An excellent brief account is that of Astrain, A., *A Short Life of St. Ignatius Loyola,* translated by Robert Hull (London, 1928).

[3] Goodier, Archbishop Alban, *The Jesuits* (New York, 1930), pp. 20–21, argues that Ignatius at heart was not a soldier but a courtier—soldiers were mercenary, courtiers served the king through loyalty.

[4] Photostat copies of the autograph copy are in most Jesuit houses. The best English version of the text is Mullan, Elder, *The Spiritual Exercises of St. Ignatius of Loyola* (New York, 1914). For the study of beginnings see Codina, Arturo, *Los Orígines de los Ejercicios Espirituales de San Ignacio de Loyola* (Barcelona, 1927). For a description of the work in its general historical setting see Pastor, L., *History of the Popes* (St. Louis, 1912–), XII, 1–24; in its relations to the history of the Company, see Astrain, Vol. I, Bk. I. Suárez, Francisco, *Opera* (Paris, 1860), Vol. XVI, "De Religione," Bk. IV, pp. 1017–1034, gives its canonical setting. Among the many commentaries in various languages the following are most useful: Meschler, Maurice, *The Spiritual Exercises of St. Ignatius* (Woodstock College, Maryland, 1889); Ambruzzi, A., *A Companion to the Spiritual Exercises of St. Ignatius* (3d ed.; London, 1930). For a synoptical example there is Blount, Charles, *Leading Meditations of the Spiritual Exercises* (London, 1928), which omits many details and emphasizes the chain of thirteen meditations. These are select works; for a full bibliography consult Sommervogel, *op. cit.,* and the sources, *Monumenta Ignatiana,* as cited.

[5] *Institutum Societatis Jesu* (see n. 14, *infra*), Vol. I, a compendium of bulls of approbations and privileges, gives 180 such from twenty-seven popes.

[6] Suárez, *op. cit.,* "De Religione," Bk. IV, pp. 1017 f.

[7] Cubberley, E. P., *A Brief History of Education* (New York, 1922), pp. 167, 172, 201.

[8] I do not intend here to convey the notion that the Catholic Church of the present day deviates from olden beliefs in these matters.

[9] This is getting at the fundamental reason behind the obedience which is indicated as the cause of their success by Fülöp-Miller, R., *The Power and Secret of the Jesuits* (New York, 1930).

[10] Compayré, Gabriel, *The History of Pedagogy,* translated by W. H. Payne (Boston, 1901), is among those who have made egregious mistakes regarding the classes of people taught by the Jesuits. According to him, p. 143, they instructed only the upper class.

[11] The official approval was given by Pope Paul III in the bull *Regimini Militantis,* September 27, 1540.

[12] Franciosi, Xavier de, *The Spirit of St. Ignatius,* translated from the French (2d ed.; London, 1906), is a good analysis.

[13] Incidentally, one portion of the Constitutions, known as the rules of modesty, or etiquette, came into the hands of George Washington, who called them his "Rules of Civility"; see Garraghan, G. J., "George Washington, Man of Character," *Mid-America,* Vol. XVII, N.S. VI, No. 1, p. 47. Similar adaptations of the rules seem to have been used in many non-Jesuit schools.

[14] *Institutum Societatis Jesu,* best edition, Florence, 1892. Vol. I contains No. 1; Vol. II contains Nos. 2, 3, 4, and 5; Vol. III contains the rest. There is also the *Epitome Instituti Societatis Jesu* in one volume; the last edition is from Rome, 1931. Sommervogel has an account of the many editions, *op. cit.,* V, 75–115, and IX, 609–611. For the commentators see *ibid.,* X, 705–710. In English, probably the best commentary is Humphrey, S., *The Religious State,* which follows Suárez, "De Religione." There are various Latin editions of Oswald, A., *Commentarius in Decem Partes Constitutionum Societatis Jesu* (Paris, 1845). Equally good is Fine, Edward, *Juris Regularis . . . Declaratio* (Prati, 1919). It is rather useless to begin a list of authors other than Jesuits who have commented upon the Institute; no one has done a scholarly work in English upon this subject, so extremely difficult for those outside the Society.

[15] Fitzpatrick, Edward A., *St. Ignatius and the Ratio Studiorum* (New York, 1933); McGucken, W., *The Jesuits and Education* (New York, 1932).

[16] Franciosi, *op. cit.,* chap. xxv.

[17] Smith, Preserved, *History of Modern Culture* (New York, 1930), p. 363, summarizes the government of the Society as a "despotic concentration of authority." Like most superficial observers he neglects the salient spiritual element of the government.

[18] *Constitutions,* Part IX, chap. iii.

[19] *Ibid.,* Part IX, chap. iv.

[20] *Ibid.,* Part IV, chap. viii.

[21] *Ibid.,* Part VIII, chap. ii.

[22] Bulla *Exposcit Debitum,* July 21, 1550.

[23] Bulla *Ecclesiae Catholicae,* June 28, 1590.

NOTES TO CHAPTER II

[1] Corcoran, T., *Renatae Litterae Saeculo a Chr. XVI in Scholis Societatis Jesu Stabilitae* (Dublin, 1927), Part I, publishes in Latin the documents regarding the beginnings of Jesuit teachers and schools.

[2] Bull of Pope Paul III, *Regimini Militantis Ecclesiae*, September 27, 1540; Astrain, Vol. I, chap. ii, has a good account of the early religious teaching of the Company.

[3] Astrain, I, 206, recounts briefly his early life; see Prat, J. M., *Histoire du P. Ribadeneira* (Paris, 1862), for his complete life and tribulations. For his own account of himself cf. *Monumenta Historica Societatis Jesu,* "Ribadeneira" (Maddrid, 1920), I, 10 ff.

[4] Herman, J. B., *La Pédagogie des Jésuites au XVIᵉ Siècle* (Louvain, 1914), p. 8.

[5] Astrain, Vol. I, chap. v.

[6] Fitzpatrick, *op. cit.,* Part I.

[7] Letter of Father Segura to the general from Havana, Nov. 18, 1568, translated and published in *Historical Records and Studies* (New York, 1935), XXV, 100.

[8] Adamson, J. W., *Pioneers of Modern Education* (Cambridge, 1905), p. 13.

[9] Cubberley, E. P., *The History of Education* (Boston, 1920), with many others, misses this point completely, pp. 336–344. Even more does Danby, R. H., *The Causes of the French Revolution,* as quoted by Cubberley, *loc. cit.,* miss the motivating force of the Jesuits. The spirit is indicated in the many letters of the generals (*Epistolae Generalium*) to the whole Society.

[10] Raumer, Karl von, *Geschichte der Pädagogik vom Wiederaufblühen klassischer Studien bis auf unsere Zeit* (Stuttgart, 1857), I, 270, manifests a bias against the Jesuits, accusing them of theft. Bernard, Henry, in his *Memoirs of Eminent German Teachers and Educators* (Philadelphia, 1863), p. 228, translates the memoir of von Raumer regarding "The Jesuits and their Schools"; the purpose of von Raumer is best stated on p. 250, that is, to warn Lutherans that "to view aright these gloomy and sinister institutions of the Jesuits with their dark, joyless, soul-destroying aims, it will be well to call to our minds the open-hearted admonitions of Luther to his beloved Germans, admonitions prompted by the love of a true pastor."

[11] See Cubberley, E. P., *Readings in the History of Education* (Boston, 1920), p. 211, for Sturm's plan; Quick, R. H., *Essays on Educational Reformers* (New York, 1890), in chap. iii for Sturm. Schwickerath, R., *Jesuit Education* (St. Louis, 1904), pp. 140–141, comes to an agreement with Paulsen, F., *Geschichte des gelehrten Unterrichts auf den deutschen Schulen und Universitäten vom Ausgang des Mittelalters bis zur Gegenwart* (Leipzig, 1896–1897), I, 412, both writers holding the improbability of Jesuit pedagogical origins from Sturm and indicating the probability of Sturm's dependence on the Brethren of the Common Life for his system.

[12] Sturm, J., *Classicarum Epistolarum*, Bk. III. As translated in Monroe, P., *A Cyclopedia of Education* (New York, 1911–1913), art. *sub* Sturm, it has just the opposite sense, namely, that Sturm copied from the Jesuits.

[13] For fuller discussions of the origins of Jesuit pedagogy as distinct from the spirit animating their efforts, see McGucken, *op. cit.*, chap. ii (gives good bibliography); Herman, *op. cit.*, chap. i;—both of whom have the Jesuit Ratio. Fitzpatrick, *op. cit.*, discusses this in the whole of Part I as introduction to his translation of the Ratio. Corcoran, T., *Renovatio Litterarum in Scholis Saeculi a C. XVI Deducta* (Dublin, 1925), has in Latin a list of pertinent documents, which are statements by the great educators of that period upon educational ideals and aims. The same author in *Renatae Litterae* publishes (1) documents pertaining to the beginnings of Jesuit teachers and schools (see reference, n. 1, above), and (2) the Ratio from 1550 to 1599 with the various Jesuit plans—the First Ratio in 1586, the Intermediate of 1591, before the *Definitiva* of 1599. Hughes, Thomas, *Loyola and the Educational System of the Jesuits* (New York, 1892), is authoritative; Schwickerath, R., *op. cit.*, gives the history and principles, with good bibliography, but is rather apologetic. Most important for the Ratio are *Monumenta Historica Societatis Jesu* as cited, but especially installments 93, 97, 99, 100, 101, and 194, which are entitled *Monumenta Paedagogica* (Madrid, 1901–1902); these are not to be confused with *Monumenta Germaniae Paedagogica*, edited by Dr. Karl Kehrback, of which Volumes II, V, IX, and XVI by Pachtler, G. M., pertain to the Jesuits and are republished in four volumes under the title *Ratio Studiorum et Institutiones Scholasticae Societatis Jesu per Germaniam olim Vigentes* (Berlin, 1887–1894), the last volume being edited by Bernard Duhr; Jouvancy, J., *Josephi Jouvencii Ratio discendi et docendi* (Paris, 1778), has the principles, but for post-sixteenth-century teachers.

[14] McGucken gives these similarities, p. 25. For a good summary of Vives see McCormick, P. J., *History of Education* (Washington, 1915), pp. 195–204. For a complete study see Watson, Foster, *Luis Vives* (Oxford, 1922). But Ignatius ordered that the writings of Vives be dropped from Jesuit school curricula (*Monumenta Ignatiana*, Series I, Vol. V, pp. 56, 421).

[15] So Pedro Ribadeneira, and other young members.

[16] Thus, Goodsell, Willystine, *The Conflict of Naturalism and Humanism* (New York, 1910), chap. i, proposing the materialistic concept of education in the opening sentence of her introduction, leaves the impression that reason awakened in the fifteenth century. Laurie, S. S., *Studies in the History of Educational Opinions from the Renaissance* (Cambridge, 1903), in chap. i, makes the "medieval house a dark prison of the intellect." Chap. viii pertains to the Jesuits, whose success is explained by their organization.

[17] On the Brethren, consult Hyma, Albert, *The Christian Renaissance* (Grand Rapids, Michigan, 1924), especially pp. 122–134. Hyma bases the whole of the Christian Renaissance upon the work of Groote and his followers. Lately there comes the complete edition of Groote's *De Navolging van Christus* so edited that the additions and changes of à Kempis' *Imitation of Christ* stand out in

254 EDUCATION IN NEW SPAIN: THE JESUITS

blue type. The editor is Van Ginneken, J., S.J., 1930, whose introduction is important for this matter. The MS translation of this whole scholarly work is before me, done into English by the Rev. Joseph Malaise, S.J. Taylor, Henry Osborn, *Thought and Expression in the Sixteenth Century* (New York, 1930), I, 142 f., gives an account of the Brethren in their cultural setting.

[18] Herman, *op. cit.,* chap. iv.

[19] Other treatments are: Schwickerath, *op. cit.,* chap. xv, p. 415; McGucken, *op. cit.,* chap. xii, p. 241. Magevney, E., *The Jesuits as Educators* (St. Mary's, Kansas, 1906), has a very short account.

[20] McGucken, *op. cit.,* p. 242, gives a detailed account of the requirements from sources.

[21] In 1550 the novices lived in the house of the professed fathers of the Society at Rome (*Monumenta Historica, Vita Ignatii Loiolae,* the chronicle written by the secretary of Ignatius, Juan de Polanco, II, 6).

[22] *Historical Records and Studies,* XXV, 140. Mention is made here of the youths who had joined the missionaries in Florida; the document is the "Brief Narrative of the martyrdom of the fathers and brothers," by Jaime Martínez. See also *ibid.,* p. 64, for editorial discussion by the Rev. Rubén Ugarte, S.J.

[23] Letter of Father Ignatius Azevedo to Francis Borgia from Brazil, March 11, 1569, published in *Monumenta Historica, S. Francis Borgia,* V, 27–30.

[24] Various items about novitiate activities and training may be gleaned from the *Monumenta Historica,* which contains the letters of Ignatius and succeeding generals, the chronicle of Polanco, letters to the generals, etc. The study of these is too great to enter upon here, but sample documents utilized are found in *Monumenta Ignatiana,* Series III, Vol. I (Rome, 1934); Series IV (Madrid, 1904), Vol. I, 171, 278–280, 411, 413; *Vita Ignatii Loiolae,* II, 6; *S. Francis Borgia,* V, 27–30, 253–254, 795, 813.

[25] The account of scholastic studies which follows is made in the manner indicated in the preceding footnote. Besides the *Ratio,* Polanco's *Vita Ignatii Loiolae* contains summaries in pp. 166, 214, 216, 221, 420–421, 444.

[26] *Institutum,* Part IV, chap. iii, or Fitzpatrick, *op. cit.,* pp. 167–174, for the translation; here the general and particular objectives are given together with rules for lectures.

[27] Laurie, S. S., *Institutes of Education* (3d ed.; New York, 1909), pp. 16 ff., indicates how important philosophy is to the formation of a conscious ideal of life.

[28] McGucken, *op. cit.,* p. 251.

[29] *Monumenta Paedagogica S. J.,* p. 651. The rules of the scholastics are contained here in pp. 650–656 *et passim.*

[30] *Ibid.,* pp. 471–478.

[31] Laurie, *op. cit.,* p. 364, on the need of such training. Among many others, Ambruzzi, A., *A Companion to the Spiritual Exercises of St. Ignatius* (Magalore, India, 1928), expresses the Catholic aim, p. 370.

[32] *Epitome Instituti S. J.,* pp. 181–186.

[33] *Ibid.,* pp. 186–196.

NOTES TO CHAPTER III

[1] Acosta, José de, *Historia Natural y Moral de las Indias* (Barcelona, 1591), translated in 1604 into English, reprinted in 1880 in the Works of the Hakluyt Society as Vols. LX and LXI, or *History of the Indies,* Vols. I and II; the present citation is from the latter, II, 396. See also Vetancurt, Augustín de, *Teatro Mexicano* (Mexico, 1870), I, 451. A short account is in Gann, T., and Thompson, J. E., *History of the Maya* (New York, 1931), p. 170.

[2] Acosta, *op. cit.,* II, 396. The natives were not stupid, and historians invariably comment upon their mental alertness. A stout defender of the native character is Clavigero, F. X., *Storia Antica del Messico* (4 vols.; Cesena, 1780–1781: English ed. by Charles Cullen, London, 1807); see especially Vol. I, Bk. VII, and Vol. II, Bk. VIII, in the English edition, pp. 328, 338, 363–373.

[3] John Amos Comenius (1592–1671), a leading European teacher, is given generous attention in educational textbooks as the foremost representative of sense realism; e.g., by Cubberley, E. P., *History of Education* (Boston, 1920), pp. 408–416. His methods were being applied in a less perfect way in America a century before his picture-book appeared in Europe.

[4] For details of this early native education consult Bancroft, H. H., *Native Races,* II, 240–251, 338–340, 401–402, 492–493, and III, 432, 437. Sahagún, Bernardino de, *History of Ancient Mexico,* translated by Fanny R. Bandelier (Fisk University Press, 1932), pp. 194–203, gives the purpose and process of native education.

[5] Acosta, *op. cit.,* II, 333.

[6] *Ibid.,* II, 404, 442.

[7] Drane, Theodosia A., *Christian Schools and Scholars* (London, 1881), pp. 552, 724, has descriptions of similar European schools.

[8] Engelhardt, Fr. Z., *Missions and Missionaries of California* (San Francisco, 1908–1915), I, 10.

[9] His picture is in Cuevas, Mariano, *Historia de la Iglesia en México* (El Paso, Texas, 1928), I, 10 (to be cited hereafter as Cuevas). Vetancurt, *op. cit.,* IV, 213, has an account of Gante and his obituary; the letter, containing much information written by Gante, is published in Cuevas, I, 159–161, and in Vera, González, *De los Primeros Misioneros en Nueva España* (Madrid, 1868). There is a brief account of Gante and a translation of the said letter in Griffen, J. A., *The Contribution of Belgium to the Catholic Church in America* (Washington, 1932), p. 7 (this work is Vol. XII of the Catholic University of America *Studies in American Church History*). Mendieta, Gerónimo de, *Historia Eclesiástica Indiana* (Mexico, 1870), pp. 220 ff., has a good deal on Gante; more recent is the fine contribution of Chavez, Ezequiel A., *El Primero de los Grandes Educadores de la América, Fray Pedro de Gante* (Mexico, 1934).

[10] Cuevas, I, 158.

[11] Mendieta, *op. cit.,* p. 222.

[12] *Ibid.,* p. 262.

[13] Letter of Gante, January 27, 1529, in Cuevas, *loc. cit.*

[14] This housing plan and the method of instruction in its physical aspects were similar to what Europe had known for centuries; for contrast between the two places consult Vetancurt, *op. cit.,* III, 22 f., and Drane, *op. cit.,* pp. 13, 110, 133, 469. The instruction was like that of the Lancastrian monitorial system established almost three centuries later, of which Cubberley, *op. cit.,* p. 624, has a description.

[15] García Icazbalceta, Joaquín, "La Instrucción Pública en México," a very readable essay on the subject of education in his *Obras,* Vol. II; translated by W. J. O'Donnell in *Historical Records and Studies,* Vol. XX (New York, 1931), where the present citation is found, p. 99. Another good survey is the master's thesis of Zepeda Rincón, Tomás, *La Instrucción Pública en la Nueva España en el Siglo XVI* (Mexico, 1933), though its sources are rather secondary. Kane, William, *An Essay Toward a History of Education* (Chicago, 1935), chap. xx, has a very notable survey of education in colonial America.

[16] Bancroft, Hubert H., *History of Mexico* (San Francisco, 1883–1888), II, 675. (This work will be cited hereafter as Bancroft.)

[17] Medina, José Toribio, *La Imprenta en México, Epítome 1539–1810* (Seville, 1893), p. 101, records Gante's *Catecismo* of 1553.

[18] Torquemada, Juan de, *Monarquía Indiana* (Seville, 1615), Bk. XX, chap. xxxiii, says of the Franciscans: "In 1531 they cared for 500 boys in nearly 20 establishments, and in others many more."

[19] Cuevas, I, 158.

[20] *Catholic Encyclopedia,* VI, 299, art. "Friars Minor in America," by Father Engelhardt.

[21] Mendieta, *op. cit.,* III, 418; Vetancurt, *Menologia,* p. 67.

[22] Cuevas, I, 396; the chapter is on the origins of public education. *Libro de Cabildo* records the grant of land for July 12, 1529.

[23] How widespread the evil of natural children was is unknown. Icazbalceta, *La Instrucción,* in the translation cited, p. 112, says it called forth a cedula as late as 1553, and his observation would lead one to suppose that the mestizo school was founded much later than 1529. There is still some confusion among writers between the earlier clinic and primary school and the later college of the same name.

[24] *Recopilación,* Lib. I, Tit. 23, Ley 14, and *Cedulario de Puga* (Mexico, 1879), II, 198–201.

[25] Icazbalceta, *La Instrucción,* as cited, p. 115.

[26] *Monumenta Historica, Vita Ignatii Loiolae,* IV, 397. Cuevas, I, 393, has Pesquera's letter to Ignatius.

[27] Alegre, Francisco, *Historia de la Compañía de Jesús en Nueva España* (Mexico, 1842), I, 180. (This work will be cited hereafter as Alegre).

[28] Cuevas, I, 386, gives the letter.

[29] Mendieta, *op. cit.,* Bk. IV, chap. xv, p. 115, has a good account of the college, and a defense of Latin teaching; and see Sahagún, Bernardino de, *Historia General de las Cosas de Nueva España* (Mexico, 1830), III, 80.

[30] Mendieta, *op. cit.,* 403; Sahagún, *op. cit.,* III, 70.

[31] Cuevas, I, 386. The college was sometimes called Santiago Tlatelolco, after the name of the adjacent convent.

[32] Sahagún, *op. cit.,* III, 84.

[33] In Cuevas, I, 388.

[34] Letter of Fray de la Cruz is to Charles V, October 20, 1541, in Cuevas, I, 389.

[35] Cuevas, I, 390.

[36] Sahagún, *op. cit.,* III, 83.

[37] Icazbalceta, as cited, p. 114. Bishop Sebastián Ramírez de Fuenleal was apparently interested in the study of Latin. In a letter to the king dated April 30, 1532, he endeavors to obtain a position for one Cristóbal de Campaña who had taught grammar for three years in Santo Domingo. The letter is in Cárdenas y Espejo, *Colección de Documentos Inéditos* (Madrid, 1870), Vol. XIII, p. 206; the remark is on p. 220 of the same.

[38] Priestley, H. I., "The Old University of Mexico," originally printed in *University of California Chronicle,* Vol. XXI, No. 4, has an excellent account of the origin and development of the University of Mexico.

[39] *Recopilación,* Lib. I, Tit. 22, pp. 110–121.

[40] By Priestley, *The Old University of Mexico;* useful also is Zepeda Rincón, *op. cit.,* pp. 99–116.

[41] Dugout, Ignace Henri, *Nos Martyrs* (Paris, 1900), a privately published catalogue which gives full statistics concerning Jesuits who were killed to 1773. Before 1572, 85 had been killed in Europe and in the missions; before 1773 the number was 907. Campbell, T. J., *The Jesuits* (New York, 1921), p. 90, refers to the early missionary martyrs.

[42] Valence, France, had witnessed the spectacle of a Jesuit, Fr. Auger, tied to the stake for burning; he was released at a critical moment: Rose, Stewart, *Ignatius Loyola and the Early Jesuits* (London, 1891), p. 342. For English and Irish Jesuits consult Foley, Henry, *Records of the English Province,* First Series (London, 1879), Vol. VII, Part I, Introduction.

[43] *Monumenta Historica, S. Francis Borgia,* Vol. IV, Letter 553.

[44] Schmitt, L., *Synopsis Historiae Societatis Jesu* (Ratisbon, 1914), summary to column 57.

[45] *Recopilación,* Lib. I, Tit. 14, where there are eleven pages of laws regarding priests going to the Indies.

[46] Such inferences are drawn by many writers, e.g., Steinmetz, B., *A History of the Jesuits* (Philadelphia, 1848); McCabe, Jos., *A Candid History of the Jesuits* (New York, 1913), p. 44. The latter is an outstanding vilification of the Society, the former of its leaders and missions.

[47] *Monumenta Historica, S. Francis Borgia,* Vol. IV, Letter 562; consult also *Archivum Historicum Societatis Jesu,* January-May, 1932, for a summary of article by P. Leturia in *Illumina* which gives this new view.

[48] Pastor, L. von, *History of the Popes* (London, 1899–1932), Vol. XVIII, chaps. i and ii.

[49] At least this is one interpretation of the terse statement of Ignatius found in *Monumenta Ignatiana,* First Series, Vol. II, p. 302, in a letter to Frs. Strada and Turriano from Rome, Jan. 12, 1549: "Al México inbíen, si le pareze, haziendo que sean pedidos, ó sin serlo."

[50] Florencia, Francisco de, *Historia de la Provincia de la Compañía de Jesús de Nueva España* (Mexico, 1694), Bk. I, chap. i, records the requests. (This work will be cited hereafter as Florencia.)

NOTES TO CHAPTER IV

[1] Bolton, H. E., *The Spanish Borderlands* (New Haven, 1921), has a survey of this, chaps. i, ii, iii, and v; Lowery, Woodbury, *Spanish Settlements Within the Present Limits of the United States,* Vol. I, 1513–1561 (Putnam, 1905), Vol. II, 1562–1574 (Putnam, 1911), *passim;* Priestley, H. I., *The Coming of the White Man* (New York, 1929), chap. iii.

[2] Shea, John G., *History of the Catholic Church in the United States* (4 vols.; Akron, 1886), I, 135–150, has a brief treatment of the missionary work; better than this is his "Ancient Florida," *in* Winsor, Justin, *Narrative and Critical History of America* (Boston, 1884–1889), II, chap. iv. Lowery, *op. cit.,* gives particular attention to the missionaries.

[3] Deaths at the hands of the natives were not peculiar to Florida; within the present limits of the United States, eleven Franciscans, eight Jesuits, and two Dominicans were violently killed before 1606. Cf. *American Catholic Historical Researches* (New York), XXVI (1909), 280; Bolton, *The Spanish Borderlands,* chap. v; and Goldt, John T., "Our Florida Martyr Priests," *Ecclesiastical Review,* LXIX, 498–513, 614–631. (Other accounts are cited just below.)

[4] There is no attempt here to explain either the constructive work of Menéndez or his policy of utilizing the Jesuits in the Florida advance; for this, consult Lowery, *op. cit.,* II, 264–275, and Appendix EE, p. 461, where there is a discussion of evidence concerning the Jesuits' attempt to find a strait to China via the Potomac and Rappahanock. This with the evidence quoted by Hughes, Thomas, *History of the Society of Jesus in North America* (New York, 1917), II, 213, regarding the Sinaloa Missions as a stepping stone to Japan, might lead one to suppose that the Jesuits in both Florida and New Spain were driving toward the Orient and were not much interested in America. More recent in this field are Kenny, Michael, *The Romance of the Floridas* (Milwaukee, 1934), p. 93, and Lanning, John T., *The Spanish Missions of Georgia* (Chapel Hill, N. C., 1935), chap. ii.

[5] Alegre, I, 18, 22, 24; Lowery, *op. cit.,* II, 339; Hughes, *op. cit.,* p. 212. Bolton and Ross, *The Debatable Land* (Berkeley, 1925), is an excellent summary.

[6] Florencia, p. 65, and Alegre, I, 66; for other letters consult Winsor, *op. cit.,* II, 282. See also *Historical Records and Studies,* Vol. XXV (New York, 1935), which contains documents and letters under the title "The First Jesuit Mission in Florida," by Rubén V. Ugarte, p. 59. Astrain, II, 640, has a letter of Rogel dated August 28, 1572.

[7] There is likely to be some dispute about the use of the word martyrdom; subjectively, their sacrifice of life was martyrdom for the Jesuits, but in the sense in which the Church uses the term the victims must have been slain out of hatred of the Faith in order to merit the title of martyr. Did the natives know what the Faith was, or did they kill the Jesuits as enemies and Spaniards? *Nos Martyrs,* pp. 10–12, gives the names and dates.

[8] Florencia, p. 65; they were Fathers Sedeño and Rogel, lay brothers Salvatierra, Carrera, and Villarreal, and the novice Salcedo.

[9] Pérez de Rivas, Andrés, *Crónica y Historia de la Provincia de la Compañía de Jesús de México en Nueva España* (written 1648–1655, published privately 1896, Mexico), I, 13 (cited hereafter as Rivas); Alegre, I, 45. Both of these Jesuit writers cite the letters of invitation, as does Florencia, but Astrain, II, 299, says he cannot find them. The purpose of the Jesuit writers in emphasizing the requests for the Company was probably to show that the fathers did not wish to intrude where they were not entirely welcome.

[10] The *Carta al Rey* is in Florencia, p. 71. Shiels, W. E., *Gonzalo de Tapia* (New York, 1934), pp. 22 ff., gives some details of Mexican life, and a translation of two cedulas.

[11] It must be remembered that the *Cabildo* was pleading a cause and hence was more likely to overstate than to understate its case. It made haste to say that the other religious orders were doing excellent work; still, that the field was too vast for them.

[12] See *Monumenta Historica S. J.,* especially the section devoted to the *Cartas* de San Francisco de Borja, for numerous letters of Borgia which bring out his spirit; also Ribadeneira, Pedro, *Vida del Padre Francisco Borgia* (Madrid, 1592). The author grew up in the Society, knew all its early members, their ideals, and their plans, by reason of his long residence and secretaryship at Rome.

[13] Alegre, I, 46–47. Letter of appointment of Borgia to Sánchez, 15 July, 1571. Bancroft, II, p. 706, gives an account of Sánchez. Alegre, II, 18, has a character sketch, as has Florencia (in Bk. VIII). Cuevas, II, 332, presents his picture. Rivas, I, 316–329, gives his life and virtues.

[14] Veitia Linaje, José de, *Norte de la Contratación de las Indias Occidentales* (Seville, 1672), I, 231.

[15] This was strictly in accord with the constitutions of the Society, *Constitutions,* Part III, chap. ii—"It is according to our vocation to travel to various places and to live in any part of the world where there is hope of God's greater glory and the help of souls."

[16] In the beginning, Ignatius as general of the Company disposed of his men directly because the members were fewer. Later the power of selecting and sending men was delegated to their respective provincials. The pope and the general may still exercise their authority of appointing Jesuits to particular duties or places.

[17] It is interesting to note the change of personnel which came over the province during the year's wait. This is indicated in the list of names given by Borgia and that of the group which sailed. Alegre, I, 47, gives the former; and Rivas, I, 18, Florencia, and others, the latter.

Pedro Sánchez (Toledo Province)	Sánchez
Father Eraso (Toledo Province)	Pedro Díaz
Brother Camargo (Toledo Province)	Camargo
Martín González (Toledo Province)	González

Lope Navarro (Toledo Province)............. Navarro (who left)
Father Fonseca (Castilla) .... Bazán
Father Concha (Castilla).................... Concha
Father Andres López (Castilla) .... Diego López
Novice Bart. Larrios (Castilla).............. Larrios
A novice theologian (Castilla).............. Juan Curiel
Brother Mantilla (Aragon)................. Mantilla (Motilla)
Brother Valenciano (Aragon) .... Mercado
                                            Diego López de Mesa
                                            Pedro López de la
                                              Parra
                                            Juan Sánchez
                                            (Sedeño)

Bancroft, following his source, Florencia, fails to distinguish between lay brothers and scholastic brothers. Curiel, Mercado, and Juan Sánchez were scholastics. Larrios, Motilla, and González were lay brothers. The rest were priests. Father Diego López was the rector.

[18] Cf. cedula, p. 69, *infra.*

[19] Sedeño is a noteworthy character as the precursor of many Jesuit advances. He was at the beginnings in Havana and Florida, was the first to Mexico, the first Jesuit to some of the cities in Nueva España, the one who closed the Havana episode in 1573 and who carried on an argument with the king about the same, and, finally, he was the pioneer Jesuit from Mexico to the Philippines, where later he was appointed the first vice-provincial.

[20] Alegre, I, 80.

[21] When he left is not stated. Salcedo was with him.

[22] Bancroft, II, 700, says he was a relative of Borgia. This was not, however, the reason the Jesuits came.

[23] Rivas, I, 15. Probably because of the brief time that elapsed between his appointment on July 15 and the sailing of the *flota* on August 10. In this interval Sánchez had to visit the king and the Council of the Indies, present his letters to the *Casa de Contratación* for the necessary provisions, gather up his companions, etc.

One of the boats of that particular *flota* was lost. It was the one the fathers had intended to take. After that every *flota* wanted a Jesuit along. (Rivas, I, 21.)

[24] Shea, J. G., "Ancient Florida," *in* Winsor, *op. cit.,* II, 270.

[25] The Society of Jesus was an international organization; therefore, with continuous wars going on, the rule against talking about them was important to the *esprit de corps.*

[26] Bancroft, II, 701, says they journeyed on foot. This traditional mode of locomotion for missionaries may have been followed part of the time to get relief from the uncomfortable pack-saddles, in between two packs, which Alegre vouches for, I, 53.

[27] Florencia, p. 100, gives September 25, and Bancroft, II, 701, follows him. Astrain and Alegre give September 28. It is probably a misprint in Florencia because he has "September 25, the feast of Saints Cosmos and Damián." Rivas also gives September 25, p. 45. The 28th is definitely settled by Juan Sánchez, one of the first comers, who later wrote the *Carta de Juan Sánchez*, a MS history of early fathers now in the Jesuit archives of Mexico. (Cf. chap. vii, *infra*, for accounts of Juan and his work.)

[28] But there is no record of the number of people in the concourse. Notable, however, is the public spirit of the townsmen and natives, who were ever on hand for civic events.

[29] Given in Florencia, but we suppose there were no stenographers to take them down accurately.

[30] Florencia, p. 103. Rivas, p. 46.

[31] Testimony of this is the list of laws regarding education in the *Recopilación*, I, 110–121 (1756 edition); also in Bayle, Constantino, *España y la Educación Popular en América* (Vitoria, 1934), chap. iii.

[32] Bourne, E. G., *Spain in America* (New York, 1904), p. 196.

[33] Bolton, H. E., *The Padre on Horseback* (San Francisco, 1932), pp. 17–18; *Rim of Christendom* (New York, 1936), p. 4.

[34] Bancroft, II, 701.

[35] Rivas, I, 46–50.

[36] See chap. ix, *infra*, for fuller account of Villaseca.

[37] According to the cedula quoted, p. 69, *supra*.

[38] Cuevas, II, 355. The three old orders then in Mexico had enjoyed from time immemorial a pontifical privilege which prohibited any other order from erecting a convent within a certain radius of any building belonging to their respective convents. The distance was, for some, 300 cannas; for others, 400 cannas. A *canna*, or reed's length, was 2.23 meters. The Society of Jesus had a privilege, granted by Pius IV (in *Etsi ex Debito*, issued 1571) allowing it to build or receive buildings not only within the 300-canna limit, but as close as 140 cannas (272.2 meters) to a convent.

[39] Rivas, I, 53.

NOTES TO CHAPTER V

[1] Before the conquest there were in Tenochtitlán 300,000 natives, according to Prescott, *Conquest of Mexico,* Bk. IV, chap. i, who follows the guess of Cortés. Rivas, I, 28, also gives this number, as does Arthur Helps; Peter Martyr, Cortés (Letters), Herrera, Torquemada, Bernal Díaz say there were 60,000 homes; Clavigero says 50,000 homes. Priestley, *The Mexican Nation,* p. 22, estimates 200,000 people. The conquest and the plague removed great numbers of these. Bancroft says, II, 17, there were 400 Spanish families in the city in 1530, and 2000 in the year 1550. In this he quotes Gómara, interpreting the latter's 2000 settlers to mean heads of families. This over the period would be an average yearly increase of 80 families. Salazar, *México en 1554,* mentions 3000 families for the year 1554, which we may judge to mean less than that number in view of the flowery eulogy he was writing. On the basis of the normal increase we would conclude that there were 3000 Spanish families in the city in 1560, which includes both settlers from Spain and Creoles; this would signify a total white population of about 18,000. Priestley, *op. cit.,* pp. 82–83, says there were 20,000 Negroes in the city, which number exceeded the total white population; some other whites, however, were classed as vagrants.

To judge from these statistics, there could not have been more than 2000 instructible youths of the white race in Mexico City by 1560, and possibly a scant 3000 by the year 1572. Rivas, *loc. cit.,* gives 6000, but this might mean at any time up to 1650.

However, looking back from the statistics given by Bancroft, III, 470–471, namely, that there was a total population in the capital of 137,000 in 1600, we might raise the estimate of whites a trifle. This figure is the total population after four great plagues had swept the land, affecting principally the natives; hence we should expect the whites to be in the majority after the decimation of the natives. Bancroft's figures for 1600 are illuminating but not soothing: 2500 Spaniards, 65,000 Creoles, 33,000 natives, 26,500 mestizos, 10,000 mulattoes; there is no mention of full-blooded Negroes.

[2] We take the maximum figures.

[3] These are deductions from n. 1 above, especially from Priestley's estimate of 18,000 Spaniards in 1560; according to this there should have been about 2000 boys of high-school age by 1572, and possibly five or six times as many natives.

[4] Bancroft, II, 567.

[5] Bolton and Marshall, *The Colonization of North America* (New York, 1920), chaps. ii, iii.

[6] Bancroft, II, 529; Cavo, Andrés, *Los Tres Siglos de Méjico durante el Gobierno Español* (Mexico, 1836–1838), I, 142.

[7] Grijalva, Juan de, *Crónica de la Orden de Nuestro Padre San Agustín en las Provincias de la Nueva España* (Mexico, 1624), pp. 67–68, mentions that five-sixths of the total population died.

[8] Cavo, *op. cit.,* p. 136, gives the three famous plagues of 1520, 1555, and 1575; there were plagues in 1545 and 1594, also. If, as is stated by the various authors, the plague of 1520 took two-thirds of the natives, that of 1545 took five-sixths, that of 1555 about one-half, that of 1575–1576 five-sixths, and the final one in 1594 an unestimated number, one might suppose that no natives remained in the year 1600.

[9] Most probably this plague was smallpox; it is remarkable how measles made havoc among native American tribes; from local descriptions the plagues apparently were typhus, yellow fever, measles, and smallpox; in England there was a terrible plague in 1498 called "sweating sickness."

[10] Clavigero, Francisco X., *Storia Antica del Messico* (Cesena, 1780–1781), English version by Charles Cullen (London, 1807), especially Dissertation 3; the Jesuit is at great pains to refute the accusations of Buffon and De Paw, who asserted that the people were "hardly more than hairy apes," and the land was full of insects, snakes, and beasts.

[11] Priestley, *The Mexican Nation,* p. 22.

[12] Acosta, *op. cit.,* I, 153; Spinden, H. J., *Ancient Civilizations of Mexico* (New York, 1928), pp. 207–208; for a short classic description of a European town of the sixteenth century, consult Hayes, Carleton J. H., *A Political and Social History of Modern Europe* (New York, 1933), I, 60.

[13] Rivas, I, 29 ff., describes Mexico City; consult also Salazar, F. C., *México en 1554* (Mexico, 1875), and González Obregón, Luis, *México Viejo, 1521–1821* (new ed.; Mexico, 1900), *passim.*

[14] The cornerstone of the present cathedral was laid in 1573; there had been a metropolitan church called a cathedral since 1535.

[15] Rivas, *loc. cit.*

[16] The heart of London of that day is revealed as a place where one sloshed rather than walked of a rainy season, and this through refuse of all sorts.

[17] Bancroft, II, 523.

[18] Florencia, Bk. III, chap. vi, whom we follow, gives his proposal address; even though we may have doubts about the beautiful form of expression, we cannot avoid judging the native a cultured man in view of his sentiments. Consult also Rivas, I, 56.

[19] The edifice, which gloried in a shingled roof, three aisles, and a congregational capacity of three hundred, was 157 feet square and was called San Gregorio de Jacalteopán (Florencia, *loc. cit.*).

[20] Rivas, I, 57.

[21] Castañeda, Carlos E., *Nuevos Documentos* (Mexico, 1929), II, p. 26; this publication of Dr. Castañeda is a continuation of Genaro García, *Documentos Inéditos o Muy Raros.* In this series by García, Vols. XIX and XXI are Dr. Felix Osores' *Noticias Bio-bibliográficas de Alumnos Distinguidos del Colegio de San Pedro, San Pablo y San Ildefonso;* the *Nuevos Documentos* are an appendix to the *Noticias,* and are the published notes of Osores, and hence they will

be cited as Osores. Dr. Castañeda utilized the *Apuntes* of Mariano Echeverría in preparing this edition, and these will be cited as Veytia.

[22] Alegre, I, 72; Florencia, Bk. III, chap. iv.

[23] Florencia, *loc. cit.*

[24] *Ibid.;* Osores, p. 30.

[25] Osores, p. 30. After it had been privileged in 1701 and 1704 to grant university degrees, it was made definitely a secular college in 1709 and in reality a state institution under the *Patronato Real.*

[26] Rivas, I, 60; Florencia, Bk. III, chap. ix.

[27] Alegre, I, 73.

[28] Florencia, p. 146; there were eleven in 1573 and nine in 1574; among those who applied was the bishop of Honduras.

[29] Rivas, I, 54.

[30] Alegre, I, 74, says it was used as such until his time.

[31] Alegre, I, 70.

[32] *Ibid.*

NOTES TO CHAPTER VI

[1] The present system of Catholic seminary education really began with the Council of Trent (1545–1563) and the word *seminary* was probably used for the first time in its present sense by Cardinal Pole in 1556. The twenty-third session of the Council (1563) declared in the form of laws binding upon all the Church that every diocese was bound to support, educate, and train a number of youths, who were to be at least twelve years of age and promising material; these afterwards and all others were to have a liberal education as a foundation for their professional studies. This course in liberal arts included what now would be a high-school training and two years of college work.

[2] Florencia, Bk. III, chap. xiii, No. 170, quotes him as saying that the learning of the priest should be as great as his virtue—and this should be as that of the saints and angels. We follow Florencia's account during this chapter, but it will be necessary to specify data taken from pages other than those which treat directly of the foundation of the college, that is, Book III, chap. xiv. The paging in Florencia goes awry and pages 156 to 160 are repeated. Rivas, pp. 68–69, is very brief on this foundation, an indication that possibly it was not so important.

[3] Florencia, p. 185, is not condemning the Latin situation, but is making his argument for the beginning of Latin studies by the Jesuits as strong as possible. Another point is that the chair of Latin referred to here was humanistic; the grammar was being taught in the convents and by private tutoring in Mexico and at the cathedrals of the other four bishoprics. Besides this there were classes in the College of Santa Cruz de Tlatelolco. In the succeeding chapter this point will be amplified.

[4] The manuscript was found, according to him, in the archives of the College of San Ildefonso. It was written in 1583. Florencia publishes it; and also Alegre, I, 75.

[5] It is important also for this, that it shows the distinction between the founders of this San Pedro y San Pablo and the founder of the Colegio Máximo de San Pedro y San Pablo.

[6] Alegre, I, 77.

[7] Florencia, Bk. III, chap. xv, gives these other founders. They were the señores Aragusel, Martín Cano, Juan de Hermosa, Alonso de Rivas, Juan Nieto, Diego de San Román, Pedro Ortiz, Juan Jaramillo, Pedro Gallo de Escalada, Dr. Damián de Torres, Melchor Pérez, Juan Ramírez de Alarcón, Alonzo Rodríguez, Diego López Alcaraz, Juan de Rentería, Alonzo de Ocampo, Juan Santos Franco, Pedro de Egurrola, Gabriel Gutiérrez, Baptista Duarte, Constantino Bravo de Lagunas, Diego de Burgos, Juan Martínez de Arrazola, and Hernando de Vargas.

[8] For classroom and house wear, a single black cassock was prescribed.

[9] "Aquí se fundo por el Padre Pedro Sánchez el Collegio Máximo de San Pedro y San Pablo en 1573. Dirección de monumentos coloniales y de Republica."

[10] In chap. viii, *infra*.

[11] Alegre, I, 171.

[12] The house did not long survive. See chart, p. 144.

[13] I should like to ascertain the basis for this argument. My surmise is that the collegians could not remain permanently in the house set apart for them because of lack of funds. Secondly, the patrons may have been seeking home leave for them too often, and thus interfering with discipline. Lastly, from a little hint in the *auto* (quoted in n. 15, *infra*), it may be concluded that the patrons were disbursing too much of the income on superfluities, too little on necessities.

[14] On Lanuchi, see reasons for his appointment in chap. vii, *infra*.

[15] The *auto* is quoted in Alegre, I, 182. Its gist: The Royal Audiencia considered the petition of Dr. Damién Torres, Pedro Gallo de Escalada, Alonzo Jiménez, and other patrons of the college. These requested that the regimen of the college be turned over to the Jesuit rector. The Audiencia requested him to have supreme charge and appoint a vice-rector to manage the college. The rector was to draft the constitutions and visit the college to see that they were enforced.

A committee composed of the Provincial, Plaza, and Pedro Sánchez of the Company, and Dr. Pedro López and Alvaro de Figueroa, was to settle the matter of collecting the income from the principal set aside by the founders and to see to its apportionment. They were to guard the resources and not to permit superfluous things, lest the college be reduced to penury or poverty. The constitutions were to be safeguarded and violators punished by penalties specified therein. Clearly the Jesuits would have chief control of the administration.

[16] Evidently the constitutions which had been drawn by the fathers of the Company bound the patrons too tightly to their obligations. Possibly personalities entered into the dispute. Certain it is that the students themselves were being taught gratis and that the Jesuits were of a mind to continue doing so.

[17]

The Rectors	*Their Period*
Lic. Francisco Núñez	July 30, 1588, to Oct. 18, 1589
Fr. Juan Rafael Gallo	to Oct. 16, 1589
Fr. Francisco de Porras	to May 4, 1591
Fr. Diego Gutiérrez de Bocanegra	to Mar. 12, 1592
Fr. Hernando Caballero	to Aug. 20, 1594
Lic. Miguel Sánchez de Trujillo	to Aug. 16, 1597
Fr. Diego Sánchez de Ávila	to Aug. 8, 1598
Dr. D. Francisco de Villagrá (*Oidor*)	to May 10, 1605
Dr. D. Juan Quesada Figueroa (*Oidor*)	to May 29, 1612

The last named did not officially give up his position until Jan. 7, 1614, because of the delay with legal signatures and arrangements after the issuance of the cedula by Philip III on May 29, 1612, which put the college under the Jesuits. Osores gives the entire list of rectors to 1830. Three Jesuits ruled, 1816–1821, after the restoration of the Society.

[18] Philip III issued a cedula on May 29, 1612, "entrusting the government and administration of the Colegio de San Pedro y San Pablo of Mexico to the Company of Jesus and its religious and reserving the patronage of it to ourselves and

our successors." (*Recopilación,* Lib. I, Tit. 23, Ley 13.) This does not signify a legal union with San Ildefonso, but rather autonomy for San Pedro y San Pablo under Jesuit control; the students of both colleges were taught in the same lecture halls by the Jesuits just as they had been previously.

[19] The building of San Pedro y San Pablo was dismantled in 1618 (Florencia, p. 177).

NOTES TO CHAPTER VII

[1] Alegre, I, 84, follows Rivas, I, 63 ff.

[2] The account is given in glowing terms in Florencia, Bk. III, chap. xiii, and Rivas, *loc. cit.*

[3] Florencia, Bk. III, chap. xviii.

[4] A short manuscript biography of Juan Sánchez is included with a number of others of the early Jesuits in a single volume labeled *MS Biog. IX.* It is in the Jesuit archives in Mexico City.

According to this he was skilled in theology, sacred and moral, as well as in plastic and pictorial arts. He wrote and directed the famous pageants of "The Persecution of Diocletian" and its successor "Constantine," which were presented when the relics of the saints arrived in Mexico from Rome; on that occasion he had the city decorated in Roman style with details of statuary, columns, and inscriptions. His mathematical knowledge helped in the planning of the aqueduct constructed from San Gregorio to the Tula River. His historical writing has been referred to already. He died in 1619.

[5] Alegre, I, 85. They were Father Vincent Lanuchi and six scholastics, who had reached Vera Cruz September 1. (Rivas, p. 66.)

[6] Florencia, Bk. III, chap. xviii.

[7] It is still the custom in Catholic seminaries for the professor to begin his course with a Latin address and then dismiss the class for the day. Viceroys were still attending the "Inicio" in 1650. (Rivas, p. 79.)

[8] Rivas, I, 63.

[9] Florencia, III, chap. xix.

[10] Corcoran, T., *Renatae Litterae,* pp. 72–101, gives the plan of studies in use in the Roman College between 1560 and 1575. It is that written and used by Fr. James Ledesma, the prefect of studies. (See chap. x, *infra,* where this remark is enlarged upon.)

[11] *Carta* of Juan Sánchez. Also Alegre, I, 108–109.

[12] Florencia, III, chap. xx, says 600 students, but the *Carta Anua* for 1575 gives 300.

[13] *Ibid.* Osores also accounts for Cano in *Documentos Para la Historia de México,* Vol. XIX. He later became a Jesuit and a college rector.

[14] Pérez de Rivas, as quoted by Florencia, Bk. III, chap. xx, No. 206.

[15] Alegre, I, 109. Of course those then in the upper divisions had been trained previously, most likely at the University.

[16] García, Genaro, *Documentos Para la Historia de México,* Vol. XV, p. 106, contains a letter from the queen, dated June 6, 1550, in which she gives orders in the king's name to the Augustinian provincial, whereby he was to have all of his men teach Castilian to the Indians and in every way promote the same. Around this question of teaching the Indians Latin a great dispute revolved; for details of the argument consult Ricard, Robert, *La conquête spirituelle du Mexique* (Paris, 1933).

[17] Cuevas, Mariano, *Orígines del Humanismo en México* (Mexico, 1933), p. 15.

[18] *Ibid.*, p. 18.

[19] *Ibid.*, pp. 20–28.

[20] *Ibid.*, pp. 29–33.

[21] See n. 4, *supra,* regarding manuscript biography of Juan Sánchez. Probably Rivas wrote it, although Cuevas, *op. cit.,* p. 37, says it is a contemporary account. In the same MS volume there is a short biography of Mercado.

[22] Alegre, I, 157–159.

[23] *Epistolae Generalium,* 1576–1599, p. 58, quoted in Astrain, III, 148.

[24] Cubberley, E., *Readings in the History of Education* (Boston, 1920), p. 222, gives the plan for Eton; p. 251, the Saxony plan; p. 207, that of the Collège de Guyenne; p. 211, that of Sturm.

NOTES TO CHAPTER VIII

[1] See chart, p. 82, *supra.*

[2] Rivas, I, 68.

[3] Florencia, pp. 164–167, 183.

[4] Rivas, *loc. cit.*

[5] *Ibid.*, I, 67 ff.

[6] *Ibid.*, I, 69.

[7] Alegre, I, 85–86. The complication arises when Osores, *Nuevos Documentos,* II, 45, states that Sánchez established San Gregorio after getting a license from the viceroy on Jan. 19, 1575; I have not come across this license.

[8] Osores, *loc. cit.*

[9] *Ibid.*, II, 42.

[10] Florencia, p. 165.

[11] *Ibid., loc. cit.*

[12] Quoted in Osores, *op. cit.*, p. 42, n. 47. The *Carta Anua* for 1576 mentions the establishment of four colleges and states that they were grouped conveniently around the Jesuit house. If this is taken literally, San Pedro y San Pablo was to the west, San Gregorio to the east, San Miguel to the north, and San Bernardo in front to the south.

[13] Osores, *op. cit.*, pp. 43, 42.

[14] For a clarification of the dispute, consult Ricard, Robert, *La conquête spirituelle du Mexique, 1521–1572* (Paris, 1933), chap. vii, particularly pp. 273 ff.

[15] Clavigero, F. X., *Storia Antica del Messico,* in English translation by Charles Cullen (2 vols.; London, 1807), II, 351. Ricard, *loc. cit.,* differs from Bancroft, I, 700, in estimating Father Clavigero; the latter is laudatory.

[16] A cedula of Philip II, Dec. 2, 1578, tells the viceroy to forbid the ordinations of mestizos, because "We have been informed that some have been ordained who have not sufficient knowledge. Ask our advice before proceeding." And in the *capitulo* to the Royal Audiencia (1582) the king explains that this pertained only to the sons of Indians and those of the Indian-Spanish unions.

[17] Clavigero, *op. cit., loc. cit.*

[18] This will be explained *infra,* p. 128.

[19] *Carta Anua* of 1576; Astrain, III, 132.

[20] *Ibid.*

[21] Florencia, p. 166.

[22] Osores, *op. cit.*, p. 38, n. 43.

[23] *Ibid.*, p. 37.

[24] Vol. I, p. 193.

[25] Vol. I, p. 219.

[26] Osores, p. 38.

[27] Alegre, II, 96.

[28] *Ibid.;* and *Recopilación,* Lib. I, Tit. 23, Ley 13.

[29] *Recopilación, loc. cit.*

[30] Florencia, p. 177.

[31] Osores, pp. 19–26, accounts for Cristo.

[32] Alegre, *loc. cit.,* has the cedula. Its gist is in this and the following paragraph.

[33] Rivas, I, 70 ff., gives the daily order, and says all the other seminaries in charge of the Jesuits of New Spain followed it. There is no need to give it here, because it is almost identical with the daily order of the Jesuit scholastics as given in chap. ii, *supra.*

[34] Osores, *Nuevos Doc.,* p. 169, lists the rectors of San Pedro y San Pablo y San Ildefonso. I disagree with this nomenclature. These were separate foundations. I disagree with the dates given for the life of the institution, namely, 1573–1829. San Ildefonso did not exist at the first-named date. Between these dates, Osores names fifty-three Jesuit rectors, eighteen from the secular clergy, and two lay rectors; the ninth Jesuit named began a long line of successive Jesuit rectors, which began in 1614 and terminated in 1767 with the fiftieth; later it was resumed by three others, 1816–1821.

[35] Osores, pp. 105–108.

[36] The table is computed from the lists of names printed in Osores, pp. 187–204; the Jesuits and most of the others might just as easily be claimed as products of the Colegio Máximo. There would have been 1788 students admitted on the twelve burses granted each year by the king during the 149 years between 1618 and 1767.

[37] Cf. *Documentos Inéditos* of Genaro García (described above, chap. v, n. 21), XIX and XXI. These two volumes total 665 pages of interesting research by a scholarly alumnus; the list in reality pertains to the whole center of Jesuit education in Mexico City.

[38] Osores, pp. 151–161.

[39] *Ibid.,* p. 119.

[40] *Ibid.,* pp. 93–104.

[41] *Ibid.,* pp. 72–92, where names and amounts are listed.

[42] *Ibid.,* pp. 163–168.

[43] *Documentos Inéditos,* Vols. XIX and XXI, where writers and their works are listed.

NOTES TO CHAPTER IX

[1] Bancroft, II, 701, appreciated the importance of this gentleman in the Jesuit foundation. Rivas, I, 83, and Florencia, Bk. V, chap. i, and Alegre, I, 175–177, devote several pages to him, as members of a province deeply grateful to a benefactor.

[2] Alegre, I, 113.

[3] This might be inferred from Alegre, I, 55.

[4] Cuevas, *Orígenes del Humanismo en México,* pp. 14–15.

[5] Priestley, *The Mexican Nation,* chap. vi, pp. 96–114, summarizes religious conditions. See also Cuevas, Vol. II, Bk. I.

[6] See his deed, quoted *infra.*

[7] Archivo General, *Temporalidades.* The tomes of manuscripts pertaining to the Colegio San Pedro y San Pablo and Colegio Máximo are numbered 180; 227; 229; 230 1.A.; 231 1.B.; 232 1.C.; 233 1.D.; 234 1.F. In the last quoted of these is the document referred to.

For a description of the 247 tomes of *Temporalidades* see *Indice del Ramo de Temporalidades,* and for a fuller description of the 42 volumes pertaining to the temporal affairs of the colleges of Mexico from 1686 to 1836, see *Boletín del Archivo General de la Nación,* Tomo III, Oct.-Nov.-Dec., Indice del Colegios, p. 512.

[8] See chap. v, *supra.*

[9] Alegre, I, 113.

[10] *Temporalidades,* Tomo 234 1.F., p. 2. This is not mentioned explicitly by the Jesuit writers Alegre and Florencia, but must have been included in the almost 150,000 pesos which they mention as Villaseca's total gift.

[11] Jesuit Archives, Mexico City, Vol. IX, MS Biog., The biography of Pedro Sánchez.

[12] Alegre, *loc. cit.*

[13] *Ibid.* Also Florencia, Bk. V, chap. i. Astrain, III, 133, quoting from the letter of Mercurian to Sánchez in Mexico, says Alegre slips on the date. Villaseca really made the foundation gift on April 29 rather than August 29. Villaseca's writing was not according to the legal form for bequests as adopted by the Society; so the general wrote out the form to be used, and the second draft was dated August 29. Rivas, p. 81, simply says the deed was drawn August 29, 1576.

[14] Even Bancroft, *op. cit.,* II, 704, n. 10.

[15] Decorme, Gerardo, *La Obra de los Jesuitas en México en la Época Colonial,* unpublished manuscript, Vol. I, p. 15, an excellent authority, gives Dec. 12, 1572. The plaque on the front of the building gives 1573. (Cf. chap. vi, n. 9, *supra.*)

[16] Decorme, *op. cit.,* I, 17.

[17] The letter is quoted in Alegre, I, 145, and in Rivas, I, 81.

[18] Cf. charts, which are drawn partly from actual observation and partly from the sources quoted in the preceding chapters. There are two old maps of the city, dating from the early eighteenth century, hanging in the Museo Nacional. While they are beautiful and large, they disagree with one another and with the sources.

[19] See chart of the ground plan. For the description of the Colegio Máximo consult Alegre, I, 105, or the translation in Shiels, *Gonzalo de Tapia,* p. 51; Florencia, Bk. III, chap. xxi, No. 206. (The page numbering in the latter is duplicated from 203 to 214.)

[20] The height is not given in the authors; this is a surmise from the size of the arches in the first patio.

[21] Alegre says "the hall for theology," but more likely there were two, and there is space for three.

[22] The stones are very similar to those around the old novitiate property at Tepotzotlán.

[23] Cf. chart for the evolution on the property, p. 144.

[24] Castañeda, *Nuevos Documentos,* p. 45; and p. 38, n. 43.

[25] Cuevas, *Historia,* II, 334.

[26] Rivas, p. 82; Alegre, I, 175. If one is curious to see how the Society commemorated founders and benefactors, he may do so by turning to Part IV of the *Constitutions.* It is in English in Fitzpatrick, *St. Ignatius and the Ratio Studiorum,* pp. 52–54.

[27] Decorme, *op. cit.,* I, 16.

NOTES TO CHAPTER X

[1] Cuevas, II, 331.

[2] Bk. III, chap. xv, n. 183.

[3] Astrain, III, 133.

[4] Astrain, III, pp. 141–144, quotes the report sent by the provincial congregation to the general in October, 1577, regarding the state of the province. These figures are contained in it. It runs contrary in some measure to what Alegre, I, 125, gives for October, 1577—"There were only thirty, or a few more, subjects in the whole province." Evidently he is excluding the novices, who numbered eleven, and the lay brothers. This would leave thirty-four.

[5] Astrain, III, 178–179.

[6] *Cartas Anuas* for that year.

[7] *Cartas Anuas* for 1599.

[8] Nor was the Province of New Spain niggardly with its men. Many of the 42 who were in the Philippines in 1599 had been sent from Mexico; some others were on their way to making a new province in the northeast of South America (*Cartas Anuas* for 1599).

[9] Cuevas, *loc. cit.*

[10] Alegre, II, 168. He died May 12, 1626.

[11] Florencia, Bk. III, p. 187, No. 208.

[12] *Ibid*. Rivas, p. 76, says Archbishop Moya was a disciple of Hortigosa.

[13] Alegre, *loc. cit.;* Cuevas, *Orígines del Humanismo,* p. 39.

[14] Alegre, II, 66–67.

[15] Florencia, *loc. cit.;* Alegre, I, 125.

[16] Alegre, I, 115.

[17] Cf. chap. vii, *supra.*

[18] Florencia, Bk. III, chap. xv, No. 182, and chap. xvii, No. 203.

[19] Rashdall, H., *The Universities of Europe in the Middle Ages* (Oxford, 1895), Vol. II, Part 1, p. 99.

[20] Drane, T. A., *Christian Schools and Scholars* (London, 1881), p. 650.

[21] *Ibid.,* p. 652.

[22] Rashdall, *op. cit.,* II, 77.

[23] *Ibid.,* pp. 65–107.

[24] *Catholic Encyclopedia,* XIII, 393, art. *sub* Salamanca.

[25] Fuente, Vicente de la, *Historia de las Universidades, Colegios . . . en España* (Madrid, 1884–1889), Bk. II, chap. xxii, and chap. lx, is concerned with the first Jesuit college in Spain.

[26] For the character of the man see Herman, J. B., *La Pédagogie des Jésuites au XVIe Siècle,* pp. 32–33; for his work, *Monumenta Paedagogica,* 338–454, or Corcoran, T., *Renatae Litterae,* pp. 76 f.

[27] Corcoran, *op. cit.*, p. 79, gives them.

[28] *Ibid.*, p. 93.

[29] Part IV, chap. xiii.

[30] Decorme, *op. cit.*, II, 513. Rivas, I, 98, surprises us with the statement that physics and zoölogy (books concerning animals) were taught at the Colegio Máximo as part of the A.B. course to students who afterwards went to the University of Mexico.

[31] Decorme, *loc. cit.*

[32] *Ibid.*

[33] *Ibid.*

[34] López was a considerable philosopher and later taught theology to the collegians of San Pedro y San Pablo. His life ended in a shipwreck in the Philippines. (Florencia, *loc. cit.*)

[35] Alegre, I, 117.

[36] *Recopilación*, Lib. I, Tit. 23, Ley 13 (Madrid ed., 1791, I, 205).

[37] Alegre, *loc. cit.*

[38] Astrain, III, 66.

[39] I, 119.

[40] Florencia, Bk. III, p. 187.

[41] Florencia, Bk. III, pp. 190 f.

[42] Florencia, Bk. III, p. 191.

[43] Alegre, I, 161, says they used the bulls of March 10, 1571, given by Pius V, and of May 7, 1578, granted by his successor, Gregory XIII. The first would be the *Cum Litterarum* (privileges of lecturers in colleges, even where there are universities of others). This is not in the *Bullarium Privilegiorum,* which does, however, contain a similar and more inclusive declaration made July 21, 1571; cf. Vol. 4, Part 3, p. 172 of the Roman edition, 1746. The bull quoted by Alegre is in the *Institutum Societatis Jesu*, I, 44. The second bull, called *Quanta in Vinea Domini* (*ibid.*, p. 74), gave the right to confer degrees.

[44] Florencia, p. 192.

[45] Florencia, *loc. cit.*

[46] *Recopilación*, Lib. I, Tit. 23, Ley 48, 2 January, 1572.

[47] Plaza came as a *visitador* in 1579 and hence really did not begin his term as provincial until 1580.

[48] Bancroft, II, 703.

[49] *Carta* of the provincial congregation, quoted in Astrain, III, 141.

[50] Florencia, *loc. cit.*, No. 209.

[51] Cf. chart in Decorme, *op. cit.*, II, 511.

[52] Astrain, III, 149, quotes this from the *Archivo de Indias* (Sevilla, 60–2–21).

[53] *Cartas Anuas*, 1599.

[54] *Ibid.*

[55] Decorme, II, 504.

NOTES TO CHAPTER XI

[1] These "firsts" are offered with the usual qualification "as far as we know."

[2] "Lugar de Alegría," according to Ibarra de Anda, *Geonomia Indígena Mexicana* (Mexico, 1932). Acosta, José de, *Historia Natural y Moral de las Indias,* p. 154, describes the cool, healthful region, and Mecham, J. Lloyd, *Francisco de Ibarra and Nueva Vizcaya* (Duke University Press, 1927), pp. 20 f., gives Michoacán its proper place in the northward expansion.

[3] Beaumont, Fray Pablo, O.F.M., *Crónica de la Provincia de los Santos Apóstoles S. Pedro y S. Pablo de Michoacán* (5 vols.; Mexico, 1874), Vol. III, chap. viii. Also Florencia, Bk. IV, chap. iv; and Alegre, I, 88, 93.

[4] Bolton and Marshall, *Colonization of North America,* p. 39; Priestley, *The Mexican Nation,* p. 58; Beaumont, *op. cit.,* III, 437.

[5] Bancroft, II, 341 f.; Beaumont, *loc. cit.*

[6] Quiroga was born in Galicia in 1470. Placed at Valladolid, N.E., by the king in 1530 as chancellor, he was horrified by the bloody acts of some of the conquistadores; he set about the task of winning the hearts of the inhabitants without resorting to the use of swords, and was asked to take the bishopric. This meant he had to be ordained and consecrated (1538). He really loved the multitudes of natives under his jurisdiction. Cf. his *Carta,* quoted in Cuevas, I, 311–312. He erected hospitals, schools, and chapels, even with his own hands. Cf. León, Nicolás, *Señor Don Vasco de Quiroga* (Mexico), pp. 156 ff. Deservedly may his name be placed near the very top of the list of outstanding clergymen and officials of colonial times (Cuevas, *op. cit.,* Vol. I, chap. xiii). González Dávila, Gil, *Teatro Ecl.* (Madrid, 1649–1655), I, 122, says he founded the Colegio de San Nicolás in Valladolid, and, p. 113, that he founded it for the Company of Jesus, both of which statements are incorrect.

[7] Alegre, I, 93.

[8] Basalenque, Diego (1577–1651), *Historia de la Provincia de San Nicolás de Tolentino, de Michoacán* (Mexico, 1st ed., 1673; 2d ed., 1886), p. 124. For the coming of the Augustinians in 1539, cf. pp. 126–127; for their founding of a University at Tiripitío, Michoacán, in 1541, cf. Bancroft, II, 735. Beaumont, *op. cit.,* III, 239, tells of the coming of the Franciscans to Pátzcuaro.

[9] Bonavit, J., *Fragmentos de la Historia del Colegio Primitivo y Nacional de San Nicolás de Hidalgo* (Morelia, 1910), p. 6. The inaccuracy of his title will be pointed out later.

[10] *Recopilación,* Lib. III, Tit. 23, Ley 12 (May 1, 1543).

[11] The substance of this paragraph is taken from the testimonial made by Quiroga to Philip II, January 24, 1565, shortly before his death; published in Cuevas, I, 397–399.

[12] Rivas, I, 12; Florencia, Bk. I, chap. i, and Bk. IV, chap. i.

[13] Rivas, I, 13; Alegre, I, 44.

[14] Astrain, III, 134.

[15] *Carta de Juan Sánchez.* It will be remembered that the other two scholastics, Mercado and Juan Sánchez, were the first to teach Latin in the capital. Morales ordained them likewise, on his way to Puebla.

[16] Rivas, p. 105; Alegre, I, 95, says 100 pesos were added for preaching; Astrain, III, 136.

[17] Bancroft, II, 774, n. 36; Rivas, p. 102.

[18] Alegre, *loc. cit.*

[19] *Carta de Juan Sánchez.*

[20] Decorme, *Obra,* I, 22.

[21] *Carta de Juan Sánchez;* also Florencia, Bk. IV, chap. iii.

[22] Alegre, I, 119–120.

[23] Bancroft, II, 775, follows Florencia, Bk. IV, chap. xiv.

[24] Alegre, *loc. cit.;* Florencia, Bk. IV, chap. vi.

[25] *Carta de Juan Sánchez.* Unfortunately he did not give the exact date of the death of Curiel. Alegre, I, 112, says it was on a Sunday in March.

[26] Alegre, I, 120–121.

[27] Bonavit, *op. cit.,* p. 16. Certainly the majority of these did not become priests.

[28] Alegre, I, 127–128, has the best account of the fire.

[29] Alegre, I, 127–138, for this material.

[30] Rivas, I, 107–108; Florencia, Bk. IV, chap. vii.

[31] Alegre, I, 146, 147, gives the donations.

[32] Astrain, IV, 391, prints the letter.

[33] *Ibid.* He adds that the separation was not effected until 1591.

[34] Bonavit, *op. cit.,* p. 7.

[35] *Ibid.,* p. 22. No reason is given for this move.

[36] Alegre, I, 185.

[37] Decorme, I, 44. The superiors in order to this time were Juan Sánchez, Diego López de Para, Mejano, and Juan Sánchez.

[38] *Cartas Anuas, 1592.*

[39] *Cartas Anuas, 1599.*

[40] Decorme, I, 47. Mexican languages also were taught at the Colegio Máximo (*Memorial* of the *visitador* Avellaneda to the general in 1592, given in full in Astrain, IV, 410 f).

[41] Astrain, V, 321, publishes this report for 1653.

[42] Decorme, II, 419.

[43] *Ibid.,* p. 511.

[44] Cuevas, *Historia,* V, 58; Clavigero was one of his teachers.

[45] *Ibid.,* I, 400. This college, however, is not a continuation of the one founded by Quiroga and later brought to Valladolid. The latter was called San Nicolás de Tolentino de Michoacán and ceased to exist in 1810 when the revolutionaries forced its closing. It was opened as a new and separate institution thirty-seven years later and then not as a seminary. Hence the error in the title given to his book by Bonavit. See n. 9.

[46] *Ibid.,* V, 74 f.

NOTES TO CHAPTER XII

[1] Rivas, I, 24; Alegre, I, 54.

[2] Rivas, *loc. cit.;* Alegre, *loc. cit.*

[3] Alegre, I, 135–136.

[4] Peña, Alberto Pérez, *El Colegio del Estado de Puebla,* Puebla, 1931, pp. 28–29.

[5] Echeverría y Veytia, Mariano F., *Historia de la Fundación de la Ciudad de la Puebla de los Angeles en Nueva España,* published in Puebla by Fidel Solis, 1931. The author, writing before 1779, says in Vol. II, p. 404, the bill of sale for this transaction was dated March 9, 1578, and that three years later the Jesuits bought the rest of the square. Alegre, I, 136, and Astrain, III, 146, give May 9. Both Alegre and Veytia say "some" houses were bought, while Astrain says "a house." Astrain's greater error lies in implying that Father Sánchez carried on negotiations with Bishop Morales, who had died two years previously.

[6] Bancroft, II, 686.

[7] *Ibid.*

[8] Veytia, *op. cit.,* II, 375.

[9] Alegre, I, 147.

[10] *Ibid.,* p. 174.

[11] *Ibid.,* p. 175.

[12] *Cartas Anuas,* 1580, quoted in Astrain, III, 146.

[13] Rivas, I, 130–133, gives a short biography of him.

[14] Alegre, I, 179.

[15] Rivas, p. 131.

[16] Alegre, I, 186.

[17] Rivas, p. 120.

[18] *Ibid.;* also Alegre, I, 178.

[19] Veytia, II, 419.

[20] Astrain, IV, 389, quotes it in part.

[21] *Ibid.*

[22] Alegre, p. 213. Date of the general's letter was January 24, 1586. Astrain, *loc. cit.;* Peña, *op. cit.,* p. 29.

[23] Veytia, II, 406; Rivas, p. 122; Alegre, I, 251, all have accounts of Covarrubias. Peña has two pictures of him, many of the state college which he is supposed to have founded, many more of the directors and faculty, none of the Jesuits.

[24] Veytia, II, 419; Alegre, I, 186.

[25] The third chapter of Peña's compilation, written by José Carreto, informs us, p. 35: "The Jesuits, not contented with being masters of the whole block, wanted to take in the street known as 6 Sur, in order to extend their college." The *Acts* of the *Ayuntamiento,* p. 175, say it was closed, but litigation continued for eleven years, until 1602, when the Jesuits lost the suit and the street was reopened.

[26] Veytia, II, 406, for description of the church, dedicated in 1600. Really the remains of the founder lie in the wall between the church and the college building.

[27] Peña, p. 61, for pictures and descriptions of the college. The building had been begun in 1583 (Alegre, I, 186).

[28] For 1582, 1584, 1592.

[29] I, 375.

[30] Rivas, p. 134.

[31] Alegre, I, 186.

[32] *Anua* of 1592.

[33] *Anua* of 1599.

[34] Letter of Avellaneda to the general, published in Astrain, IV, 417.

[35] Alegre, I, 253, gives the will dated May 16, 1592. May 25 was the date of the death. Peña, pp. 29–30, gives details relative to the haciendas.

[36] Alegre, I, 198, 200.

[37] Pereyra, C., *La Obra de España en América* (Madrid, 1920), p. 162.

[38] Astrain, V, 321, publishes the catalogues.

[39] Rivas, I, 133.

[40] Veytia, II, 423–424.

[41] Rivas, I, 134.

[42] *Ibid.*, p. 135.

[43] Veytia, *loc. cit.*

[44] Astrain, VI, 462.

[45] Decorme, *Obra,* II, 511.

NOTES TO CHAPTER XIII

[1] Cubberley, E., *A Brief History of Education* (1922), p. 171.

[2] Cubberley, E., *The History of Education* (1920), p. 324.

[3] Rivas, pp. 110–111. Unfortunately, seven chapters of his manuscript which pertained to Oaxaca and Guadalajara have been lost.

[4] Burgoa, Francisco de, O.P., *Palestra Historial de Virtudes y Exemplares Apostólicos* (Mexico, 1670), pp. 6 ff., and his Vol. II, *Geográfica Descripción*, p. 129, describe the land and peoples.

[5] Cuevas, I, 336.

[6] Florencia, Bk. IV, chap. viii, for running account.

[7] Rivas, p. 112; Florencia, Bk. IV, chap. ix; Burgoa, I, 68–81.

[8] Rivas, *loc. cit.*, attributed their scruple to the machinations of the Evil One.

[9] Rivas, p. 114. A *regidor* carried the missives.

[10] Rivas, p. 338, gives a short biography of this important father. Pedro Díaz had been a professor at the University of Alcalá before entering the Society. He became master of novices, twice rector of the Colegio Máximo, and the provincial under whom the Sinaloa missions were begun. He helped to found the colleges of Guadalajara and Campeche.

[11] Florencia, Bk. IV, chap. ix. (His paragraph numbers are awry at this section.)

[12] Decorme, *Obra*, I, 24.

[13] González Dávila, *Teatro Eclesiástica*, I, 227. He does not give the date of the foundation of San Bartolomé. Bancroft, II, 694–695, says, "Ledesma left a distinguished name as a writer and patron of education." He was formerly a lecturer in the University of Mexico, the same whom we have mentioned on the occasion of the debut of the Jesuits in those halls.

[14] Particularly from Francisco de Alabez and Julián Ramírez.

[15] Astrain, IV, 139.

[16] Florencia, *loc. cit.*, especially p. 240.

[17] Astrain, IV, 401, prints the letter in full. This contradicts Florencia, who makes the general statement (p. 240) that all was well with the school from the start, and that about twenty subjects (*mas, ó menos*) were there from the outset. Twenty Jesuits never resided in Oaxaca at one time in the sixteenth century.

[18] *Epistolae Generalium*, Aquaviva to Mendoza, September 9, 1586. For convenience we give the Mexican provincials:

1571—Pedro Sánchez	1594—Esteban Páez
1579—Juan de la Plaza	1599—Francisco Báez
1585—Antonio Mendoza	1600—Ildefonso Castro
1590—Pedro Díaz	1608—Martín Peláez

[19] Florencia, *loc. cit.*, and chap. x.

[20] *Cartas Anuas* for 1592 and 1599.

[21] Florencia, Bk. IV, chap. ix, p. 241.

[22] González Dávila, I, 179–180.

[23] Alegre, I, 81.

[24] Alegre, I, 200–208, for the running account. Rivas, p. 359, for a biography of Concha.

[25] *Epistolae Generalium*, Ysleta Archives, Aquaviva to Mendoza, April 18, 1590, says, "I am sending the patent by which I accept the Colegio de Guadalajara."

[26] *Ibid.*, letter of Avellaneda (the *visitador*) to Aquaviva. (See chap. xii, n. 34, *supra*.)

[27] *Cartas Anuas*, 1592.

[28] *Epist. Gen.*, Aquaviva to Díaz, March 15, 1593, mentions that there should be an outside priest in charge of it.

[29] González Dávila, I, 180. Also see chap. v, *supra*, for an account of Santos as founder of Santa María de Todos Santos.

[30] Alegre, I, 299.

[31] *Cartas Anuas*, 1592.

[32] Alegre, III, 90–92. While Fr. Salvatierra, rector of Santo Tomás, was awaiting word to go to California, he was busy about a project of founding a collegial seminary. Having received sufficient donations from a number of benefactors, he obtained license, June 25, 1695, for the new establishment. Thus began to flourish the Seminary of San Juan Bautista.

[33] Decorme, II, 511.

[34] Alegre, I, 165–169.

[35] *Ibid.*, p. 179.

[36] *Ibid.*, pp. 190–191.

[37] *Ibid.*, p. 209.

[38] For this last there is a fine document in the MS collection in the Jesuit Archives in Mexico City. It is in the Vol. *III, MS Ant.*, and is similar to the *Cartas Anuas* with which it is bound. Astrain refers (Vol. IV, Introd., p. xviii) to Chirino, Pedro, *Relación de las islas Filipinas y de lo que en ellas han trabajado los Padres de la Compañía de Jesús* (Rome, 1604), which is a valuable document for this topic. A number of manuscript sources in the Newberry Library, Chicago, are being catalogued. For a further history of Sedeño and Alonzo Sánchez consult Pastells, P. Pablo, *Historia General de Filipinas* (Barcelona, 1926), Vol. II, pp. cxxx ff.

[39] Alegre, I, 336 ff., gives completely the *Relación* of this journey and beginning, by Medrano.

[40] Alegre, I, 392.

[41] *Ibid.*, p. 225

[42] Decorme, I, 42.

[43] *Cartas Anuas*, 1592.

[44] Alegre, I, 270.

[45] *Ibid.*; and Decorme, *loc. cit.*

NOTES TO CHAPTER XIV

[1] Bancroft, II, 704, nodded when he said the Casa Profesa was a house of novices.

[2] See chap. ii, *supra,* for further details.

[3] Decorme, *Obra,* I, 36; Alegre, I, 153; Rivas, p. 233. The last named, who was twice rector there, offers a fifty-page account of the Casa and its fruits.

[4] Rivas, *loc. cit.*

[5] See chap. v, *supra.*

[6] Alegre, I, 208.

[7] Valle, R. H., *El Convento de Tepotzotlán,* Mexico, 1924, pp. 7–9. This is a valuable monograph on the history of the town and its institutions; 130 pages, with copious illustrations.

[8] Alegre, I, 188.

[9] Valle, *loc. cit.*

[10] For the following quotations, Bolton, H. E., "The Mission as a Frontier Institution in the Spanish-American Colonies," *Am. Hist. Rev.,* Vol. XXIII, No. 1, Oct., 1917, p. 43.

[11] Bolton, *op. cit.,* gives this characterization to the later institutions of this type.

[12] Alegre, I, 170.

[13] Ribas, Andrés Pérez de, *Historia de los Triúnfos de Nuestra Santa Fé* (Madrid, 1645), Bk. XII, chap. iv.

[14] If the Indian boys of twelve or so, of the earlier times, were as bright as the barefoot lad now showing visitors around the ancient and empty Jesuit novitiate and church at Tepotzotlán, the Jesuits could justly be proud of their neophytes. Eager and cheerful, the boy gives intimate details of the fathers, their rooms, the altars, statuary, pictures, patios, and bells. He reminds one of the *temastianes,* the little catechists of frontier times.

[15] Valle, *op. cit.,* p. 16.

[16] *Epistolae Generalium,* Aquaviva to Mendoza, Sept. 9, 1586, refers to it.

[17] Alegre, I, 198.

[18] Decorme, II, 416–417.

[19] Letter of Zarfate to the provincial, Nov. 20, 1594. (In Alegre, I, 281.)

[20] Alegre, I, 305, 357.

[21] Rivas, II, 249.

[22] From the *Epistolae Generalium* for the dates given.

NOTES TO CHAPTER XV

1 *Epistolae Generalium,* Aquaviva to Páez, June 10, 1598, orders the *Definitiva* to be followed.

2 Decorme, *Obra,* I, 49–104, is the basis of the following data.

3 *Ibid.,* p. 504.

4 Rippy, J. Fred, *Historical Evolution of Hispanic America* (New York, 1932), p. 61. A good survey of the transfer of culture appears at p. 36.

5 Engelhardt, Z., "The Earliest Books in the New World." This is the introduction to *Doctrina Breve,* a facsimile of Zumárraga's early publication, printed by the United States Catholic Historical Society, Monograph Series, X, New York, 1928. Our reference is to p. 11. Priestley, *The Mexican Nation,* in his chap. ix, has an authoritative discussion of printing and books.

6 García Icazbalceta, *Bibliografía Mexicana* (Mexico, 1886), in Vol. I, Introduction, has a history of this.

7 See Icazbalceta, *op. cit.,* for descriptions, or Beristain y Sousa, José Mariano, *Biblioteca Hispano-Americana Septentrional* (Amecameca, 1883). Cuevas, II, 399, begins a chapter on printing with a good classification of the output.

8 Icazbalceta, *La Instrucción Pública,* p. 137.

9 *Ibid.,* 130. And in *Bibliografía Mexicana,* I, 229, the viceroy Enríquez' permission is recorded; there, too, is a list of books specified for printing.

10 Quesada, Vicente G., *La Vida Intelectual en la América Española* (Buenos Aires, 1910), pp. 3–34, gives the list of laws and a discussion of the same. The treatment is anti-Spanish.

11 Leonard, Irving A., "A Shipment of Comedias to the Indies," *Hispanic-American Historical Review,* Vol. II, No. 1, Jan., 1934, p. 39.

12 *Ibid.*

13 *Ibid.*

14 Icazbalceta, *La Instrucción* . . . p. 135 f.

15 *Ibid.,* p. 137, has a discussion. See also Coester, Alfred, *The Literary History of Spanish America* (New York, 1916), in which there is a short account. Quesada, *op. cit.,* utilizes Icazbalceta, *La Instrucción.* Pimentel, Francisco, *Historia Crítica de la Literatura y de las Sciencias en México,* I, 42 f., handles the poets.

16 Bolton, H. E., *Rim of Christendom,* 22, note.

17 Icazbalceta, *La Instrucción,* p. 143.

18 Inglis, A., *The Principles of Secondary Education* (New York, 1918), gives this definition.

19 Bolton, H. E., "The Epic of Greater America," Presidential address delivered before the American Historical Association, December, 1932.

INDEX